D0205491

# James A. Garfield
## A BIBLIOGRAPHY

James A. Garfield (1831–1881). Photo courtesy Ohio Historical Society

# James A. Garfield
## A BIBLIOGRAPHY

Compiled by
**ROBERT O. RUPP**

**Bibliographies of the Presidents of the United States,
Number 20**
*Mary Ellen McElligott, Series Editor*

**GREENWOOD PRESS**
Westport, Connecticut • London

**Library of Congress Cataloging-in-Publication Data**

Rupp, Robert O.
James A. Garfield : a bibliography / compiled by Robert O. Rupp.
p.   cm.—(Bibliographies of the presidents of the United States,
ISSN 1061–6500 ; no. 20)
Includes bibliographical references and index.
ISBN 0–313–28178–5 (alk. paper)
1. Garfield, James A. (James Abram), 1831–1881—Bibliography.
I. Title.  II. Series.
Z8324.18.R87  1997
[E687]
016.9738′4′092—dc21      97–33146

British Library Cataloguing in Publication Data is available.

Library of Congress Catalog Card Number: 97–33146
ISBN: 0–313–28178–5
ISSN: 1061–6500

First published in 1997

Greenwood Press, 88 Post Road West, Westport, CT 06881
An imprint of Greenwood Publishing Group, Inc.

Printed in the United States of America

The paper used in this book complies with the
Permanent Paper Standard issued by the National
Information Standards Organization (Z39.48–1984).

10 9 8 7 6 5 4 3 2 1

*TO*
Abigail, Emily and Thaddeus

# Contents

# Foreword

Nothing in the American constitutional order continues to excite so much scholarly interest, debate, and controversy as the role of the presidency. This remains the case in spite of the complaint, so common in the historical profession a generation ago, about the tyranny of "the presidential synthesis" in the writing of American history.

This complaint had its point. It is true enough that the deep currents in social, economic, and intellectual history, in demography, family structure, and collective mentalities, flow on without regard to presidential administrations. To deal with these underlying trends, the "new history" began, in the 1950s and 1960s, to reach out beyond traditional history to anthropology, sociology, psychology, and statistics. For a season social-science history pushed politics and personalities off the historical stage.

But in time social-science history displayed its limitations. It did not turn out to be, as its apostles had promised, a philosopher's—or historian's—stone. "Most of the great problems of history," wrote Lawrence Stone, himself a distinguished practitioner of the new history, "remains as insoluble as ever, if not more so." In particular, the new history had no interest in public policy—the decisions a nation makes through the political process—and proved impotent to explain it. Yet one can reasonably argue that, at least in a democracy, public policy reveals the true meaning of the past, the moods, preoccupations, values, and dreams of a nation, more clearly and trenchantly than almost anything else.

The tide of historical interest is now turning again—from deep currents to events, from underlying trends to decisions. While the history of public policy requires an accounting of the total culture from which national decisions emerge, such history must center in the end on the decisions themselves and on the people who make (and resist) them. Historians today are returning to the insights of classical history—to the recognition that the state, political authority, military power, elections, statutes, wars, the ideas, ambitions, delusions, and wills of individuals make a difference to history.

This is far from a reversion to "great man" theories. But it is a valuable corrective to the assumption, nourished by social-science history, that public policy is merely a passive reflection of underlying historical forces. For the ultimate fascination of history lies precisely in the interplay between the individual and his environment. "It is true," wrote Tocqueville, "that around every man a fatal circle is traced beyond which he cannot pass; but within the wide verge of that circle he is powerful and free; as it is with man, so with communities."

The *Bibliographies of the Presidents of the United States* series therefore needs no apology. Public policy is a powerful key to an understanding of the past; and in the United States the presidency is the battleground where issues of public policy are fought and resolved. The history of American presidents is far from the total history of America. But American history without the presidents would leave the essential part of the story untold.

Recent years have seen a great expansion in the resources available for students of the presidency. The National Historical Publications Commission has done superb work in stimulating and sponsoring editions, both letterpress and microform, of hitherto inaccessible materials. "Documents," as President Kennedy said in 1963, "are the primary sources of history; they are the means by which later generations draw close to historical events and enter into the thoughts, fears and hopes of the past." He saluted the NHPC program as "this great effort to enable the American people to repossess its historical heritage."

At the same time, there has been a rich outpouring of scholarly monographs on presidents, their associates, their problems, and their times. And the social-science challenge to narrative history has had its impact on presidential scholarship. The interdisciplinary approach has raised new questions, developed new methods and uncovered new sources. It has notably extended the historian's methodological arsenal.

This profuse presidential literature has heretofore lacked a guide. The *Bibliographies of the Presidents of the United States* series thus fills a great lacuna in American scholarship. It provides comprehensive annotated bibliographies, president by president, covering manuscripts and archives, biographies and monographs, articles and dissertations, government documents and oral histories, libraries, museums, and iconographic resources. The editors are all scholars who have mastered their presidents. The series places the study of American presidents on a solid bibliographical foundation.

In so doing, it will demonstrate the wide sweep of approaches to our presidents, from analysis to anecdotage, from hagiography to vilification. It will illustrate the rise and fall of presidential reputations—fluctuations that often throw as much light on historians as on presidents. It will provide evidence for and against Bryce's famous proposition "Why Great Men Are Not Chosen Presidents." It will remind us that superior men have somehow made it to the White House but also that, as the Supreme Court said in *ex parte Milligan*, the republic has "no right to expect that it will always have wise and humane rulers, sincerely attached to the principles of the Constitution. Wicked men, ambitious of power, with hatred of liberty and contempt of law, may fill the place once occupied by Washington and Lincoln."

Above all, it will show how, and to what degree, the American presidency has been the focus of the concerns, apprehensions and aspirations of the people and the times. The history of the presidency is a history of nobility and of pettiness, of courage and of cunning, of forthrightness and of trickery, of quarrel and of consensus. The turmoil perennially swirling around the White House illuminates the heart of American democracy. The literature reflects the turmoil, and the *Bibliographies of the Presidents of the United States* supply at last the light that will enable scholars and citizens to find their way through the literature.

Arthur Schlesinger, Jr.

# Editor's Preface

Individuals who rise to the highest elected office offered by the American people hold a special fascination. Their backgrounds, their philosophies over time, the way they "rise" are matters of enduring observation, commentary, and analysis. The Greenwood *Bibliographies of the Presidents of the United States*, splendidly begun by the late Carol Fitzgerald in 1988, provides to both the specialist and generalist a comprehensive guide to every aspect of those unique individuals.

Each volume records the mundane and the critical—from early education, to contemporary news and political analysis, family reminiscences, scholarly analysis and revision, partisan attacks, official papers, personal manuscripts, visual records, and, for administrations of our day, the film and video record.

The Greenwood series offers the possibility of complete access to every instant of the Chief Executive's career or preparation. Taken together, the volumes provide chronological, precise, and detailed accounts of how each President has risen, administered, and withdrawn—and how scholars, pundits, and the American people have weighed that progress.

Mary Ellen McElligott

# Introduction and Acknowledgments

While his presidency was limited to 200 days, James A. Garfield had a full public life which intersected with much of American history. The variety of categories in this bibliography attests to the wide range of Garfield's public experiences which spanned from a college campus and the state legislature in Ohio, to Civil War battlefields in Kentucky and Tennessee, to the halls of Congress, and then to the White House in Washington, D.C.

In addition to his record of public service, Garfield had a dramatic—if not melodramatic—personal life worthy of Horatio Alger, who would, in fact, write one of his campaign biographies. Born in a log cabin, raised in rural poverty, deprived of a father before the age of two, Garfield became a preacher, a professor, a college president, a brigadier general, a Congressional leader and a presidential nominee—all before he attained the age of fifty.

It is no wonder that Rutherford B. Hayes would write in 1880 that Garfield "is the ideal candidate because he is the ideal of self-made man," noting that "the boy on the tow path has become in truth the scholar and the gentleman by his own unaided work." Indeed Garfield's life personified his era's belief in a time when the nation promoted the American dream and the values of family, education, and self-help.

In arranging the literature relating to Garfield, this bibliography uses categories which roughly follow a chronological order, starting with his childhood and education. Specific events in his military and long political career are highlighted in special sections. These include the Civil War battles of Sandy Creek and Chickamauga and certain Congressional reform efforts and scandals. A separate category on the Compromise of 1877 reflects Garfield's role in the disputed election of 1876 both as an observer in Louisiana and as a member of the Electoral Commission.

An intellectual in politics, always enamored with statistics and process, Garfield entered the House of Representatives in 1863 and stayed for almost two decades.

Over time his views evolved, for example, from the professor and college president who in 1861 embarked on the crusade of the Civil War to the young Congressman who in 1863 questioned the radical credentials of Abraham Lincoln. As a responsible party leader, Garfield was more comfortable promoting administrative reform than ideological crusades. Concerning himself with party, process, and economy, he in some ways resembled a Gladstone without Ireland.

The category on the political studies in this period highlights Garfield's role in reshaping the Republican party, whose divisions often broke along personality, generational, and ideological lines. As a Congressional party leader in the Gilded Age, Garfield represented the second generation of emerging party leaders who helped forge the successful modern Republican party of McKinley, which was more interested in future development and fiscal stability than in past dogma.

Although Garfield had few legislative accomplishments, he enjoyed the distinction of having few public enemies in an era of political feuds, and of having never lost an election in a time when turnover in Congress was the rule, not the exception. Elected to the United States Senate in 1880, Garfield appeared ready to continue his legislative career when he won the Republican presidential nomination without openly seeking it, and upon winning the presidential election in 1880, became the only sitting House member to become a chief executive of the United States.

Special categories in this bibliography are assigned to both the dramatic 1880 Republican convention and the close presidential election that followed. At the Chicago assembly Garfield won on the 36th ballot after the delegates deadlocked between the leading contenders—Senator James G. Blaine, leader of the "Half-breed" faction, and former president Ulysses S. Grant, supported by the "Stalwarts" faction led by Senator Roscoe Conkling.

The unexpected nomination of Garfield set the stage in November for a contest featuring two former Union generals—one a career soldier, Democratic nominee William S. Hancock, and the other who had become a career politician, Garfield. In one of the closest popular votes in American history, Garfield carried the country with a plurality of less than 8,000 votes, or less than one-tenth of one percent of the votes cast.

In addition to the survey of the standard partisan tracts and campaign biographies, the presidential election category features a section on the "Morey letter" which might be described as the first "October surprise" in presidential electioneering. Released by the opposition in the final days of the campaign, the letter allegedly signed by Garfield supported the importation of Chinese labor—a stand which would infuriate many voters on the West Coast. This forgery prompted Republicans to send a special train to California carrying documents to refute the charge.

The 1880 campaign also introduced the "front-porch" campaign as Garfield gave short, crafted speeches to selected delegations which visited his home in Mentor, Ohio. This innovation would later be expanded by other successful Ohio presidential candidates, William McKinley and Warren G. Harding.

When Garfield entered the White House in March of 1881, he was the last president to have been born in a log cabin as well as one of most politically experienced presidents in decades. But the executive record of this Washington-tested career politician never came to fruition as Garfield was shot on July 2, 1881 only 120 days after his inauguration.

Garfield's very short term makes most historians reluctant to evaluate his presidency. And since Garfield's months as chief executive featured few initiatives, one can speculate that neither the period, the political equilibrium, nor his personality were conducive to dramatic initiatives even had he served out his term. Bold ambitions and actions in the Gilded Age were more often found in the business rather than in the political community.

Although his truncated administration of 200 days witnessed no legislation, since the House of Representatives was not in session, the bibliography does reflect the actions of his cabinet during the spring of 1881. These included the Postmaster General's discovery of a scandal over the Star Route service which the Attorney General investigated, the Secretary of Navy's tentative steps to rebuild the Navy, and the Secretary of State's launch of an ambitious attempt to focus on Latin America.

The category on his brief administration also highlights his dramatic patronage battle with Senator Conkling of New York which rapidly evolved into an issue of constitutional dimension. Garfield's battle over senatorial courtesy involved a tangled web of patronage, Presidential-Congressional turf wars, and party division (the respective leaders of the "Stalwart" and "Half-Breed" factions—Conkling and Blaine—had not spoken to each other for years).

Since Garfield was known more for his conciliatory nature than his firm decision making, he surprised observers by insisting on the appointment of William H. Robertson as collector of the port of New York City. Referring to the Senate, Garfield announced, "They may take him [Robertson] out of the Senate head first or feet first; I will never withdraw him." In the end the new president was victorious, prevailing over party faction and Senate obstruction.

Ironically the day after total victory in the Senate and the vanquishment of his foe (Conkling could not regain the Senate seat after a dramatic resignation), Garfield was shot on July 2, 1881 in the Washington train station while departing for a summer vacation.

Even Garfield's death was dramatic, as the country watched for eighty days as the wounded president battled for his life. The many citations in the section on his medical treatment reflect the public focus on his personal health. The press reported to an anxious nation details about his medical condition, the temperature of his room at the White House, and finally about the effort in the last days to aid his recovery by moving him to a New Jersey seaside resort. The section also highlights the extended public debate after his death about his medical treatment. National attention and fascination also focused on the trial of his assassin and the subsequent debate about the legitimacy of the unsuccessful insanity defense.

The genuine outpouring of national grief that followed Garfield's death is reflected in the sections on eulogies and memorials which document, among other things, the successful effort to provide an impressive public memorial in Cleveland for the slain president.

The bibliography examines not only the events, but also the people whose lives intersected with Garfield and made up his rich political and personal life. These include cabinet members, politicians, and political associates as well as private individuals and family members. And although Garfield did little public writing, he left a private diary and an extensive record of public speeches which are surveyed in a special section.

When he lay dying, James R. Garfield asked his secretary, Almon Rockwell, "do you think my name will have a place in human history?" To which Rockwell replied: "Yes, a grand one, but a grander place in human hearts." The passing years, however, were not kind to either Garfield or the Gilded Age. The twentieth president and the period in which he served were forgotten by most of the public and scorned or dismissed by most of the historians.

However, more recent citations throughout the bibliography reflect the renewed interest of historians in the Gilded Age and the growing acknowledgment that this period of transformation was more complex, diverse, and important than the previous stereotypes allowed. As this age has become seen as more important, so has Garfield. And while his potential as president remains a question mark, his life provides an important perspective on an important time of transition.

Special acknowledgment must be given to the strong support provided by the library staff at West Virginia Wesleyan College and especially thanks to Sue Martin Roth in interlibrary loan and Judy Martin, who both provided valuable help in locating bibliographical material. I would also like to thank West Virginia Wesleyan College for the partial financial support through a Faculty Innovation Grant.

Special thanks are also given to Joann Capch at the Lake County Historical Society and to the staffs at the Ohio Historical Society, the Hayes Memorial Library, the Maumee Valley Historical Society, and the Library of Congress.

Thanks are also due to editors Carol Bondhus Fitzgerald who provided early support for the project and Mary Ellen McElligott who assisted with the manuscript, preparation. Also I would like to acknowledge Garfield biographer, Allan Peskin, whose kindness to my inquiries provided needed insight and whose studies of Garfield provided a rich resource for scholars of this period. Any mistakes in commission and omission are, of course, mine.

This volume has been prepared for future researchers with the hope that they will feel compelled by the admonition of the head of Hiram College and later 20th president of the United States to a student in 1857, "Do you not feel a spirit stirring within that longs to know-to-do and to dare-to-hold converse with the great world of thought?" And the final thank you is to my family for their patience and support as they boldly answer Garfield's question.

# Chronology

**1831**

November 19. Born to Eliza Ballou Garfield, Orange, Ohio. Fifth child in a family of five.

**1833**

May 8. Father, Abram Garfield, dies.

**1848**

August–October. Works on a canal boat.

**1849**

March 6. Attends classes at Geaugua Academy in Chester, Ohio.

November 13. Teaches one term at a one-room schoolhouse in Solon.

**1850**

March 4. Baptized in the Chagrin River after joining the Disciples of Christ church.

**1851**

Attends newly founded Western Reserve Eclectic Institute (name later changed to Hiram College) in Hiram, Ohio.

**1853**

Begins preaching in area churches.

**1854**

July 11. Enters Williams College in Williamstown, Massachusetts.

**1856**

August 7. Graduates with honors from Williams College.

**1857**

Professor and president of Hiram College.

**1858**

November 11. Marries Lucretia Rudolph in Hiram.

**1859**

October 11. Elected to Ohio Senate, representing Portage and Summit counties.

**1860**

July 3. Daughter, Eliza Arabella Garfield, born.

**1861**

January 26. Admitted to the Ohio bar.

August 21. Commissioned as Lieutenant Colonel of 42nd regiment of Ohio Volunteer Infantry.

November 27. Promoted to Colonel.

**1862**

January 10. Defeats Confederate forces at the battle of Middle Creek during the Big Sandy Valley campaign in eastern Kentucky.

January 11. Promoted to Brigadier General.

April 7. Sees limited action at Shiloh, Tennessee.

July 30. Returns to Hiram on sick leave.

September 2. Nominated for Congress by district convention.

September 25. Reports to Washington. Assigned to the court-martial case of General Fitz-John Porter.

October. Elected to U.S. House of Representatives from the 19th Congressional District. Term to start in December 1863.

## 1863

February 12. Appointed chief of staff under General Rosecrans.

September 19. Takes an active role in the battle of Chickamauga, Tennessee.

September 20. Appointed Major General.

October 11. Son, Harry Augustus Garfield, born.

December 1. Daughter, Eliza "Trot," dies.

December 5. Resigns from army at Lincoln's request to take his Congressional seat. Holds the seat for the next 17 years (1863 to 1880).

## 1864

January 14. Makes his first speech in Congress. Serves on the Committee on Military Affairs.

November 22. Degree of Master Mason conferred, Columbus, Ohio.

## 1865

October 17. Son, James Rudolph Garfield, born.

December 12. Appointed to Way and Means Committee.

## 1867

January 16. Daughter, Mary "Mollie" Garfield, born.

February 26. Successfully promotes the short-lived Department of Education.

July 13. He and Crete sail to Europe for a four-month tour.

December 5. Chairs Committee on Military Affairs.

## 1869

December. As chair of the Committee on Banking and Currency (1869–1871), he heads investigation into the "Black Friday" Gold Panic.

## 1870

August 3. Son, Irvin McDowell Garfield, born.

## 1871

December. Appointed chair of first Committee on Appropriations (1871–1875) where he begins establishing control of the budget process.

## 1872

November 21. Son, Abram Garfield, born.

## 1874

October 13. Faces his only serious electoral challenge to his Congressional seat when he defends himself on Credit Mobilier and "salary grab" issues.

December 26. Son, Edward "Neddie" Garfield, born.

## 1875

December. Appointed member of Ways and Means Committee.

## 1876

July. Begins service as Republican minority leader in the House (1876–1880).

October 25. Son, Edward, dies.

October 31. Purchases land and farmhouse in Mentor, Ohio.

November 10. Sent by President Grant as one of the "visiting statesmen" to witness counting of Louisiana presidential vote.

## 1877

January. Selected as member of the Electoral Commission which ultimately chooses Hayes as the 19th President.

April. Moves to the Mentor house which will be enlarged and during the 1880 campaign given the name "Lawnfield."

## 1879

March 29. Gains national attention for his "Revolution in Congress" speech attacking Democratic attempts to challenge election laws.

## 1880

January 13. Elected by Ohio General Assembly to the U.S. Senate for term beginning March 4, 1881.

June 8. Nominated for President on the 36th ballot by Republican Convention in Chicago.

November 5. Elected President of United States.

November 8. Resigns from House of Representatives.

December 23. Declines Senate seat as President-Elect.

**1881**

March 4. Inaugurated as president.

March 5. Appoints his cabinet.

March 14. Appoints Stanley Matthews as Associate Justice.

March 23. Appointment of William H. Robertson as collector of Port of New York prompts prolonged patronage fight with Senator Roscoe Conkling, leader of the "Stalwart" faction of the Republican party.

April 9. Discovery of Star Route fraud at Post Office Department.

May 16. New York senators Conkling and Thomas Collier Platt resign over their dispute with the President over federal appointments.

May 18. Collector Robertson confirmed by Senate.

July 2. Shot by disappointed office seeker while passing through the train station at Washington, D.C.

September 6. After two months at the White House the wounded president is taken to Elberon, New Jersey, in hope of aiding recovery.

September 15. After initial rally, suffers setback.

September 19. Dies from wound while resting in Elberon, New Jersey.

September 20. Body lies in state in the Rotunda for two days.

September 26. Burial services at Lakeview Cemetery in Cleveland.

# 1
# Manuscript and Archival Resources

**A. Unpublished Personal and Administrative Papers of James A. Garfield**

**1.** Garfield, James A. Papers. Library of Congress. Collection of 484 containers hold approximately 77,000 documents covering the years 1839–1884. Material includes family, personal, and official correspondence, diary, speeches, legal papers, scrapbooks, and other material relating to his career and death. Available on microfilm.

**2.** Garfield, James A. *James A. Garfield Papers, Index.* Washington, D.C.: Library of Congress, 1973.

**3.** _____. *Presidential Microfilm: James A. Garfield Papers.* Washington, D.C.: Library of Congress, 1973. 177 reels of microfilm including index.

1. Diaries, 1848–1881. 21 vols. Reels 1–3.

2. Family and General Correspondence. Reels 5–124.

3. Speeches and Memoranda. Reels 126–133.

4. Law Cases, Notebooks, Scrapbooks, Miscellany. Reels 133–177.

**4.** _____. Papers. University of Chicago Library. 1880–1881. ca. 350 items, some facsimiles. Material relating to the 1880 campaign and his assassination, including guide.

**5.** _____. U.S. Presidents' Papers, 1753–1935. Duke University Library, Durham, N.C. 8 Garfield items.

**6.** _____. Papers. Hiram College, Hiram, Ohio. 5 feet. Concentrates on his association with the college as a student, teacher, president. Covers the years 1851–1881 and includes commemorative material from 1881 to present.

**7.** _____. Papers. Ohio Historical Society, Columbus. 1853–1881. 203 items. (microfilm, 1 reel). Correspondence, memorandum book (1853–1857), printed material concerning his death, and letters concerning Hiram College. Unpublished inventory.

**8.** _____. Papers. Historical Society of Western Pennsylvania, Pittsburgh. 1863–1878. 45 items. Letters and speeches. Some photocopies.

**9.** _____. Andre deCoppet Collection, 1566–1942. Firestone Library, Princeton University, Princeton, N.J. 15 items.

**10.** _____. Almon Ferdinand Rockwell Papers. 1852–1900. Library of Congress .3 feet (ca. 2,000 items). Includes 90 letters from Garfield and material concerning their joint investments and Garfield's assassination.

**11.** _____. Almon Ferdinand Rockwell Papers. 1880–1888. Western Reserve Historical Society, Cleveland. 15 items including letters from Lucretia Garfield to friend of Garfield dating back to the Civil War.

**12.** _____. John Sherman Papers. Mansfield-Richland County Public Library, Mansfield, Ohio. 1839–1921. 46 Garfield items.

**13.** _____. William Henry Smith Papers. Indiana Historical Society, Indianapolis. 21 letters (1880–1881) from Garfield to Rutherford Hayes.

**14.** _____. Henry B. Boynton Papers, 1854–1887. Western Reserve Historical Society, Cleveland. .2 linear feet. Includes journal started by William A. Boynton while a student at Hiram and continued by brother, Henry B. Boynton. Their cousin, Garfield, is frequently cited. Also includes letters from Garfield, 1856–1880, as well as the record book of their debating club, Philomathian Society, of which Garfield was an officer.

**15.** _____. John M. Stull Papers. Western Reserve Historical Society, Cleveland. Vertical file. Useful for the giant presidential rally at Warren, Ohio.

**16.** _____. David Gaskill Swaim Papers. 1861–1874. Western Reserve Historical Society, Cleveland. 2 volumes. Contains approximately 140 letters from Garfield covering the years 1861–1874.

**17.** New York Genealogical and Biographical Society Library, New York. Six political broadsides on the 1880 campaign.

**18.** Brooklyn Historical Society, Brooklyn, N.Y. October 1, 1876. Military appointment.

**19.** Garfield, James A. Boston Public Library. 3 items.

## B. Published Personal and Administrative Papers of James A. Garfield

**20.** Brown, Harry James, and Frederick D. Williams, eds. *The Diary of James A. Garfield.* 4 vols. East Lansing: Michigan State University Press, 1967–1981. Well-edited volumes cover the years from 1848 to 1881, providing Garfield's immediate observations of events, as well as his views on issues. Important source on Gilded Age politics as well as Garfield.

**21.** Fisher, Everett. "The Garfield Centennial." *Manuscripts* 33, no.2 (Spring 1981): 138–43. Discusses his efforts to buy documents from collectors.

**22.** Hinsdale, Burke A., ed. *The Works of James Abram Garfield.* 2 vols. Boston: J. R. Osgood, 1882–1883. Compilation by his friend includes ninty-nine pieces. Most were speeches delivered in the House of Representatives. Others were contributions to magazines such as *Century*, *Atlantic Monthly*, and *North American Review*.

**23.** Hinsdale, Mary L., ed. *Garfield-Hinsdale Letters: Correspondence between James Abram Garfield and Burke Aaron Hinsdale.* Ann Arbor: University of Michigan Press, 1949. Correspondence from 1857 to 1881 between Garfield and his successor to the presidency of Hiram College.

**24.** Merritt, Arthur H., ed. "Two Unpublished Letters of James A. Garfield, Written While a Student at Williams College." *New-York Historical Society Quarterly* 31 (July 1947): 129–38. The recipient was Amos Sutton, head of Western Reserve Eclectic Institute (Hiram College).

**25.** Norris, James D., and James K. Martin, eds. "Three Civil War Letters of James A. Garfield." *Ohio History* 74 (Autumn 1965): 247–52. Letters written in 1862 to Frederick Augustus Williams, a student and friend who captained the company raised at Hiram and who later died during the Kentucky campaign.

**26.** Norris, James D., and Arthur H. Shaffer, eds. *Politics and Patronage in the Gilded Age: The Correspondence of James A. Garfield and Charles E. Henry.* Madison: State Historical Society of Wisconsin, 1970. This friend and key political advisor was a Hiram graduate and a veteran of the 42nd regiment. Garfield appointed him to be U.S. Marshall for the District of Columbia.

**27.** Shaw, John, ed. *Crete and James: Personal Letters of Lucretia and James Garfield.* Lansing: Michigan State University Press, 1994. 400 of the more than 1,200 letters found in the Garfield Papers. The letters, written between 1853–1881, focus on their marital relationship.

**28.** Smith, Theodore Clarke, ed. *The Life and Letters of James Abram Garfield.* 2 vols. New Haven: Yale University Press, 1925. Reprint; Hamden, Conn.: Archon Books, 1968. Vol. 1, 1831–1877; Vol. 2, 1877–1882. Some of Garfield's letters are included; however, the quotations are often garbled in this dated authorized biography.

**29.** Taylor, John M., ed. "Presidential Letters." *Manuscripts* 22 (Fall 1970): 262–65. Three letters show, among other things, his changing appraisals of Andrew Carnegie.

**30.** Williams, Frederick D., ed. *The Wild Life of the Army: Civil War Letters of James A. Garfield.* East Lansing: Michigan State University Press, 1964. Most were addressed to Garfield's wife and his circle of close friends, including J. Harrison Rhodes, his teacher at Hiram.

## C. Unpublished Personal and Administrative Papers of Associates of James A. Garfield

### 1. Members of the Cabinet March 4–September 19, 1881

*Arthur, Chester A.*      *Vice-President*

**31.** Arthur, Chester A. Papers. Library of Congress. 1,430 items, of which fewer than 300 are personal letters.

**32.** _____. *Chester A. Arthur Papers, Index.* Washington, D.C.: Manuscript Division, Library of Congress, 1959. 13 p. Index to the papers.

**33.** _____. *Presidential Microfilm: Chester A. Arthur Papers.* Washington, D.C.: Library of Congress, 1961. 7 reels plus index.

1. General Correspondence and Related Manuscripts, 1843–1938. 4 boxes. Reels 1–3;

2. Arthur-Dun Manuscripts, 1862–1887. 1 box. Reel 3;

3. Arthur transcripts, 1872–1926. 1 box. Reel 3;

4. Addenda. Reels 1–7.

**34.** _____. Papers. New York State Library, Albany. 200 Arthur papers.

**35.** Reeves, Thomas C. "The Search for the Chester Alan Arthur Papers." *Wisconsin Magazine of History* 55 (Summer 1972): 310–29. Biographer describes the six-decade search for the papers, which escaped the destruction ordered by Arthur in 1886.

**36.** Shelley, Fred. "The Chester A. Arthur Papers." *Library of Congress Quarterly Journal of Current Acquisitions* 16 (May 1959): 115-22. Account of Arthur's destruction of his papers and remnants salvaged.

*Blaine, James G.*      *Secretary of State*

**37.** Blaine, James G. James G. Blaine Family Papers. Library of Congress. 1777–1945. 49 containers. Available on microfilm.

**38.** _____. Papers. Maine Historical Society, Portland. Miscellaneous personal and political papers of the leader of the "Half-breed" Republican faction who was Secretary of State under two presidents (Garfield, Harrison) and was unsuccessful presidential nominee once (1884).

**39.** _____. Papers. Maine State Archives, Augusta. 1861–1865. ca. 200 letters in record of Adjunct General of Maine, Civil War correspondence, relating to the war and Washington politics.

**40.** _____. Israel Washburn Papers, 1841–1883. Washburn Norlands Library, Livermore Falls, Maine. 1841–1883. 40 letters in the collection discuss Washington politics during the Civil War. Inventory available.

*Hunt, William Henry      Secretary of the Navy*

**41.** No collection of papers exist for this Southern Unionist who served as state attorney general of Louisiana (1876) and as associate judge of the U.S. Court of Claims (1878–1881) before his cabinet appointment.

*James, Thomas Lemuel      Postmaster General*

**42.** No formal papers or correspondence. James served as postmaster for New York (1873–1881) before his appointment where he uncovered the Star Routes mail scandal.

*Kirkwood, Samuel Jordan      Secretary of the Interior*

**43.** Kirkwood, Samuel Jordan. Papers. 1841–1893. Iowa State Historical Department, Des Moines. 8 volumes of this politician who also served as governor during the Civil war and U. S. Senator after his cabinet post.

**44.** _____. Papers. 1843–1915. Iowa State Historical Department, Des Moines. 5 boxes. Includes autobiographical and biographical accounts and letters.

*Lincoln, Robert Todd      Secretary of War*

**45.** Lincoln, Robert Todd. Collection. Illinois State Historical Library, Springfield. 1865-1912. 46 volumes containing copies of approximately 20,000 pieces of his outgoing personal and business correspondence. Microfilm copy available.

**46.** Nicolay, John G. Papers. Library of Congress. 1859–1913. 1 volume and 16 boxes. Includes correspondence of the biographer's daughter, Helen Nicolay, with Robert Todd Lincoln.

**47.** Hickey, James T. "His Father's Son: Letters from the Robert Todd Lincoln Collection of the Illinois State Historical Library." 73, no. 3 (Autumn 1980) 137–58.

**48.** _____. "Lincolniana." *Journal of the Illinois State Historical Society.* 72, no. 1 (Spring 1979): 71. Brief description of the collection.

**49.** _____. "Robert Todd Lincoln and the 'Purely Private' Letters of the Lincoln Family." *Journal of the Illinois State Historical Society* 74, no. 1 (Spring 1981) 59–79. Author relates his discovery in 1975 of the papers in the home of Robert Todd Lincoln.

> *MacVeagh, Wayne Isaac     Attorney General*

**50.** MacVeagh, Wayne Isaac. Papers. Historical Society of Pennsylvania, Philadelphia. 1833–1950. 3,500 items. Includes many letters from his father-in-law, Simon Cameron, Pennsylvania senator. At the time of his appointment by Garfield, this past (1870–72, Turkey) and future (1893–95, Italy) ambassador was a railroad lawyer who had opposed Grant's renomination in 1876 and in 1880.

> *Windom, William     Secretary of the Treasury*

**51.** Windom, William. Scrapbooks. 1881–1889. Minnesota Historical Society, St. Paul. Prepared by his private secretary, C. M. Hendley. No official collection of papers exists for the Minnesota senator (1870–1881, 1881–1883) who served as Treasury Secretary in administrations of Garfield and Benjamin Harrison.

### 2. Supreme Court Justices

> *Chase, Salmon Portland     Chief Justice and early political mentor of Garfield's*

**52.** Chase, Salmon Portland. Papers. Library of Congress. 1755-1898. 108 volumes of letters and 4 volumes of letterbooks and a diary for the years 1861–1863.

**53.** _____. Papers. Cincinnati Historical Society. 1849–1873. 246 items, most relating to politics.

**54.** _____. Papers. Ohio Historical Society, Columbus. 1825-1871. 4 feet. Correspondence relating mostly to his governorship.

**55.** _____. Papers. Historical Society of Pennsylvania, Philadelphia. 1824–1882. Ca. 15,000 papers including biographical notes of J. W. Shuckers plus a number of memorandum booklets and letterpress books from the Civil War period.

> *Matthews, Stanley     Appointed Associate Justice by Garfield on May 12, 1881*

**56.** Matthews, Stanley. Papers. Rutherford B. Hayes Library, Fremont, Ohio. 1803–1889. 11 boxes, in part microfilm of letters in the Cincinnati Historical Society and the State Historical Society of Wisconsin. Chiefly family correspondence supplemented by memoranda, court opinion, and biographical sketches of Garfield appointee who was a friend of Hayes and an Ohio senator.

**57.** _____. Papers. Cincinnati Historical Society. 92 items. Letters to his wife describing military experience.

**58.** _____. Papers. State Historical Society of Wisconsin, Madison.

### 3. Members of Congress

_Allison, William Boyd_      _Iowa Republican representative_

**59.** Allison, William Boyd. Papers. State Historical Society of Iowa, Des Moines. 1825-1908. ca. 200,000 items. Correspondence, news clippings, scrapbooks chiefly relating to congressional service.

**60.** _____. Papers. University of Iowa Libraries, Iowa City. 1895-1916. 3 feet.

**61.** _____. Rutherford B. Hayes Library, Fremont, Ohio. 14 items and 30 pages of transcripts of correspondence.

_Bayard, Thomas Francis_      _Delaware Democratic senator_

**62.** Bayard, Thomas Francis. Papers. Library of Congress. 1780–1898. 239 containers, most on the years 1860–1898. No microfilm available.

**63.** _____. Papers. Historical Society of Delaware, Wilmington. 1838–1942. 225 items. Scrapbooks and political and personal correspondence.

_Cameron, James Donald_      _Pennsylvania Republican senator who was a supporter of Grant in 1880_

**64.** Cameron, J. Donald. Simon Cameron Papers. Historical Society of Dauphin County, Harrisburg, Pa. 1824–1892. 4,100 items. Microfilm, 10 reels. Guide.

**65.** Cameron, Simon. Papers. Library of Congress. 1738–1919. 29 containers. Microfilm, 22 reels.

**66.** Miles-Cameron Family Papers. Library of Congress. 1738–1919. 5 containers.

_Chandler, William E._      _New Hampshire Republican senator and close Garfield friend_

**67.** Chandler, William E. Papers. Library of Congress. 1864–1917. 167 containers. Contains 7 volumes of the most important Chandler correspondence.

**68.** _____. Papers. New Hampshire Historical Society, Concord. 1829–1917. 22 feet. ca. 25,000 items, including 50 diaries covering 1880–1917.

_Conkling, Roscoe_      _New York Republican senator and political antagonist of Garfield_

**69.** Conkling, Roscoe. Papers. Library of Congress. 1769–1985. 1 container. 150 items. Also available on microfilm. 1 reel. Conkling left virtually no significant papers.

**70.** _____. Papers. Library of Congress. 1822–1962. 1 container. In Harold Jonas Collection of Conkling material. Some transcripts and photocopies.

**71.** _____. Correspondence. New-York Historical Society, New York. 1863–1886. 23 items.

**72.** _____. Papers. Syracuse University Library, Syracuse, N.Y. 1863–1884. 40 letters, 13 from the Gerrit Smith Papers.

**73.** _____. Papers. New York State Library, Albany. 11 items in various collections.

*Cox, Jacob Dolson*        *Ohio Republican representative*

**74.** Cox, Jacob Dolson. Papers. Library of Congress. 1868–1940. 2 containers.

**75.** _____. Papers. Oberlin College Library, Oberlin, Ohio. 1861–1898. 560 items includes correspondence, diaries, and military papers.

**76.** _____. Papers. Ohio Historical Society, Columbus. 1866–1868. 2 feet. Gubernatorial papers.

*Cox, Samuel Sullivan*        *Democratic representative from Ohio*
                             *and New York*

**77.** Cox, Samuel Sullivan. Papers. Brown University, Providence. 1852–1887. 1,000 items. Political correspondence, 1861–1863 and 1883–1886.

**78.** _____. Papers. 1855-1897. Ohio Historical Society. Columbus. 4 reels. Originals in Brown University.

*Edmunds, George Franklin*        *Vermont Republican senator and a leader*
                                 *of the "Half-Breed" faction*

**79.** Edmunds, George Franklin. Various Collections. University of Vermont, Burlington. 1864–1898. .5 feet personal correspondence plus miscellaneous items. He destroyed all his papers.

*Hewitt, Abram S.*        *New York Democratic representative and party*
                         *leader in the 1876 and 1880 elections*

**80.** Hewitt, Abram S. Columbia University Libraries, New York. ca. 1840–1850. 14 volumes. Most of Hewitt's papers were lost in an office fire.

**81.** _____. New-York Historical Society, New York. 27 items. Includes letter-books while mayor of New York.

**82.** _____. Cooper-Hewitt Collection. Cooper Union Library, New York. 1803–1933. 6,000 items relating to this iron manufacturer, New York mayor, and U.S. representative.

**83.** _____. Peabody Institute Archives, Johns Hopkins University, Baltimore. 13 feet. Correspondence relating to the library.

**84.** Nevins, Allan. Papers. Columbia University Libraries, New York. 1915–present. ca. 50 boxes by historian and Hewitt biographer.

*Hoar, George Frisbie      Massachusetts Republican senator*

**85.** Hoar, George Frisbie. Papers. Massachusetts Historical Society, Boston. ca. 1851–1904. Several boxes.

**86.** _____. Papers. Massachusetts State Library, Boston. 26 letters to governors of Massachusetts.

**87.** _____. Papers. Houghton Library, Harvard University, Cambridge, Mass. 118 items.

**88.** _____. Rutherford B. Hayes Library, Fremont, Ohio. Papers, 1878–1903. 16 items.

*Ingalls, John James      Kansas Republican senator and a Williams
College graduate*

**89.** Ingalls, John James. Papers. Kansas State Historical Society, Topeka. 52 items.

*Kelley, William D.      Pennsylvania Republican representative and an
adversary of Garfield on the currency question*

**90.** Kelley, William D. Papers. Columbia University Libraries, New York. 1681–1936. In Kelley family papers. 1,800 items.

**91.** _____. Historical Society of Pennsylvania, Phildelphia. ca. 600 items. Family and political correspondence.

*Logan, John Alexander      Illinois Republican senator and supporter of
Grant in 1880. Future vice-presidential
candidate*

**92.** Logan, John Alexander. Illinois State Historical Library, Springfield. ca. 26 feet. Includes letters on the Fitz-John Porter case.

**93.** _____. Library of Congress. 1847–1925. In Logan Family Papers. 154 containers.

*Mahone, William      Virginia Independent senator*

**94.** Mahone, William. Papers. Duke University, Durham, N.C. 1856–1895. ca. 100,000 items. Political and business correspondence, letterbooks, and scrapbooks.

**95.** _____. Papers. Special Collections, University of Virginia Library, Charlottesville. Ca. 30 letters of Mahone in various collections.

*Platt, Thomas C.*       *New York Republican senator and ally of Conkling*

**96.** Platt, Thomas C. Papers. Historical Manuscripts Collection, Yale University, New Haven. Most of his papers were destroyed after his death in 1910. This collection consists of newsclippings and 1,000 letters.

**97.** _____. New York State Library, Albany. 21 items.

*Plumb, Preston*       *Kansas Republican senator*

**98.** Plumb, Preston B. Papers. Kansas State Historical Society, Topeka. ca. 1862–1910. 2 boxes of Civil War and Senate items.

*Schenck, Robert Cumming*       *Ohio Republican representative*

**99.** Schenck, Robert Cumming. Papers. Miami University Library, Oxford, Ohio. 1851–1884. ca. 9 feet. Personal, business, and congressional papers and correspondence.

**100.** _____. Papers. Ohio Historical Society, Columbus. 1802–1902. 24 reels of microfilm of the original manuscripts at Miami University.

*Sherman, John*       *Ohio Republican senator and cabinet member whom Garfield nominated at the 1880 presidential convention*

**101.** Sherman, John. Papers. Library of Congress. 1836–1900. 619 containers. Also two reels of microfilm of private papers, 1848–1893.

**102.** _____. Papers. Ohio Historical Society, Columbus. 1841–1892. 25 feet. Personal and political correspondence, especially relating to the Civil War.

**103.** _____. Papers. Rutherford B. Hayes Library. Fremont, Ohio. 1846–1896. 1 box of mostly political correspondence. 1 reel of microfilm of originals in Library of Congress. Materials related to Rutherford B. Hayes collection. Has guide.

**104.** _____. Papers. Mansfield-Richland County Public Library, Mansfield, Ohio. 1839–1921. 46 items. Includes some correspondence with Garfield.

**105.** _____. Papers. Syracuse University Library, Syracuse, N.Y. 1852–1898. 64 letters.

**106.** _____. New-York Historical Society, New York, N.Y. 15 items.

**107.** Bateman, Warner M. Papers. Western Reserve Historical Society, Cleveland. 24 boxes. As manager of Sherman's nomination efforts in 1880, his collection is valuable for the 1880 Republican presidential nomination convention that selected Garfield.

**108.** Smith, William Henry. Papers. Indiana Historical Society, Indianapolis. 42 letters.

*Vallandigham, Clement L.*        *Ohio Democratic representative*
                                  *and leading Copperhead*

**109.** Vallandigham, Clement. Papers. Western Reserve Historical Society, Cleveland. 219 items, most written to his grandmother; only 12 are in his handwriting.

**110.** Boys, Alexander S. Papers. Ohio Historical Society, Columbus. 3 letters written by Vallandigham.

**111.** Marble, Manton. Papers. Library of Congress. 11 letters written to a New York lieutenant of Tilden.

*Wade, Benjamin Franklin*        *Ohio Republican senator*

**112.** Wade, Benjamin F. Papers. Library of Congress. 1832–1886. 18 containers. Correspondence on Ohio and national politics by this senator who served from 1851–1869. Available on microfilm.

**113.** _____. Papers. Ohio Historical Society, Columbus. Miscellaneous letters in various collections.

### 4. Associates

*Black, Jeremiah Sullivan*       *Lawyer involved in Milligan case*
                                  *and Electoral Commission dispute*

**114.** Black, Jeremiah Sullivan. Papers. Library of Congress. 1755-1898. Good materials on the Milligan case and the Credit Mobilier scandal. An Attorney General (1857–1860) before the war, this noted legal scholar was an advisor to President Johnson in 1868 and the counsel for Tilden in 1877 before the Electoral Commission.

*Depew, Chauncey M.*             *New York Republican orator, anti-Conkling*
                                  *politician and future U.S. senator*

**115.** Depew, Chauncey M. Papers. Yale University Library, New Haven, Conn. 1879–1928. 23 volumes and 40 boxes. ca. 12,000 items.

**116.** _____. Papers. New-York Historical Society, New York. 1879–1923. 28 items.

**117.** _____. Papers. Syracuse University Library, Syracuse, N.Y. 1866–1927. 38 items.

**118.** _____. George Washington University, Washington, D.C. ca. 1865–1926. 15 feet. ca. 500 items.

*Hay, John Milton*               *Illinois attorney who was Abraham Lincoln's*
                                  *secretary who turned down the same job for Garfield*

**119.** John Hay. Papers. Library of Congress. 1859–1914. 15 volumes and 110 boxes.

**120.** _____. Papers. John Hay Library, Brown University, Providence, R.I. 1856–1905. 5,700 pieces including correspondence as well as journals and literary manuscripts.

**121.** _____. Papers. Illinois State Historical Library. Springfield. 700 pieces.

**122.** _____. Papers. Henry H. Huntington Library, San Marino, Calif. 52 items. Correspondence with editors of *Century*.

**123.** _____. Houghton Library, Harvard University, Cambridge, Mass. 10 volumes. 1842–1911. Includes materials associated with his Lincoln biography.

*Hinsdale, Burke Aaron*     *Ohio friend of Garfield, educator and president of Hiram College*

**124.** Hinsdale, Burke Aaron. Papers. 1857–1901. Western Reserve Historical Society, Cleveland. 6 containers. Collection of letters, writings, speeches, and sermons includes research notes about Garfield's career.

**125.** Garfield-Hinsdale Letters. Photocopies and typescript copies of the correspondence between Garfield and Hinsdale from 1857–1881. 3 boxes. Used in preparation of **23**. Originals are in Garfield Papers at the Library of Congress.

*Hopkins, Mark*     *Massachusetts educator and president of Williams College*

**126.** Hopkins, Mark. Family Letters. Williams College, Williamstown, Mass. 500 letters. Majority of letters from Hopkins to family.

**127.** _____. Papers. Williams College, Williamstown, Mass. 750 letters. Most relate to his work as college president.

**128.** _____. Letters. Massachusetts Historical Society, Boston. 40 letters to his mother covering years 1828–1853.

**129.** Amos Lawrence Papers. 50 letters from Hopkins to Lawrence written between 1844–1852. Also four copybooks of complete correspondence.

*Ingersoll, Robert G.*     *Controversial Illinois Republican orator; defense lawyer in the Star Route trials*

**130.** Ingersoll, Robert G. Papers. Library of Congress. 135 boxes and 2 portfolios.

**131.** _____. Papers. Georgetown University Archives, Washington, D.C. 200 items.

**132.** _____. Papers. Illinois State Historical Library, Springfield. 17,000 pieces.

*Kelly, John        Leader of Tammany Hall in New York City*

**133.** New-York Historical Society. New York. 7 letters. These personal and official letters are the only papers left by this prominent machine politician.

*Morton, Levi Parsons        New York politican who declined the offer to be the vice-presidential nominee in 1880, but was elected vice-president in 1888*

**134.** Morton, Levi P. Papers. New York Public Library, New York. 1868–1920. 39 volumes, 15 boxes. Correspondence, speeches, and scrapbooks. Includes official gubernatorial correspondence.

**135.** _____. Papers. George Regents Research Library, Syracuse University Library, Syracuse, N.Y. 175 items chiefly relating to his term as governor.

*Reid, Whitelaw        Ohio native and later influential editor of the* New York Tribune *who was a Garfield advisor*

**136.** Reid, Whitelaw. Papers. Library of Congress. 343 containers. Diaries, outgoing correspondence, 1869–1912.

*Wells, David Ames        Connecticut Free trade proponent and acquaintance of Garfield*

**137.** Wells, David A. Papers. Library of Congress. 1795–1899. 23 vols. and 1 box.

**138.** _____. Papers. New York Public Library, New York. 1846–1895. 1 box. ca. 1846–1895.

### 5. Former Presidents

*Grant, Ulysses S.*

**139.** Grant, Ulysses S. Ulysses S. Grant Papers. Library of Congress. 1856–1892. 47,500 items mostly on his military career. Grant left comparatively few personal papers.

**140.** _____. *Ulyssess S. Grant Papers, Index.* Washington D.C.: Manuscript Division, Library of Congress, 1965. 83 p.

**141.** _____. *Presidential Microfilm: Ulysses S. Grant Papers.* Washington, D.C.: Manuscript Division, Library of Congress, 1965. 32 reels. Includes correspondence and other related materials, 1844–1922, Reels 1–3; letterbooks, speeches and memoirs,1863–1885, Reels 4–6; headquarters records, Reels 6–30; 1861–1869, military records and miscellaneous documents and scrapbooks, 1870–1892, Reel 30.

**142.** _____. Papers. Illinois State Historical Library, Springfield. 200 items.

**143.** _____. Papers. Rutherford B. Hayes Library, Fremont, Ohio. 225 items.

*Hayes, Rutherford B.*

**144.** Hayes, Rutherford. Papers. Rutherford B. Hayes Library. Fremont, Ohio. Papers. 1835–1893. 160 feet. Papers and correspondence concerning his family and personal affairs, military service, business and law practice, political career, and other activities.

**145.** _____. Papers. Library of Congress. 1856–1892. 2 containers. Also has 10 reels of microfilm available at Rutherford B. Hayes Library.

**146.** _____. Ohio Historical Society, Columbus. 1868–1880. 1 reel of microfilm. Selected Hayes correspondence collected by William H. Smith.

**147.** _____. Papers. Ohio State University Libraries, Columbus. 1887–1892. 63 items. Letters relating to Ohio State University.

**148.** Bryan, Guy Morrison. Papers. Eugene C. Barker Texas History Center, University of Texas at Austin. 1838–1901. 3 feet.

**149.** Williams, Charles Richard. Rutherford B. Hayes Library, Fremont. Book manuscripts. 1914–1926. Ca. 5 feet manuscripts and page proofs of Williams's two books on Hayes. See also **5**.

*Lincoln, Abraham*

**150.** Lincoln, Abraham. Papers. Library of Congress. 194 volumes and boxes. Library holds 42,000 Lincoln items, 18,000 of which were part of a collection bequeathed by Robert Todd Lincoln, which include 900 separate memoranda of Abraham Lincoln, copies of letters, and drafts of speeches.

**151.** _____. *Abraham Lincoln Papers, Index.* Washington, D.C.: Manuscript Division, Library of Congress, 1959.

**152.** _____. *Presidential Microfilm: Abraham Lincoln Papers.* Washington, D.C.: Manuscript Division, Library of Congress, 1960. 97 reels.

> 1. General Correspondence and Related Documents. 1833–1916. 194 vols. Reels 1–94;
>
> 2. Additional Correspondence. 1858–1865. 1 box. Reels 95-97;
>
> 3. Miscellaneous. 1837–1897. 1 box. Reel 97.

**153.** _____. Papers. Illinois State Historical Library, Springfield. 1832–1865. 6,000 items.

**154.** _____. Papers. University of Chicago Library. 1608–1918. 4 boxes of papers relating to Lincoln and his family.

## D. Published Administrative and Personal Papers of Associates of James A. Garfield

### 1. Members of the Cabinet March 4–September 19, 1881

*Blaine, James G.*        *Secretary of State*

**155.** Hamilton, Gail (Pseud. of Mary Abigail Dodge). *Biography of James G. Blaine*. Norwich, Conn.: Henry Bill Publishing Co., 1895. This eulogistic book by a family member consists mostly of Blaine's correspondence.

### 2. Supreme Court Justices

*Chase, Salmon Portland*        *Chief Justice of U.S. Supreme Court*

**156.** Chase, Salmon Portland. Diary in *American Historical Association Report for the Year, 1902,* Washington, D.C.: American Historical Association, 1903. 11–527. Significant papers from 1862–1864 when Chase served as Garfield's mentor in Washington.

**157.** Donald, David, ed. *Inside Lincoln's Cabinet, The Civil War Diaries of Salmon P. Chase*. New York: Longmans, Green & Co., 1954. Important source; mentions efforts to help Garfield get a commission, as well as the Washington reaction to Chickamauga.

**158.** Niven, John, ed. *Salmon P. Chase Papers. Volume 1. Journals, 1829–1872.* Kent, Ohio: Kent State University Press, 1993. The first in a planned publication series, this volume contains the diary journal, which has references to Garfield from 1862–1870.

**159.** "Some Letters of Salmon P. Chase 1848–1865." *American Historical Review* 34 (April 1929): 536–56. 16 letters held by the State Historical Society of Wisconsin were written to the future senator and Supreme Court justice, Stanley Matthews.

*Matthews, Stanley*        *Ohio Appointed Associate Justice by Garfield.*

See **56–58** above.

### 3. Members of Congress

*Conkling, Roscoe*        *New York Republican senator*

**160.** Conkling, Alfred R. *The Life and Letters of Roscoe Conkling: Orator, Statesman, Advocate*. New York: Charles L. Webster and Co., 1889. Excerpts from speeches and a few letters.

*Hewitt, Abram S.*        *New York Democratic representative*

**161.** Nevins, Allan, ed. *Selected Writings of Abram S. Hewitt*. Morningside Heights, N.Y.: Columbia University Press, 1937. Includes "Secret History of

Disputed Election, 1876–1877." 155-94. This account was written in 1878 and amplified in 1895. Both accounts are in the Cooper-Hewitt Papers.

*Ingalls, John James*        *Kansas Republican senator*

**162.** Ingalls, John James. *A Collection of the Writings of John James Ingalls. Essays, Addresses, and Orations.* Kansas City, Mo.: Hudson-Kimberly Co., 1902.

*Sherman, John*        *Ohio Republican senator*

**163.** Thorndike, Rachel Sherman, ed. *The Sherman Letters: Correspondence between General and Senator Sherman from 1837 to 1891.* New York: Charles Scribner's Sons, 1894. Both Sherman brothers lived in Washington from 1877 to 1881, and their correspondence provides a unique perspective on the happenings in the capital. During the summer of 1881 John lived in Ohio and received frequent bulletins on Garfield's condition.

*Vallandigham, Clement L.*        *Ohio Democratic representative*

**164.** Vallandigham, Clement L. *Speeches, Arguments, Addresses, and Letters of Clement L. Vallandigham.* New York: J. Walter & Co., 1864.

### 4. Associates

*Hay, John, Milton*        *Illinois attorney. Lincoln's secetary and Garfield acquaintance*

**165.** Dennett, Tyler, ed. *Lincoln and the Civil War in the Diaries and Letters of John Hay.* New York: Dodd, Mead & Co., 1939. Covers April 1861 to December 1870.

**166.** Hay, Clara S., ed. *Letters of John Hay and Extracts from His Diary.* 3 vols. Washington, D.C.: By the editor, 1908.

**166a.** [Hay, John]. *The Addresses of John Hay.* New York: Century Co., 1906.

**167.** Thayer, William R. *The Life and Letters of John Hay.* 2 vols. Boston: Houghton Mifflin Co., 1915. Vol. 1, 441–50.

*Hinsdale, Burke Aaron*        *Ohio educator and president of Hiram College*

See **123**.

*Ingersoll, Robert G.*        *Illinois Republican orator and lawyer*

**168.** Ingersoll, Robert G. *The Works of Robert G. Ingersoll.* 12 vols. Dresden edition. New York: C. P. Farrell, 1900. Vol. 9, 347–403. Brooklyn Speech in the 1880 election. Vol. 10, 39–532. Includes closing arguments to jury in two Star Route trials.

**169.** Wakefield, Eva Ingersoll, ed. *The Letters of Robert G. Ingersoll.* New York: Philosophical Library, 1951. Letters preserved by his family were selected and prepared for publication in this 700–page book by his granddaughter.

### 5. Former Presidents

*Grant, Ulysses S.*

**170.** Simon, John. Y., ed. *The Papers of Ulysses S. Grant.* Carbondale: Southern Illinois University Press, 1967–.

*Hayes, Rutherford B.*

**171.** Williams, Charles Richard, ed. *Diary and Letters of Rutherford Birchard Hayes.* 5 vols. Columbus: Ohio State Archaeological and Historical Society, 1922–1926. Covers Hayes's entire life. Editing has omitted many entries.

**172.** Williams, T. Harry. *Hayes: The Diary of a President 1875–1881.* New York: David McKay, 1964. Volume is more true to the manuscripts than other publications.

*Lincoln, Abraham*

**173.** Lincoln, Abraham. *The Collected Works of Abraham Lincoln.* Edited by Roy P. Basler et al. New Brunswick, N.J.: Rutgers University Press, 1953–1955. Seven volumes. Vol. 5, 382; Vol. 6, 213, 225; Vol. 7, 333, 375.

## E. Contemporary Newspapers and Periodicals

### 1. Ohio Newspapers by City

**174.** Canton *Stark County Democrat*—Democrat

**175.** Chillocothe *Scioto Gazette*—1880–1900–Independent Whig

**176.** Cincinnati *Commercial*—1843–1883—Unites with *Gazette* in 1883

**177.** Cincinnati *Enquirer*—1840–1900–Republican. Important Ohio paper

**178.** Cincinnati *Gazette*—1827–1900–Republican. Whitelaw Reid paper during the Civil War

**179.** Intentionally Omitted.

**180.** Cleveland *Leader*—Republican pro-Garfield paper was in touch with the affairs of his district. Especially important for 1874 election.

**181.** Cleveland *Plain Dealer*—1845–1886–Democrat

**182.** Cleveland *Herald*—1819–1885–joins *Leader* in 1885–Republican

**183.** Columbus *Ohio State Journal*—1837–1900–Republican

**184.** Columbus *Ohio Statesman*—Chief voice of the Ohio Democrats during the Civil War

**185.** Dayton *Journal*—1826–1904–Republican

**186.** Dayton *Daily Herald*—1837–1900–Democrat

**187.** [Jefferson] *Ashtabula Sentinel*—Republican. Editor was W. C. Howells, father of the novelist and Garfield friend, William Dean Howells.

**188.** Lisbon *Ohio Patriot*—1809–1900–Democrat—[Town name change—1895]

**189.** Lisbon *Buckeye State*—1852–1900–Republican

**190.** Mount Vernon *Democratic Banner*—1837–1900–Democrat

**191.** *Painesville Telegraph*—Republican weekly. Garfield's family's hometown paper, located in the county seat of Lake County.

**192.** *Portage County Democrat*—1868–1900–Democrat

**193.** *Portage County Republican*—1878–1881–Republican

**194.** [Ravenna] *Ohio Star*—1830–1854–Important in antebellum period. Unites with *Portage County Home Companion and Whig* in 1854.

## 2. National Papers by City

**195.** *Albany Journal*—1842–1900–Republican

**196.** Albany *Morning Express*

**197.** *Atlanta Constitution*—1868–1900

**198.** Auburn (New York) *News & Bulletin*—gave Garfield good coverage

**199.** Auburn *Daily Advertiser*

**200.** Baltimore *Sun*

**201.** Boston *Daily Globe*—1877–1900–Independent Democrat. September 27, 1881 is Garfield Memorial edition.

**202.** Boston *Evening Transcript*—1830–1900–Independent Republican

**203.** Boston *Herald*—1846–1900–Independent

**204.** Buffalo *Commercial Advertiser*—daily—1895–1885

**205.** *Buffalo Express*—This staunchly Republican daily had a wide circulation in western New York and northwestern Pennsylvania.

**206.** Chicago *Herald*—1881–1894–consolidate with *Times*

**207.** Chicago *Times*—Democrat—1854–1894–Independent

**208.** Chicago *Tribune*—Republican

**209.** Chicago *Daily News*—1875–1900–Independent

**210.** Detroit *Advertiser and Tribune*—Republican

**211.** Detroit *Free Press*—Democrat–Independent

**212.** Detroit *Evening News*—Independent

**213.** Hartford *Courant*—Republican

**214.** Hartford *Times*—Democrat

**215.** Indianapolis *Journal*—1842–1900–Republican

**216.** Louisville *Courier-Journal*—1868–1900–Democrat

**217.** Louisville *Commercial*—1869–1900–Republican

**218.** Manchester (N.H.) *Union*—1850–1900–Democratic in 1850

**219.** New Orleans *Times-Democrat*

**220.** [New York] *Commercial Advertiser*—daily—1797–1900

**221.** [New York] *Evening Post*—1806–1881—daily—Independent-supported Garfield

**222.** *New York Herald*—Republican. Edited by James Gordon Bennett, a Conkling supporter in 1881.

**223.** *New York Sun*—Democrat-Independent-ex-Democrat editor, Charles Dana. Important for its attacks on Garfield during the Credit Moblier and later charges.

**224.** *New York Times*—Mugwump

**225.** *New York Tribune*—Republican. Edited by Horace Greeley in the 1850s and then Whitelaw Reid. Except in 1873, this paper supported Garfield and was his chief exponent in 1880 and 1881. Counterpoint to the *Herald,* which was pro-Conkling.

**226.** *New York Truth*—1879–1884

**227.** New York *World*—Leading Democratic newspaper. Important for the 1880 campaign.—Joseph Pulitzer.

**228.** Philadelphia *Inquirer*—1829–1900–Republican

**229.** Philadelphia *Press*—1857–1900–Republican

**230.** Philadelphia *Record*—1870–1900–Democrat

**231.** Philadelphia *Evening Telegraph*—1864–1880–Republican

**232.** Philadelphia *Times*—1875–1900–Republican

**233.** *Rochester Democrat and Chronicle*—Democratic

**234.** San Francisco *Chronicle*—1871–1900–Independent

**235.** San Franciso *Bulletin*—1855–1900–Independent-Republican

**236.** Springfield (Mass.) *Republican*—1824–1900–Independent

**237.** Washington *National Republican*— daily—1860–1888

**238.** *Congressional Globe*—1833–1873–Includes frequent references to the debates in Congress.

**239.** *Congressional Record*—1873–1881–Includes frequent references to the debates in Congress.

**240.** Washington *Chronicle*—daily—1861–1877

### 3. National Periodicals

**241.** *American Monthly Review of Reviews*

**242.** *Arena*

**243.** *Atlantic Monthly*

**244.** *Century Magazine*

**245.** *The Forum*

**246.** *Frank Leslie's Illustrated News*—This periodical did a pictorial essay on the death on Garfield.

**247.** *Harper's Monthly Magazine*

**248.** *Harper's Weekly*—Pro-Garfield

**249.** *The Independent*

**250.** *International Monthly*

**251.** *McClure's Magazine*

**252.** *The Nation*—New York. This reform magazine defended Garfield in 1873 and supported him in 1880 but often with reservations and criticisms.

**253.** *North American Review*

**254.** *Police Gazette*—This periodical also used a series of engravings to present the Garfield shooting and death in dramatic fashion.

**255.** *Scribner's Magazine*

# 2
# Writings and Speeches of James Garfield

## A. Published Articles in Chronological Order

**256.** Garfield, James A. "A Century of Congress." *Atlantic Monthly* 40 (July 1877): 49–64. Cites the crippling effect of patronage on the President's power and refers to the "evil invasion" of Congress.

**257.** _____. "The Army of the United States." *North American Review* 126 (March/April 1878) Pt.1:193–216; (May/June 1878) Pt.2: 442–65. Argues that cutbacks undermine the efficiency and morale of the Army.

**258.** _____. "Symposium on Negro Suffrage: Ought the Negro to Be Disfranchised? Ought He to Have Been Enfranchised?" *North American Review* 128 (March 1879): 244–50. Garfield answers "No" to the first and "Yes" to the second question. Symposium with eight notables, including James Blaine.

**259.** _____. "National Appropriations and Misappropriations." *North American Review* 128 (May 1879): 572–86. Advocates budgetary reform.

**260.** _____. "My Campaign in East Kentucky." *North American Review* 143 (December 1886): 525–35. According to James R. Gilmore (pen name "Edmund Kirke"), this narrative of the military campaign was written in the third person by Garfield for use in **359**.

**261.** _____. "My Public Life, by President Garfield." *North American Review* 144 (May 1887): 451–61. Dictated this summary of his career in Congress after he saw the proofs of James Gilmore's commissioned biography.

**262.** _____. "My Experience as a Lawyer." *North American Review* 144 (1887): 565–71. Discusses his law preparation and his trials, including two Supreme Court cases in autobiographical notes given to biographer James Gilmore.

**263.** _____. "My Personal Finances." *North American Review* 145 (July 1887): 40–45. Reveals that he was "comparatively poor" with a net worth of $25,000. This information was initially given to his biographer, Gilmore, who wanted to respond to the accusations of corruption.

## B. Other Published Writings

**264.** Balch, William Ralston, comp. *Garfield's Words: Suggestive Passages from the Public and Private Writings of James Abram Garfield.* Boston: Houghton, Mifflin & Co., 1881.

**265.** _____. *Maxims of James Abram Garfield: General, Patriotic, Political.* Philadelphia: n.p., 1880. 24-page pamphlet arranged by various subjects.

**266.** Carpenter, C. S., comp. *James A. Garfield: His Speeches at Home, 1880.* Oneonta, N.Y.: C.S. Carpenter Publisher, 1880. Nineteen short speeches Garfield gave during the campaign.

**267.** Cohen, Max, comp. *Garfield Souvenirs: The President's Courageous Sayings During His Critical Illness, and "Gems" of Press and Pulpit.* [Washington]: M. Cohen, 1881. Pamphlet contains what he said and what was said about him in the press and pulpit during the summer of 1881.

**268.** Frost, Elizabeth, ed. *The Bully Pulpit: Quotations from America's Presidents.* New York: New England Publication Associates, 1988. Includes twenty-eight Garfield quotes on various subjects.

**269.** Garfield, James A. *The Great Speeches of James Abram Garfield: Twentieth President of the United States, with a Memorial Supplement.* St. Louis: J. Burns, 1881. This first and most complete collection of Garfield's speeches divides them in terms of Congressional debates, political speeches, and miscellaneous addresses. A memorial supplement to the 500-page collection contains description of services and 15 addresses.

**270.** *The Republican Manual with Biographical Sketches of James A. Garfield and Chester A. Arthur.* New York: American Book Exchange, 1880.

**271.** Smith, E. V. *General Garfield as a Statesman and Orator; Paragraphs from His Speeches in Congress and on the Stump.* New York: National Republican Committee, 1880. Thirty-page pamphlet containing excerpts from 30 speeches. Also in **270**.

## C. Pre-Presidential Speeches

### 1860s

**272.** Garfield, James A. *Oration Delivered by Hon. J. A. Garfield at Ravenna, July 4, 1860.* n.p., 1860? Given in the 1860 campaign season, this speech discusses heroes in politics.

**273.** _____. *A Discourse Delivered at Hiram, Ohio. March 3, 1861 Occasioned by the Death of Elder John T. Smith by J. A. Garfield*. Cleveland: Fairbanks, Benedict & Co., 1861. Garfield's eulogy as minister at the funeral of a church member.

**274.** _____. *Speech of Hon. James A. Garfield, of Ohio, on the Confiscation of Property of Rebels: Delivered in the House of Representatives, January 28, 1864*. Washington: L. Towers, 1880. Uses historical analogies to argue that the southern states have by their rebellion cut themselves off from the rights of the Constitution.

**275.** _____. *Free Commerce Between the States. Speech of Hon. James A. Garfield, of Ohio, Delivered in the House of Representatives, March 24th and 31st, 1864, the House Having Under Consideration the Bill to Declare the Raritan and Atlantic Railroad, a Legal Structure for Commerce Between New York and Philadelphia*. New York: n.p., 1864.

**276.** _____. "Treason in Congress. Remarks in the House, April 1864 in Answer to a Speech by Alexander Long in Favor of Recognizing the Southern Confederacy." See **270**. 292. Spirited attack against the Copperheads and secession.

**277.** _____. "The Death of Slavery: Speech in the House of Representatives, January 13, 1865, on the Constitutional Amendment to Abolish Slavery." See **269**. 40–49. This intense attack on slavery represents "one more blow in hopes of hastening its doom."

**278.** _____. *Freedmen's Bureau: Restoration of the Rebel States: Speech of Hon. James A. Garfield, of Ohio in the House of Representatives, February 1, 1866*. Washington: L. Towers, 1880. Urges support arguing that the nation did more than "break off the chains of the slaves, it added four million citizens to the Republic who must be protected."

**279.** _____. *A Protest Against the Destruction of Jury Trials; Speech of James A. Garfield in the Famous Milligan Case*. Charleston, W.V.: n.p., 1922. Speech made in the Supreme Court, March 8, 1866, in the Milligan case.

**280.** _____. "Public Debt and Specie Payments. Speech in the House of Representatives, March 16, 1866." See **270**. 261–64. States that he would not link his name to the fate of a paper currency and predicts ruin if his party does.

**281.** _____. *Remarks of Hon. James Garfield in the House of Representatives, April 14, 1866, on the First Anniversary of the Death of Abraham Lincoln*. N.p., 1866. Composed on short notice at the request of the House leadership, this two-page speech was given at the memorial service in the House.

**282.** _____. "A National Bureau of Education. Speech in the House of Representatives, June 8, 1866." See **269**. 97–104. Advocates the bureau as a way of "shielding the coming generation from ignorance and vice."

**283.** _____. "Refusal to Return Fugitive Slaves. Speech in the House of Representatives, Feb. 8, 1867." See **270**. 265-66. In his support of Reconstruction he cites his experience in Kentucky.

**284.** _____. *An Address Delivered before the Literary Society of the Eclectic Institute at Hiram, Ohio. June 14, 1867. By Hon. James A. Garfield.* Cleveland: Fairbanks, Benedict & Co., 1867. Discusses needed reforms in education to make a liberal arts education more practical and current.

**285.** _____. *Remarks of Hon. Jas. A. Garfield of Ohio on the Impeachment of Andrew Johnson in the House of Representatives, March 2, 1868.* Washington: Philip & Sollomons, Printers, 1881. Although he had voted against the proposition earlier, he now argues that the President "leaves no choice."

**286.** _____. *The Currency. Speech of James A. Garfield . . . in the House of Representatives, May 15, 1868.* Washington: F. & J. Rives & G. A. Bailey, 1868. A major address on his fiscal policies and the need to return to specie payment.

**287.** _____. "Arlington Oration. Delivered at Arlington Cemetery, May 30, 1868." See **269**. 463–67.

**288.** _____. "Taxation of the United States. Speech in the House of Representatives, July 5, 1868." See **270**. 266–67. Attacks the policy proposed by the Democrats on the public debt.

**289.** _____. *Elements of Success: Address of James A. Garfield, Spencerian Business College, Washington, D.C., June 29, 1869.* Washington: Spencerian Business College, 1882. In this defense of business colleges he declares that work opportunities are "more valuable" to women than the ballot box.

### *1870s*

**290.** _____. *Investigation into the Causes of the Gold Panic. Report of the Majority of the Committee on Banking and Currency. March 1, 1870.* Washington: Government Printing Office, 1870. Full report of the investigation chaired by Garfield and the Democratic minority report. 461–83.

**291.** _____. "Democratic Responsibility for the Rebellion. Speech in the House of Representatives, March 14, 1870." See **270**. 268–269. Blames Democrats for the expenses of war.

**292.** _____. "The Tariff. Speech in the House of Representatives, April 1, 1870." See **270**. 267–68. Maintains his moderate stance advocating "protection which leads to ultimate free trade."

**293.** _____. "Bank-Notes and Greenbacks. Speech in the House of Representatives, June 7, 1870." See **269**. 153–80. Warns against the "great temptation" to overissue paper money in lieu of taxation.

**294.** _____. "A Non-Exportable Currency. Speech in the House of Representatives, June 15, 1870." See **270**. 271–272. Response to Pennsylvania Congressman Kelley's claim that the nation has an uncertain paper currency.

**295.** _____. *Oration on the Life and Character of Gen. George H. Thomas Delivered before the Society of the Army of the Cumberland . . . at the Fourth Annual Reunion at Cleveland—November 25, 1870*. Cincinnati: R. Clarke & Co., 1871. 52 p. Praises the skill of Thomas and cites his life as an illustration of the power of hard work.

**296.** _____. *Speech of Hon. James A. Garfield, of Ohio, on the McGarrahan Claim Delivered in the House of Representatives, Feb. 20, 1871*. Washington: n.p., 1871.

**297.** _____. "The Constitutional Amendments. Speech in the House of Representatives, April 4, 1871." See **269**. 207–36. Praises the 14th and 15th amendments as "guaranties of liberty."

**298.** _____. *Review of the Transactions of the Credit Mobilier Company, and an Examination of that Portion of the Testimony Taken by the Committee of Investigation and Reported to the House of Representatives at the Last Session of the Forty-second Congress, Which Relates to Mr. Garfield*. Washington: Capitol News Stand, 1873. Rpt. 1880. 34-page pamphlet.

**299.** _____. *The Future of the Republic, Its Dangers and Its Hopes. An Address, Delivered Before the Literary Societies of Hiram College, July 2, 1873. By the Hon. James A. Garfield*. Cleveland: Nevins Brothers, 1873. Speculates on the potential threat posed by railroads.

**300.** _____. *Discovery and Ownership of the Northwestern Territory and Settlement of the Western Reserve: Address Delivered at Burton Before the Historical Society of Geauga County, Ohio. September 16, 1873, by Hon. James A. Garfield*. Cleveland: Western Reserve and Northern Historical Society, 1874.

**301.** _____. "Deaths of Chief Justice Chase and Professor Agassiz. Delivered at a Meeting of the Board of Regents of the Smithsonian Institute, December 19, 1873." See **269**. 477–80. Public remarks on his political mentor and on America's famous scientist—both board members of the Smithsonian.

**302.** _____. *Currency and the Public Faith: Speech of Hon. James A. Garfield, of Ohio, Delivered in the House of Representatives, April 8, 1874*. Washington: Government Printing Office, 1874. Argues against fluctuating standards of currency.

**303.** _____. *Appropriations of the First Session of the Forty-third Congress, Speech in the House of Representatives, June 23, 1874*. Washington: Government Printing Office, 1874.

**304.** _____. *Tested and Sustained: Remarks of Hon. James A. Garfield, to His Constituents, at Warren, Ohio, September 19, 1874, in Reply to Attacks Upon His Official Character.* Washington: Republican Congressional Committee, 1880.

**305.** _____. *Amnesty: Speech of Hon. James A. Garfield, of Ohio, in reply to Hon. B. H. Hill, of Georgia, in the House of Representatives, Wednesday, January 12, 1876.* N.p., 1876. While wishing the best for the veterans of the South, he can never forgive "disloyal" Northerners, specifically Vallandigham.

**306.** _____. *To the Republican Voters of the Nineteenth District.* Washington: Gibson Brothers, 1881. Reprint of his 1873 "Reply to Voters" in which he explained his vote for an appropriation bill that included a retroactive salary clause.

**307.** _____. *Can the Democratic Party be Safely Intrusted with the Administration of the Government? Speech of Hon. James A. Garfield, of Ohio, in the House of Representatives, Friday, August 4, 1876.* Washington: n.p., n.d. Maintains that the party cannot be trusted because of its earlier advocacy of slavery and other discredited doctrines.

**308.** _____. "The Democratic Creed. Speech at London, Ohio September 19, 1877." See **270**. 278–79. Accuses his opponents of lacking ideas and praises the Republicans as being "a party of aggressive ideas."

**309.** _____. *Repeal of the Resumption Law: Speech of Hon. James A. Garfield, of Ohio, Delivered in the House of Representatives. Friday, November 16, 1877.* Washington: R. O. Polkinhorn, 1877. Argues that the resumption will not help the rich or hurt the poor.

**310.** _____. *Lincoln and Emancipation: Speech of the Hon. James A. Garfield, of Ohio, Delivered in the House of Representatives, February 12th, 1878.* Washington: Darby & Duvell, 1888. Speech on the Francis Carpetner painting.

**311.** _____. *The New Scheme of American Finance, A Reply to Hon. W. D. Kelley; Speech of Hon. James A. Garfield, of Ohio, Delivered in the House of Representatives, Wednesday, March 6, 1878.* Washington: R. O. Polkinhorn, 1878. A reply to Kelley's publicized attack of March 5, 1878 on Garfield's speech on resumption given on November 16, 1877.

**312.** _____. "The Tariff: Speech of Hon. James A. Garfield, of Ohio, in the House of Representatives, June 4, 1878." See **269**. 294–307. Defense of the protective tariff and an attack on the proposal from the Committee on Ways and Means.

**313.** _____. "The Press. Delivered at Cleveland, July 11, 1878, to the Ohio Editorial Association." See **269**. 512–22. Discusses the faults, benefits, and responsibilities of the press.

**314.** _____. "The Absurdity of Fiat Money. Speech at Flint, Michigan, October 22, 1878." See **270**. 282–83. Ridicules money reform as a promise to get more cloth "if you shorten the yard-stick."

**315.** _____. "Effects of Resumption. Address in Chicago, January 2, 1879." See **270**. 281–82. Successful resumption would restore prosperity.

**316.** _____. *Revolution in Congress. Speech of Hon. James A. Garfield, in the House of Representatives, Saturday, March 29, 1879.* Washington: R. O. Polkinhorn, 1879. Charges Democrats with holding the government hostage by attaching a rider to the appropriations bill barring federal troops from supervising Southern elections. The most important speech of his career—half a million copies were distributed to Northern voters.

**317.** _____. *Revival of State Sovereignty in Congress. Speech of Hon. James A. Garfield, of Ohio, in the House of Representatives, June 27, 1879.* Washington: n.p., 1879.

**318.** Republican Party (Wisconsin) State Convention (1879 July 23; Madison). *Proceedings of the Republican State Convention; and Speeches of Hon. Zach. Chandler, Gen. James A. Garfield, and Others at the Celebration of the Twenty-fifth Anniversary of the Republican Party in Wisconsin, at Madison, July 23d, 1879.* Milwaukee: State Central Committee, Aikens & Cramer, 1879.

**319.** [Vaughter, John B.] *Prison Life in Dixie: Short History of the Inhuman and Barbarous Treatment of Our Soldiers by Rebel Authorities, by Sergeant Oats (pseud) to Which Is Added the Speech of General J. A. Garfield, Delivered at the Andersonville Reunion, at Toledo, Ohio, October 3, 1879.* Cleveland: Central Book Concern, 1880.

**320.** Garfield, James A. *Speech of Hon. James A. Garfield, of Ohio. Delivered at Cleveland, Ohio, October 11, 1879.* Washington: n.p., 1880. This election appeal urges young men not to "pitch your tent among the dead" and vote for a Democratic party which has dead ideas.

### 1880

**321.** Garfield, James A. "On the Occasion of His Election to U.S. Senate. Delivered at Columbus, Ohio, January 14, 1880." See **269**. 387–89. In his remarks Garfield asserts that he will follow personal principles.

**322.** _____. *Obedience to the Law the Foremost Duty of Congress: Speech of Hon. James A. Garfield, of Ohio, in the House of Representatives, March 17, 1880.* Washington: n.p., 1880. Also entitled "The New Nullification."

**323.** *Reports of James A.* Garfield, for the Minority of the Committee on Ways and Means, House of Representatives, on Duties on Hoop, Band, and Scroll Iron, and Upon Certain Other Articles, May 11 and 24, 1880. Washington: n.p., 1880.

**324.** Garfield, James A. "Nomination of Hon. John Sherman. Delivered Before the Republican National Convention, in Chicago, June 5, 1880." See **269**. 390–96. This classic nomination speech brought Garfield critical attention at the convention that later would nominate him.

**325.** _____. "Hiram Commencement. Delivered at Hiram College, June 11, 1880." See **269**. 523–25. Describes the college as an institution that promotes the doctrine of self-help.

**326.** _____. *A Soldiers' Monument: Speech of Hon. James A. Garfield at Painesville, Ohio, July 3, 1880 on the Completion of a Soldiers' Monument.* N.p., 1880. Speaks of the monument as "a lesson of sacrifice for what we love."

**327.** Carpenter, C. S., comp. *James A. Garfield. His Speeches at Home, 1880.* Oneonta, N.Y.: C.S. Carpenter, 1880. This 50-page pamphlet contains 18 speeches that Garfield made to selected audiences during the campaign.

**328.** Garfield, James A. "At Chautauqua. Delivered before Chatauqua Circle, August 9, 1880." See **269**. 530–31. In his praise of the organization, Garfield makes no political statements.

**329.** _____. "Reunion of His Old Regiment. Delivered at Ashland, Ohio, August 25, 1880." See **269**. 532–35. Refers to a regiment as a family.

**330.** _____. "Army of the Cumberland. Delivered at Twelfth Annual Reunion, Toledo, Ohio, September 21, 1880. See **269**. 536–38. Recalls Generals Thomas and Sheridan and the battle of Chickamauga.

**331.** _____. "Address to the First Voters' Battalion of Cleveland. Delivered at Mentor, October 8, 1880." See **269**. 397–99. Remarks welcoming to his home 400 young voters from Cleveland.

**332.** _____. "Remarks to Classmates. Delivered at Washington on the Night Previous to His Inauguration." See **269**. 529. One page of remarks he made when he met his classmates and his teacher, Mark Hopkins.

### D. Presidential Speeches and Addresses

**333.** Israel, Fred L., ed. *The State of the Union Messages of the Presidents, 1790–1966.* New York: Chelsea House, 1971. 1422. Garfield died prior to delivery of any annual messages.

**334.** Lott, Davis Newton, ed. *The Inaugural Addresses of the American Presidents.* New York: Holt, Rinehart & Winston, 1961. 143–48. Address with side notes.

**335.** Podell, Janet, and Steven Anzovin, eds. *Speeches of the American Presidents.* New York: H. Wilson Co., 1988. 240–53. Contains "Revolution in Congress" (242–47) and his Inaugural Address (248–53). Editors assert that the former made him a presidential contender and the latter was "uncharacteristically dry and platitudinous."

**336.** Richardson, James D., ed. *Messages and Papers of the Presidents, 1789–1897.* 10 vols. Washington: Government Printing Office, 1896–1899. Vol. 8, 1–32.

# 3
# Biographical Publications

**337.** Alger, Horatio. *From Canal Boy to President: The Boyhood and Manhood of James A. Garfield*. Boston: DeWolfe, Fiske, 1881. Written by the famous author as an inspiration for young readers, this book contains fictitious dialogue and nothing on his administration.

**338.** Balch, William Ralston. *The Life of James Abram Garfield, Late President of the United States. . . .* Louisville: W. W. Peniston, 1881. Reissue of Brisban's 1880 popular campaign biography. See **341**.

**339.** Bancroft, William Dixon. *McKinley, Garfield, Lincoln: Their Lives—Their Deeds—Their Deaths—With a Record of Notable Assassinations and a History of Anarchy*. Chicago: United States Newspaper Syndicate, 1901. 301–60. Laudatory sketch of his life.

**340.** Bates, Richard O. *The Gentleman from Ohio: An Introduction to Garfield*. Durham, N.C.: Moore Co., 1973. This favorable review of his life relies on his published letters and limited bibliographical sources.

**341.** Brisbin, James S[anks]. *From the Tow-path to the White House: The Early Life and Public Career of James A. Garfield . . . Record of a Wonderful Career Which Is Like that of Abraham Lincoln, . . . Including Also a Sketch of the Life of Hon. Chester A. Arthur*. Boston: D. L. Guernsey, 1880. This popular campaign biography includes contemporary sources and also incidents of fictitious dialogues. Was reissued after the assassination as **338** using the name of a local writer, William R. Balch.

**342.** Brown, Emma Elizabeth. *The Life and Public Services of James A. Garfield . . . Together with Notable Extracts from His Speeches and Letters*. Boston: Lathrop, 1881. This eulogistic narrative emphasizes Garfield as a practical and practicing Christian.

**343.** Bundy, Jonas Mills. *The Life of Gen. James A. Garfield.* New York: A. S. Barnes & Co., 1880. Written by the editor of the *New York Evening Mail* at Garfield's request, it is the best of the campaign biographies, includes details that came from interviews at the candidate's home in Mentor.

**344.** _____. *The Nation's Hero: In Memoriam, The Life of James Abram Garfield...With an Account of the President's Death and Funeral Obsequies.* New York: A. S. Barnes & Co., 1881. Bundy's book was reissued with a thirty-page addition discussing the administration and assassination.

**345.** Caldwell, Robert Granville. *James A. Garfield: Party Chieftain.* New York: Dodd, Mead, 1931. Dated biography that portrays him more as a drifting politician than a statesman.

**346.** Coffin, Charles Carleton. *The Life of James A. Garfield: With a Sketch of the Life of Chester A. Arthur.* Boston: J. H. Earle, 1880. New Hampshire journalist who had met Garfield during the Civil War produced this well-written though rushed campaign biography.

**347.** Conwell, Russell Herman. *The Life, Speeches and Public Services of Gen. James A. Garfield of Ohio.* Indianapolis: F. L. Horton, 1880. This laudatory campaign biography has an introduction by Mark Hopkins. The author first met him at Shiloh and after the nomination often visited him in Mentor to gather information.

**348.** Doenecke, Justus D. *The Presidencies of James A. Garfield & Chester A. Arthur.* American Presidency Series. Lawrence: Regents Press of Kansas, 1981. This revisionist study challenges the foreign policy as well as the presidential stereotypes. Sees Garfield as weak, but contends that both he and Arthur helped contribute to the revival of the presidency.

**349.** Fallows, Rev. Samuel. *Life of William McKinley: Our Martyred President, with Short Biographies of Lincoln and Garfield.* Chicago: Regan Printing House, 1901. Chap. 25. 333–343. Has a short biographical sketch and the 1886 dedication speech of the Garfield statue in Congress.

**350.** Fuer, Howard B., ed. *James A. Garfield, 1831–1881; Chester A. Arthur, 1830–1886; Chronology-Documents-Bibliographical Aids.* Presidential Chronology Series. Dobbs Ferry, N.Y.: Oceana, 1970. Contains a brief bibliography, a chronology, and some edited documents.

**351.** Fuller, Corydon E. *Reminiscences of James A. Garfield, with Notes Preliminary and Collateral.* Cincinnati: Standard Co., 1887. Written by a close friend from Hiram, this book contains series of letters from Garfield as well as important early information.

**352.** Goebel, Dorothy B., and Julius Goebel, Jr. *Generals in the White House.* Freeport, N.Y.: Books for Libraries Press, 1945. 212–22. This hostile account of Garfield's activities as a soldier asserts that he lacked the "quality of steadfastness."

**353.** Green, Francis Marion. *A Royal Life; Or, the Eventful History of James A. Garfield, Twentieth President of the United States.* Chicago: Central Book Concern, 1882. A former pupil and longtime friend, Green in 1868 composed a sketch of then General Garfield.

**354.** [Hope, Evita]. *New World Heroes: Lincoln and Garfield: The Life Story of Two Self-made Men, Whom People Made Presidents.* London: W. Scott, 1884. 151–358. Finds lessons for British youth in the lives of these presidents who worked their way up from lowly positions.

**355.** Hosterman, Arthur David. *Life and Times of James Abram Garfield: Twentieth President of the United States.* Springfield, Ohio: Farm and Fireside, 1882. Inspirational contemporary biography written for children.

**356.** Houdek, John Thomas. "James A. Garfield and Rutherford B. Hayes: A Study in State and National Politics." Ph.D. dissertation, Michigan State University, 1971.

**357.** Kennedy, E. B. "Life of General J. A. Garfield." In *Our Presidential Candidates and Political Compendium . . .* Newark, N.J.: F. C. Bliss & Company, 1880. Chap. 2. 25–68. Flattering account.

**358.** Key, William S. *Life and Works of President Garfield, with an Account of His Tragic Death.* London: Simpkin, Marshall, 1882.

**359.** Kirke, Edmund, [pseud. of Gilmore, James R.]. *The Life of James A. Garfield: Candidate for the Presidency with Extracts from His Speeches.* New York: Harpers Brothers, 1880. The author, who met Garfield in 1863, wrote a biographical sketch after visiting Ohio. After the nomination he wrote one of the earliest and shortest campaign biographies by adding some press clippings to his notes and the sketch.

**360.** Leech, Margaret, and Harry J. Brown. *The Garfield Orbit.* New York: Harper & Row, 1978. Concentrating on the years before 1863, this biography focuses on his personal life during his youth with special emphasis on his relationship with women. Brown completed Leech's unfinished manuscript.

**361.** *Life and Death of James A. Garfield.* New York: Butler Brothers, 1881. Part of the Electric series of popular dime novels, this pamphlet concentrates on his assassination and reflects the popular interest in the slain President.

**362.** Lossing, Benson John. *A Biography of James A. Garfield.* New York: H. S. Goodspeed & Co., 1882. This inspirational biography was intended for American youth.

**363.** McCabe, James Dabney. *From the Farm to the Presidential Chair, Being an Accurate and Comprehensive Account of the Life and Public Services of Gen. James A. Garfield, To Which Is Added the Life of Gen. Chester A. Arthur.* Philadelphia: National Publishing Co., 1880. This campaign biography includes one chapter on Arthur.

**364.** _____. *Our Martyred President: The Life and Public Service of Gen. James A. Garfield . . . Together with the History of His Assassination . . .* Chicago: W. M. Farrar, 1881. This revision of **363** includes three additional chapters covering the assassination.

**365.** McClure, James Baird, ed. *General Garfield from the Log Cabin to the White House, Including His Early History, War Record, Public Speeches, Nominations, Inauguration, Assassination, Death, and Burial.* Chicago: Rhodes and McClure, 1881. An expanded revision of **366**.

**366.** _____. *Stories and Sketches of Gen. Garfield, Including His Early History, War Record, Public Speeches . . . and All the Interesting Facts of His Great Career.* Chicago: Rhodes & McClure, 1880. This campaign biography contains many praiseworthy anecdotes attesting to the candidate's character.

**367.** Mason, Captain F. H. *The Life and Public Service of James A. Garfield . . . Biographical Sketch.* London: Tribune and Co., 1881. Sympathetic sketch prepared for European audience by a journalist who was a former student of and a staff officer for Garfield.

**368.** Nevin, David Jenkins. *Biographical Sketches of Gen'l James A. Garfield and Gen'l Chester A. Arthur: Republican Nominees for the Presidency and Vice-Presidency of the United States.* Philadelphia: Presidential Printing and Publishing Co., 1880. Standard campaign biography.

**369.** Ogilvie, John S. *The Life and Death of James A. Garfield: From the Tow Path to the White House.* New York: J. S. Ogilvie and Co., 1882. Half of this four-hundred-page biography is an account of the assassination, trial, and national response.

**370.** Peskin, Allan. *Garfield: A Biography.* Kent, Ohio: Kent State University Press, 1978. The definitive biography makes extensive use of existing manuscripts to trace his personal and public life.

**371.** _____. "Garfield." *The American Presidents: The Office and the Men.* Ed. Frank N. Magill. Massachusetts: Salem Press, 1986. 397–400.

**372.** Phelps, William Walter. "James A. Garfield" in *The Presidents of the United States, 1789–1914.* Ed. James Grant Wilson. Vol. 3: 161–94. New York: Scribners, 1914. Flattering review.

**373.** Quad, M. *The Comic Biography of James A. Garfield; Prepared from Carefully Selected Stock and Warranted Perfectly Fresh. Edited by Detroit Free-Press Man.* New York: Chic Publishing Company, 1880. This anti-Garfield campaign pamphlet with numerous cartoons ridicules his political career by emphasizing his scandals and his use of "bloody shirt" rhetoric.

**374.** Reid, J. A., and R. A. Reid. *. . . Garfield's Career: From the Tow-path to the White House; His Seventy-nine Days' Struggle for Life, the Public Obsequies.* Providence, R.I.: J. A. & R. A. Reid Publishers, 1881. Biographical pamphlet.

**375.** Rennick, Susan. *Buckeye Boys Who Have Become Presidents: Six Sons of Ohio and Their Part in the Nation's History*. Chicago: L. W. Walter Company, 1911. 121–60.

**376.** Riddle, Albert Gallatin. *The Life, Character and Public Service of Jas. A. Garfield*. Cleveland: W. W. Williams, 1880. This campaign biography by a close friend of Garfield was made by making a few additions to the biographical sketch in **405**.

**377.** Ridpath, John Clark. *The Life and Work of James A. Garfield: Embracing an Account of the Scenes and Incidents of His Boyhood; The Struggle of His Youth; His Valor as a Soldier; His Career as a Statesman; His Election to the Presidency; And the Tragic Story of His Death*. Cincinnati: Jones Brothers and Co., 1881. An adoring biography that is a good source of information on the early years.

**378.** Rutherford, William G. *President Lincoln and James Garfield: The Story of Their Lives*. London: Sunday School Union, 1890.

**379.** Stoddard, William Osborn. "James A. Garfield: Twentieth President." In *The Lives of the Presidents*, vol. 9: *Rutherford Birchard Hayes, James A. Garfield and Chester Alan Arthur*. New York: F. A. Stokes & Brothers, 1889. A dated account without notes.

**380.** Taylor, John M. *Garfield of Ohio: The Available Man*. New York: Norton, 1970. State Department official using material in Library of Congress portrays Garfield as a man of contradictions.

**381.** Thayer, William M. *From Log-Cabin to the White House: Life of James A. Garfield, Boyhood, Youth, Manhood, Assassination*. Boston: James H. Earle, 1881. This campaign biography by the author of the popular work on Lincoln stresses the similarities of the two presidents.

**382.** Weisenberger, Bernard A. "James A. Garfield/Chester Arthur." In *The Presidents: A Reference History*. Ed. Henry Graff. New York: Charles Scribner's Sons, 1984. 325–36.

# 4

# Childhood

**383.** Booraem, Hendrick. *The Road to Respectability: James A. Garfield and His World, 1844–1852.* Lewisburg, Pa.: Bucknell University Press, 1988. Investigates Garfield's adolescence.

**384.** Boynton, Henry B. "Early Life of Garfield." *Hiram College Advance* 6 (June 1896): 198–99. Written by a relative of Garfield's.

**385.** Bridge, William Dawson. *Genealogy of the John Bridge Family in America, 1632–1924.* Rev. ed. by Reverend Bridge. Cambridge, Mass.: Murray Printing Co., 1924. 411–24. First published in 1884, this book includes a section on the Garfield family, starting with Edward Garfield, who came to America in the 1630s.

**386.** *Burke's Presidential Families of the United States of America.* London: Burke's Peerage Limited, 1975. 347–57. Contains short biography (347–53) and discussion of Garfield's lineage back to 1575 (354–57).

**387.** Cottom, Robert Irving, Jr. "To Be Among the First: The Early Career of James A. Garfield, 1831–1868." Ph.D. dissertation, Johns Hopkins University, 1975. Uses an emphasis on psychoanalysis in reviewing Garfield's first 35 years.

**388.** Hatcher, Harlan. *The Western Reserve: The Story of New Connecticut in Ohio.* Indianapolis: Bobbs-Merrill, 1949. Background on the region, containing only a few references to Garfield.

**389.** Henry, Frederick Augustine. *Captain Henry of Geauga: A Family Chronicle.* Cleveland: Gates Press, 1942. Chaps. 5–8, 11. Provides some insight and anecdotes about Garfield at Hiram, in the war, and in Ohio politics by an author who knew him at Hiram and served with him in Kentucky.

**390.** Henry, Reginald Buchanan. *Genealogies of the Families of the Presidents.* Rutland, Vt.: Turtle Co., 1935. 249–50.

**391.** Historical Society of Geauga County, Ohio. *Pioneer and General History of Geauga County, With Sketches of Some Pioneers and Prominent Men.* Burton, Ohio: Historical Society of Geauga County, 1880. Provides limited background on the county.

**392.** _____. *Pioneer and General History of Geauga County.* Cleveland: Geauga County History and Memorial Society, 1953. 68–71. General overview of the county; provides only a few scattered citations on Garfield.

**393.** Hoar, George Frisbie. *President Garfield's New England Ancestry: Read at the Annual Meeting of the American Antiquarian Society, in Worcester, Oct. 21st, 1881.* Worcester, Mass.: C. Hamilton, 1882. Paper prepared by the Massachusetts senator who was a political associate of Garfield's.

**394.** Hoff, Rhoda. *They Grew up to Be Presidents.* New York: Doubleday, 1971. 85–89. General account of Garfield's childhood.

**395.** Howells, William Dean. *Years of My Youth & Three Essays.* New York: Harper & Brothers, 1916. 204–7. Howells's father was an Ohio editor and an acquaintance of Garfield's. Provides anecdotes about the author's meetings with Garfield.

**396.** Jackson, Ronald Vern. *James Abram Garfield and Lucretia Rudolph Ancestry.* Bountiful, Utah: Accelerated Indexing Systems, 1980. Traces lineage back 300 years.

**397.** Lake County Historical Society. *Here Is Lake County, Ohio.* Cleveland: Howard Allen, 1964. 90, 96–97. County history contains only a few citations on Garfield, but does provide a catalogue of important people and places in Garfield's region.

**398.** Lottick, Kenneth V. "Cultural Transplantation in the Connecticut Reserve." *History and Philosophical Society of Ohio Bulletin* 17 (1959): 154–66. Reemphasizes the New England origins that Garfield often acknowledged.

**399.** _____. "The Western Reserve and the Frontier Thesis." *Ohio Historical Quarterly* 70 (1961): 45–57. Supports Garfield's expressed belief that the Western Reserve was an "extension of Connecticut's social, political and educational structure."

**400.** Null, Anne. "The Garfield Log Cabin." *Western Reserve Historical Society News* 29 (May-June 1975): 2–6. Notes that the cabin presently located at Lawnfield is not an "authentic" replica of the original, which stood 1830–1854. Includes pictures of the cabin and James Hope's popular print.

**401.** Perry, Enos J. *The Boyhood Days of Our Presidents.* Chicago: Adams Press, 1971. 161–69. Folksy anecdotes.

**402.** Peskin, Allan. "The Western Reserve's Favorite Son." *Western Reserve Magazine* 7 (September-October 1980): 39–47. Discusses Garfield's close identification with the Western Reserve as a source of his strength. Notes that his unglamorous boyhood laid the "foundations for political success."

**403.** Pessen, Edward. *The Log Cabin Myth: The Social Backgrounds of the Presidents.* New Haven, Conn.: Yale University Press, 1984. This debunking book has to contend with Garfield—the last president literally born in a log cabin. Asserts that Garfield was not really poor because he had a good education and his mother did not live off charity.

**404.** Porter, Edward Griffin. *Concerning President Garfield's Ancestry: A Communication from the Rev. Edward G. Porter, Read at the October Meeting of the Massachusetts Historical Society.* Cambridge: Cambridge University Press, 1881. Includes a memorandum Garfield wrote in 1858 on his mother's recollection of their family history and a copy of Edward Garfield's 1668 will.

**405.** Riddle, A. G. *Williams' History of Geauga and Lake Counties, Ohio, with Illustrations and Biographical Sketches of its Pioneers and Most Prominent Men.* Philadelphia: Williams Brothers, 1878. Includes an extended biographical sketch of Garfield based on notes from him and interviews with several of his friends.

**406.** Shackleton, Robert. "The Western Reserve." *New England Magazine* 14 (1896): 334–38. This portrait of the Western Reserve in the 1890s emphasized its resemblance to New England. Calls the Reserve a "virtual new Connecticut."

**407.** Smith, Bessie White. *The Boyhoods of the Presidents.* Boston: Lathrop, Lee and Shepard, 1924. 188–97. Limited value.

# 5
# Education

## A. Hiram College

**408.** Allmendinger, David F., Jr. "The Dangers of Ante-bellum Student Life." *Journal of Social History* 7 (Fall 1973): 75–85. This examination of student disorder in colleges such as Amherst provides insight since Hiram resembled the New England college model.

**409.** Davis, Harold Eugene. *Garfield of Hiram: A Memorial to the Life and Services of James Abram Garfield; Published on the Occasion of the Centennial of His Birth, November 19, 1931.* Hiram Historical Society Publication. Hiram: Hiram Historical Society, 1931. A reprint of **1389** with additional quotations.

**410.** _____. *Hinsdale of Hiram: The Life of Burke Aaron Hinsdale: Pioneer Educator, 1837–1900.* Washington: University Press of Washington, 1971. 126–37. Discusses his years at college where Garfield was his mentor and close friend.

**411.** Fletcher, William Harold. "Amos Sutton Hayden: Symbol of a Movement." Ph.D. dissertation, University of Oklahoma, 1988. Examination of the church leader who served as Hiram's first president and mentor for Garfield, who succeeded him in 1857.

**412.** Garfield, James A. "The Material and the Spiritual, A Sermon . . . Garfield Preached at Hiram College in 1857 as Reported by (Hiram Student) Alanson Wilcox." Newspaper clipping, n.d. Pamphlet Collection-PA Box 81. Ohio Historical Society, Columbus. Warns against materialism and urged attention to the spiritual.

**413.** "Garfield House Is Their Home." *Western Reserve Magazine* 2 (1974): 6–10. Built in 1852, this house in 1860 was purchased by Garfield, who made renovations. The house then belonged to Hinsdale, the new college president.

**414.** Green, Francis Marion. *Hiram College and Western Reserve Eclectic Institute: Fifty Years of History, 1850–1900*. Cleveland: O. S. Hubbell Printing Co., 1901. Written by an alumnus who was a student of Garfield's.

**415.** Harper, Martha M. "James Abram Garfield, Educator." M.A. thesis, Hiram College, 1927. Discussion of Garfield's desire for education.

**416.** Hinsdale, Burke Aaron. "The History of Popular Education in the Western Reserve." *Ohio Archaeological and Historical Publications* 6 (January 1898): 45–58. Notes that the overabundance of teachers in the area made it a "nursery of school teachers" as many (including Garfield) left to seek jobs elsewhere.

**417.** _____. *President Garfield and Education: Hiram College Memorial*. Boston: J. R. Osgood, 1882. Contains Garfield's twelve educational addresses including "College Education" (277–312) and "Some Tendencies in American Education" (335–39). Also has an essay on Garfield's relationship to Hiram and **1389**.

**418.** Hinsdale, Ellen C. "The Garfield-Hinsdale House: A House of Memories, II." *Pickup from the American Way*. Hiram Historical Society (1947), 13–20. These reminiscences by the daughter of the Hiram's president include stories of Garfield's visit to 1880 commencement.

**419.** Hiram College. *First Annual Catalogue of Hiram College*. Hiram: Fairbanks, Benedict and Co., 1868.

**420.** Hiram College. *James Abram Garfield, 1831–1881: Addresses Delivered at a Service of Memory, on the Occasion of the One Hundredth Anniversary of His Birth*. Hiram, Ohio: Hiram College, 1931. Reprint of *Hiram College Bulletin*, vol. 23, no. 4, November, 1931.

**421.** Osgood, Elliott I. *In the Days of Old Hiram*. Hiram, Ohio: Hiram Historical Society, 1931. This pamphlet on the college's history has a few comments on Garfield.

**422.** Rudolph, Adelaide, and Ellen C. Hinsdale. *Two Early Hiram Houses: The Garfield-Hinsdale House, A House of Memories*. Hiram, Ohio: Hiram Historical Society, 1947. A relative of Lucretia Garfield's discusses the first house owned by the Garfields and her memories of visiting it as a child.

**423.** Starr, Michael E. "The Hiram College Garfield Commemorative Lectures." *Hayes Historical Journal* 3, no.4 (Fall 1981): 5–9. This introduction to the lectures provides a brief review of Garfield's life.

**424.** Trudley, Mary Bosworth. *Prelude to the Future: The First Hundred Years of Hiram College*. New York: Associated Press, 1950. Centennial history includes coverage of its most famous graduates.

## B. Williams College

**425.** Durfee, Calvin. *A History of Williams College*. Boston: A. Williams, 1860. Contemporary account.

**426.** Perry, Arthur Lathan. *Williamstown and Williams College*. Norwood, Mass.: The author, 1899. Massive but partisan and dated history.

**427.** Rudolph, Frederick. *Mark Hopkins and the Log: Williams College, 1836–1872*. New Haven: Yale University Press, 1956. Well-written biography on an influential educator.

**428.** Spring, Leverett W. *A History of Williams College*. Boston: Houghton Mifflin, 1917. Short history of the college.

**429.** Williams College Class of 1856. *Williams College, Class of 1856 (Class History)* N.p., 1898. 6–16. A section on James Abraham (*sic*) Garfield includes reminiscences by some classmates.

**430.** Wilson, Carroll A. "Familiar Small College Quotations, II: 'Mark Hopkins and the Log.'" *Colophon*, n.s. 3 (1938): 194–209. Questions the accuracy of Garfield's famous 1871 quote—"The ideal college is Mark Hopkins on one end of a log and a student on the other."

## C. Education Views

**431.** Gallaudet, Edward Miner. *President Garfield's Connection with the National Deaf-Mute College, Washington, D.C.* Washington: Gibson Brothers, printers, 1882. The college's president recounts Garfield's support and visits to the institution. Reprint from *American Annals of the Deaf and Dumb*, January 1882.

**432.** Rudolph, Frederick. *The American College and University*. New York: Alfred A. Knopf, 1962. 243. This history of American higher education that notes Garfield's defense of the old-time college values and teaching placed him at odds with post-Civil War trends.

**433.** Sawyer, Robert W. "James A. Garfield and the Classics." *Hayes Historical Journal* 3 (Fall 1981): 47–56. Discusses Garfield's love of the Greek language and his struggle between an academic and political career.

# 6
# Antebellum Years and Ohio Politics

**434.** Howard, Victor B. "The 1856 Election in Ohio: Moral Issues in Politics." *Ohio History* 70 (1971): 24–44. Asserts that the Republican victory marked "the successful political uprising" of evangelical churches focusing on slavery as a moral issue.

**435.** Land, Mary. "John Brown's Ohio Environment." *Ohio State Archaeological and Historical Quarterly* 57 (January 1948): 24–47. Discussion of the strong antislavery feelings in the Western Reserve.

**436.** Monroe, James. *Oberlin Thursday Lectures, Addresses and Essays*. Oberlin, Ohio: E. J. Goodrich, 1897. Author recounts his days in the Ohio legislature and in Congress, including observations on Garfield.

**437.** North, Ira L. "A Rhetorical Study of the Public Speaking of James A. Garfield, 1851–1859. Ph.D. dissertation, Western Reserve University, 1958.

**438.** Porter, Lorle A. "The Lecompton Issue in Knox County Politics: Division of the Democracy, 1858." *Ohio History* 81 (Summer 1972): 157–92. This study of the press provides a good look at the bitter divisions of Ohio politics.

**439.** Riddle, A. G. "Rise of the Anti-Slavery Sentiment in the Western Reserve." *Magazine of Western History* 6 (June 1887): 145–56. A general and dated review of the chronological rise of antislavery feeling in the area.

**440.** Wyatt-Brown, Bertram. "Reform and Anti-Reform in Garfield's Ohio." *Hayes Historical Journal* 3 (Spring 1982): 63–78. Explains Garfield's bitter outrage at slavery and the South as part of a challenge to traditional custom by a secular order.

# 7
# Military Career

## A. Civil War Histories and Generals

**441.** Dana, Charles A. *Recollections of the Civil War, With the Leaders at Washington and in the Field in the Sixties*. New York: D. Appleton & Co., 1898. Chaps. 8–10. Critical observations of Rosecrans in Tennessee by the person sent by Secretary of War Stanton to observe the general.

**442.** Eaton, Clement. *A History of the Southern Confederacy*. New York: Collier Books, 1961.

**443.** Faust, Patricia L. *Historical Times Illustrated Encyclopedia of the Civil War*. New York: Harper & Row, 1986. Entries on Rosecrans (642–43), Marshall (476), and Chickamauga battle (136–38).

**444.** Fiske, John. *The Mississippi Valley in the Civil War*. Boston: Houghton-Mifflin Co., 1900. Chap. 2–Shiloh; Chap. 7–Chickamauga.

**445.** Foote, Shelby. *The Civil War: A Narrative; Fredericksburg to Meridan*. New York: Random House, 1963. 712–57. Account of Chickamauga.

**446.** Gilmore, James R. (Edmund Kirke, pseud.). *On the Border*. Boston: L. C. Page & Co., 1890.

**447.** _____. *Down in Tennessee, and Back by Way of Richmond*. New York: Carlton, Publisher, 1864. Observations by the author, who met Garfield in Tennessee during the war.

**448.** _____. *Personal Recollections of Abraham Lincoln and the Civil War*. Boston: L. C. Page, 1898. 118–31, 222–26. A close acquaintance of Garfield's provides insight on the military involvement of the future President as well as Rosecrans.

**449.** Greeley, Horace. *The American Conflict: A History of the Great Rebellion in the United States of America.* Hartford, Conn.: O. D. Case and Company, 1871. 42–44, 414–23.

**450.** *Harper's Pictorial History of the Great Rebellion.* 2 vols. New York: Harper, 1868.

**451.** Hazen, W. B. *A Narrative of Military Service.* Boston: Ticknor & Co., 1885. Author was an officer at Chickamauga.

**452.** Jones, Archer. *Confederate Strategy from Shiloh to Vicksburg.* Baton Rouge: Louisiana State University Press, 1961. This favorable reinterpretation of Confederate leaders investigates Johnston's "western plan" for defense of the region.

**453.** Keifer, Joseph Warren. *Slavery and Four Years of War: A Political History of Slavery Together with a Narrative of the Campaigns and Battles of the Civil War in which the Author Took Part: 1861–1865.* 2 vols. New York: G. P. Putnam's Sons, 1900.

**454.** MacCartney, Clarence Edward. *Grant and His Generals.* New York: McBride Co., 1953. Grant's view of Thomas.

**455.** Nevins, Allan. *The War for the Union.* 4 vols. New York: Scribner, 1959–1971. Vol. 2:75-87. Shiloh; Vol. 3:198–206. Chickamauga.

**456.** Riddle, Albert Gallatin. *Recollections of War Times: Reminiscences of Men and Events in Washington, 1860–1865.* New York: G. P. Putnam's Sons, 1895.

**457.** Shannon, Fred Albert. *The Organization and Administration of the Union Army: 1861–1865.* 2 vols. Cleveland: Arthur H. Clark Co., 1928. Alleges that an "air of bias" surrounded military commissions, causing officers to be dismissed without resort to official court martial procedure. See **492** for contrary view.

**458.** Wakelyn, Jon. *Biographical Dictionary of the Confederacy.* Westport, Conn.: Greenwood Press, 1977. Bragg (105–6) and Marshall (311–12).

**459.** *The War of the Rebellion: A Compilation of the Official Records of the Union and Confederate Armies.* 128 vols. Washington: Government Printing Office, 1880–1901. Classic official study of the Civil War.

**460.** Warner, Ezra J. *Generals in Blue: Lives of the Union Commanders.* New Orleans: Louisiana State University Press, 1964. Short biographical sketches of Garfield (166–67), Rosecrans (410–11), and Thomas 500–01.

**461.** _____. *Generals in Grey: Lives of the Confederate Commanders.* New Orleans: Louisiana State University Press, 1964. Short biographical sketches of Bragg (30–31) and Marshall (212–13).

**462.** Williams, Kenneth P. *Lincoln Finds a General: A Military Study of the Civil War.* 5 vols. New York: Macmillan, 1949–1950.

**463.** Williams, T. Harry. *Lincoln and His Generals*. New York: Alfred A. Knopf, 1952. Includes a discussion of his strained relationship with Rosecrans.

## B. Garfield as General and Ohio's Role

**464.** Cox, Jacob Dolson. *Military Reminiscences of the Civil War*. 2 vols. New York: C. Scribner's Sons, 1900. Vol. 1:6–7, 200, 483–84; Vol. 2: 8–16, 396–98. Garfield's intimate friend provides observations at the start of the war and at Chickamauga.

**465.** Marshall, S. L. A. "Garfield as a General." *Civil War Times Illustrated*, September, 1968: 4–6, 45–47. Military historian describes Garfield as an "ideal type of American civilian soldier."

**466.** Mason, F. H. *The Forty-Second Ohio Infantry: A History of the Organization and Services of that Regiment in the War of the Rebellion with Big Sketches of Its Full Officers*. Cleveland: Cobb, Andrews & Co., 1876. 75–92. Account of the regiment's activities in Kentucky.

**467.** *Official Roster of the Soldiers of the State of Ohio in the War of the Rebellion, 1861–1866*. Vol. 4 Akron: Werner Co., 1886–1895.

**468.** Peskin, Allan. "James A. Garfield." In *For the Union: Ohio Leaders in the Civil War*. Ed. Kenneth W. Wheeler. [Columbus]: Ohio State University Press, 1968. Reviews Garfield's military role, noting that he was one of only four major generals who had no military experience.

**469.** Reid, Whitelaw. *Ohio in the War: Her Generals, and Her Soldiers*. 2 vols. Cincinnati: Moore, Wilstach and Baldwin, 1868. Vol. 1: 739–64; Vol.2: 266–70. This contemporary review of the military and political events during the war includes an early biographical account of Garfield and a discussion of the 42nd Regiment.

**470.** Roseboom, Eugene H. *The Civil War Era: 1850–1873*. Vol. 4 of *The History of the State of Ohio*. Ed. Carl Wittke. Columbus: Ohio Historical Society, 1944. Standard state history.

**471.** Schurtleff, G. W. "A Year with the Rebels." *Sketches of War History, 1861–1865. Papers Read Before the Ohio Commandery of the Military Order of the Loyal Legion of the United States*. Cincinnati: R. Clark, 1888. Vol. 4 Among other stories, relates Garfield's election loss to Eratus Taylor as colonel of the 7th regiment.

**472.** Tourgee, Albion W. *The Story of a Thousand*. New York: S. McGerald and Son, 1896. Chs. 18–19. This history of the 105th regiment of the Ohio Volunteer Infantry has two chapters on Chickamauga. Author served in this unit until December 1863.

## C. Kentucky Campaign

**473.** Copeland, James E. "Where Were the Kentucky Unionists and Secessionists?" *Register of the Kentucky Historical Society* 71 (1973): 344–63. Finds geographic differences within the state on secession. The secessionist sentiment was strongest in the western part of the state and weakest in the south-central and northeast.

**474.** Coulter, E. Merton. *The Civil War and Readjustment in Kentucky.* Chapel Hill: University of North Carolina Press, 1926. Focuses on the politics of the war rather than the military battles.

**475.** _____. "Humphrey Marshall." *DAB* (1933), vol. 12:309–11.

**476.** Guerrant, Edward O. "Marshall and Garfield in Eastern Kentucky." In *Battles and Leaders of the Civil War*. Eds. Robert Underwood Johnson and Clarence Clough Buel. New York: Thomas Yoseloff, Inc., 1887–1888. 1: 393–97. Critical review of Marshall by his adjutant-general. An eyewitness account from the "*Century* War Series."

**477.** Johnson, R. N., and C. C. Bull. *Battles and Leaders of the Civil War.* New York: Thomas Yoseloff Co., 1886. Vol. 1:87–88.

**478.** Levin, H, ed. *The Lawyers and Lawmakers of Kentucky.* 1897: rpt. Easley, S.C.: Southern Historical Press, 1982. 174–80. Short biographical sketch of Garfield's opponent in the Sandy Valley, Kentucky campaign.

**479.** Peskin, Allan. "The Hero of the Sandy Valley: James A. Garfield's Kentucky Campaign of 1861–1862." *Ohio History* 72 (January and April 1963): 3–24, 139–49. Details Garfield's successful efforts in stopping the Confederate "miniature invasion" of eastern Kentucky.

**480.** Schuster, Richard. *The Selfish and the Strong.* New York: Random House, 1958. Novel based on Garfield's Kentucky campaign.

## D. General Fitz-John Porter's Court-martial

**481.** Cox, Jacob Dolson. *Second Battle of Bull Run as Connected with the Fitz-John Porter Case.* Cincinnati: Peter G. Thompson, 1882. Garfield associate believes that Porter was guilty. Includes documents as well as views in 1880 of Garfield, who served at Porter's court-martial in 1862.

**482.** Eisenschiml, Otto. *The Celebrated Case of Fitz-John Porter: An American Dreyfus Affair.* New York: Bobbs-Merrill Co., 1950. Asserts that the general never forgave Garfield for his voting against him at the military trial and refusing to support Porter's fight for vindication—referred to as the "Third Battle of Bull Run."

**483.** *Fitz-John Porter Case. Official Reports of Investigations: 1862, House Reports*, 37th Cong., 3rd sess., No. 71, 1862; and in *Senate Reports*, 46th Cong., 1st sess., No. 37, 1879.

**484.** Grant, Ulysses. "An Undeserved Stigma." *North American Review* 135 (December 1882): 536–46. Grant reviews the battle and suggests restoration for Fitz-John Porter.

**485.** Lord, Theodore A. *A Summary of the Case of General Fitz-John Porter*. San Francisco: Croker & Co., 1883. Believes that Porter was a scapegoat for General Pope, who was beaten by his own mistakes.

**486.** McDonough, James L. *Schofield: Union General in the Civil War and Reconstruction*. Tallahassee: Florida State University, 1972. Book ends at 1868 before the general chaired the review board on Porter.

**487.** Porter, Fitz-John. Papers. Library of Congress. Manuscript refers to his trial and dismissal from service for "alleged negligence at Second Bull Run."

**488.** Porter, Lucia Chauncey. Correspondence, 1853–1917. United States Military Academy, West Point, N.Y. 429 items. Most of collection by his daughter is concerned with responses by former Civil War officers to her requests for help in clearing her father.

**489.** *Report of the Board of Officers in the Case of Fitz-John Porter, Late Major-General of Volunteers*. Washington: Army and Navy Gazette, 1879. Board of officers convened at West Point in June, 1878 to hear charges against the general.

**490.** Ropes, John C. "The Hearing in the Case of Fitz-John Porter." In the *Papers of Military History of Massachusetts*. Vol. 2: *The Virginia Campaign of 1862 Under General Pope*. Ed. Theodore F. Dwight. Boston: Houghton Mifflin and Company, 1895. 349–86. Concurs with the decision of the review board.

**491.** Schofield, [J. M.]. *Forty-six Years in the Army* New York: Century Club, 1897. 241–43. Brief reference to the review board he chaired.

**492.** Swart, Stanley L. "The Military Examination Board in the Civil War: A Case Study." *Civil War History* 16 (1970): 227–45. This examination of one commission challenges critics who believed that the military commissions were unfair.

**493.** Weld, Stephen M. "The Case of Fitz-John Porter." In the *Papers of Military History of Massachusetts*. Vol. 2: *The Virginia Campaign of 1862 Under General Pope*. Ed. Theodore F. Dwight. Boston: Houghton Mifflin and Company, 1895. 221–62. Argues that the case should be reopened.

## E. Army of the Cumberland: Chickamauga

### 1. Battle Accounts

**494.** Cist, Henry M. *The Army of the Cumberland*. New York: C. Scribner's Sons, 1970. Staff officer reviews the performance of Rosecrans and Thomas.

**495.** Cozzens, Peter. *This Terrible Sound: The Battle of Chickamauga*. Urbana: University of Illinois Press, 1992. A thorough, well-written account of the "barren victory" that "sealed the fate of the South," includes detailed maps and bibliography.

**496.** Fitch, John ("An Officer," pseud.) *Annals of the Army of the Cumberland*. Philadelphia: J. B. Lippincott & Co., 1863. Hastily assembled contemporary account of the army contains chapters on Rosecrans and Thomas.

**497.** Gracie, Archibald. *The Truth About Chickamauga*. Boston: Houghton-Mifflin, 1911. Hostile book by an amateur historian who charges that a cover up promoted Union heroism and undermined the magnitude of this Confederate victory.

**498.** Hill, Daniel H. "Chickamauga—The Great Battle of the West." In *Battles and Leaders of the Civil War*. Ed. Robert Underwood Johnson and Clarence Clough Buel. New York: Thomas Yoseloff, Inc., 1887–1888. Vol. 3:393–97. Confederate officer is critical of Bragg.

**499.** Smith, Theodore Clarke. "General Garfield at Chickamauga." *Proceedings of the Massachusetts Historical Society* 48 (February 1915): 268–80. Upholds Garfield's critical view of Rosecrans.

**500.** Stanley, David Sloane. *Personal Memoirs*. Cambridge: Harvard University Press, 1917. Hostile assessment of Garfield as chief of staff.

**501.** Tucker, Glenn. *Chickamauga: Bloody Battle in the West*. Indianapolis: Bobbs-Merrill, 1961. Detailed examination of the battle is critical of Garfield as well as most officers except Thomas.

**502.** Van Horne, Thomas B, and Edward Ruger. *History of the Army of the Cumberland: Its Organization, Campaigns, and Battles*. Vol. 1. Cincinnati: Robert Clarke & Co., 1875. rpt. Wilmington, N.C.: Broadfoot, 1988. Chap. 20, 310–85. Written by a chaplain who also served as unofficial historian.

**503.** Woods, Joseph T. *Steedman and His Men at Chickamauga*. Toledo: Blade Printing Co., 1876. A Union veteran recounts the action of his division under the command of General Steedman.

### 2. Generals at Chickamauga

*Bragg, Braxton*          *Louisiana Confederate commander*

**504.** Bragg, Braxton. Papers. Duke University, Durham, N.C. 49 items. Correspondence on military affairs.

**505.** _____. Papers. Southern Historical Collection, Wilson Library, University of North Carolina at Chapel Hill. 11 items. Military letters and telegrams.

**506.** _____. Papers. United States Military Academy, West Point, N.Y. ca. 15 miscellaneous items.

**507.** _____. Papers. Misssouri Historical Society, St. Louis. 21 letters written to his wife during the Civil War.

**508.** _____. Papers. Galveston and Texas History Center, Rosenberg Library, Galveston, TX. 5 folders, ca. 1849–1878.

**509.** Donald, David, ed. _Divided We Fought: A Pictorial History of the Civil War, 1861–1865_. New York: Macmillan, 1952. 229. Bragg is described as a "tense dawdler."

**510.** Dowdey, Clifford. _The Land They Fought For: The Story of the South as the Confederacy, 1832–65_. Garden City, N.Y.: Doubleday, 1955. 227–28. Hostile assessment of Bragg as "a warrior who couldn't make up his mind."

**511.** Lanza, Frederic Logan. "Braxton Bragg." _DAB_ (1928) vol. 20:585–87.

**512.** McWhiney, Grady. _Braxton Bragg and Confederate Defeat. Volume 1: Field Command_. New York: Columbia University Press, 1969. Balanced account of this controversial general.

**513.** Seitz, Don C. _Braxton Bragg_. Columbia, S.C.: State Co., 1924. Chaps. 6–8. 202–302. Sympathetic and dated account.

**514.** Spiller, Roger J., ed. _Dictionary of American Military Biography_. Westport, Conn.: Greenwood Press, 1984. Vol. 1:111–14.

**515.** Stout, L. H. _Reminiscences of General Braxton Bragg_. Hattiesburg, Miss.: Brook Farm, 1942. Written in 1876 by a surgeon who served in Confederate Army, this pamphlet presents a favorable view of the general.

**516.** Williams, T. Harry. "The Military Leadership of the North and South." In _Why the North Won the Civil War_. Ed. David Donald. Baton Rouge: Louisiana State University Press, 1960. 34. Asserts that Bragg lacked the will.

_Rosecrans, William S._     _Ohio General to whom Garfield served as Chief of Staff_

**517.** Lamers, Williams M. _Edge of Glory_. New York: Harcourt, Brace & World, 1961. Well-researched, balanced account of this controversial general portrays him as a man of ability but with questionable personality traits.

**518.** Mulhane, Lawrence W. "Major Gen. William Starke Rosecrans." _American Catholic Historical Society of Philadelphia_ 35 (Sept. 1924): 242–66. Defends him as a hero and the father of the Cumberland Army.

**519.** Piatt, Donn. "The General Who Heard Mass Before Battle." *The Collector* 1 (June 1942): 55–58. Discusses the general who converted to Catholicism at West Point.

**520.** "Report of the Joint Committee on the Conduct of the War, Part III. Rosecrans's Campaigns." *Senate Document #142*, 38th Cong. 2nd sess. 1864.

**521.** Rosecrans, William Starke. "Mistakes of Grant." *North American Review* 141 (December 1885): 580–99. Defends his record against Grant's written criticisms.

**522.** _____. Papers. University of California at Los Angeles Library. 110 boxes of correspondence, memorabilia, letters of his and his family.

**523.** Society of the Army of the Cumberland. *Burial of General Rosecrans, Arlington National Cemetery, May 17, 1902*. Cincinnati: Robert Clarke Co., 1903. 88–89. Quotes from Rosecrans's account that he went back to Chattanooga at Garfield's urging.

**524.** Spaudling, Oliver L. "William Starke Rosecrans." *DAB* (1935): vol. 16:163–64.

**525.** Taylor, John M. "'With More Sorrow Than I Can Tell': A Future President Turns on His Commander." *Civil War Times Illustrated* (January 1981): 20–29. Traces the uneasy relationship between Garfield and Rosecrans, who was fired after Chickamauga.

*Thomas, George H.*        *Union general credited with saving Chickamauga*

**526.** Cleaves, Freeman. *Rock of Chickamauga: The Life of General George H. Thomas*. Norman: University of Oklahoma Press, 1948. 137–77. General review of his role at the battle.

**527.** Coppee, Henry. *Life of George H. Thomas*. New York: D. Appleton and Company, 1898. Dated sketch.

**528.** Johnson, Richard W., Brig.-Gen. U.S.A. (Retired). *Memoir of Maj. George H. Thomas*. Philadelphia: J. B. Lippincott & Co., 1881.

**529.** McKinney, Francis F. *Education in Violence: The Life of George H. Thomas and the History of the Army of the Cumberland*. Detroit: Wayne State University Press, 1961. Defends Thomas and is hostile to Garfield.

**530.** O'Connor, Richard. *Thomas: Rock of Chickamauga*. New York: Prentice-Hall, 1948. Sympathetic portrayal of Thomas.

**531.** Piatt, Donn, and H. V. Boynton. *General George H. Thomas: A Critical Biography*. Cincinnati: R. Clarke & Co., 1891. Eulogistic view of Thomas and hostile portrayal of Grant.

**532.** Spaudling, Oliver L. "George Henry Thomas." *DAB* (1936) vol. 18: 432–34.

**533.** Thomas, George H. Papers. Huntington Library. San Marino, Calif. 30 letters. 1848–1870. Microfilm copy at New York Public Library, New York. 1 reel-115 frames.

**534.** Thomas, Wilbur. *General George H. Thomas: The Indomitable Warrior.* New York: Exposition Press, 1964. Believes that the general was slighted.

**535.** Van Horne, Thomas B. *The Life of General George H. Thomas.* New York: Charles S. Scribner's Sons, 1882. Biography by the chaplain who was made official historian of the army by Thomas and permitted access to many documents and dispatches.

# 8
# General Works on Politics

## A. National Politics and Parties in the Gilded Age

**536.** Beard, Charles A., and Mary R. Beard. *The Rise of American Civilization.* New York: Macmillan, 1928. Vol 2. Labels period 1865 to 1897 as the "Age of Negation."

**537.** Blodgett, Geoffrey. "A New Look at the American Gilded Age: Politics in a Cultural Context." *Historical Reflections* 1 (Winter 1974): 231–44. Critiques the traditional negative view of the period. Also appears in Walker Howe, *Victorian Age.* Philadelphia: University of Pennsylvania Press, 1976. 95-108.

**538.** Bryce, James. *The American Commonwealth.* New York: Macmillan, 1919. Vol. 2. This classic commentary on Gilded Age politics disparages both parties and politics.

**539.** Curtis, Francis. *The Republican Party: A History of Its Fifty Years: Existence and Record of Its Measures and Leaders, 1854–1904.* 2 vols. New York: G. P. Putnam's Sons, 1904. 2:74–95.

**540.** DeSantis, Vincent, ed. *Gilded Age: Eighteen Seventy-seven to Eighteen Ninety-six.* Arlington Heights, Ill.: Harlan Davidson, 1973.

**541.** _____. "The Political Life of the Gilded Age: A Review of the Recent Literature." *History Teacher* 9 (November 1975): 73–106. Finds traditional negative view of the Gilded Age politics persisted in 1975.

**542.** _____. "The Republican Party Revisited, 1877–1897." In *Gilded Age: A Reappraisal*, edited by Wayne Morgan. Syracuse: Syracuse University Press, 1963. Defends the Republican party against the stereotype of corrupt politicians, Union veterans, and businessmen.

**543.** Edison, William G. "Who Were the Stalwarts?" *Mid-America* 52 (October 1970): 235-61. This roll-call analysis of seven Stalwart senators challenges traditional stereotypes.

**544.** Friedman, Leon. "The Democratic Party, 1860–1884." In **545** 2: 885-986. Describes this period as the "darkest" in the party's history.

**545.** Friedman, Leon, ed. *History of U.S. Political Parties: Vol. 2, 1860–1910: Gilded Age of Politics.* New York: Chelsea House Publishers, 1973.

**546.** Ginger, Ray. *Age of Excess: The United States from 1877 to 1914.* New York: Macmillan, 1965. Chap. 6. 98–128. Skeptical look at the "politics of complacency."

**547.** Gould, Lewis L. "New Perspectives on the Republican Party, 1877–1913." *American Historical Review* 77 (October 1972): 1074–83. This review article notes how recent biographies have "refurnished some damaged reputation" of some post-1877 Republican leaders.

**548.** _____. "The Republican Search for a National Majority." In **542**. 171–87. Argues that Garfield benefitted from upward mobility within a receptive party.

**549.** Hicks, John D. *The American Nation: A History of the United States from 1865 to the Present.* 2 vols. Boston: Houghton Mifflin Company, 1943. Chap. 19, 263–73. Notes that the Democratic trouble in 1880 "was prosperity."

**550.** House, Albert V. "Republicans and Democrats Search for New Identities, 1870–1890." *Review of Politics* 31 (1969): 466–76. Revisionist view finds a "trace of conscience" among the professional political operatives.

**551.** Jensen, Richard. *The Winning of the Midwest: Social and Political Conflict, 1888–1896.* Chicago: University of Chicago Press, 1971. Although the book starts with the 1888 election, the first chapter provides insights into the partisanship of the decade.

**552.** Josephson, Matthew C. *The Politicos, 1865–1896.* New York: Harcourt Brace, 1938. Survey disparages the political leaders of the era as irresponsible spoilsmen.

**553.** Keller, Morton. *Affairs of State: Public Life in Late Nineteenth Century America.* Cambridge, Mass.: Harvard University Press, 1977. This examination of government and law between 1864–1900 provides insight into Garfield's political world.

**554.** Kelley, Robert. "Ideology and Political Culture from Jefferson to Nixon." *American Historical Review* 82 (June 1977): 531–62. Important analysis places Garfield in the context of the American political tradition.

**555.** _____. *The Trans-Atlantic Persuasion: The Liberal and Democratic Mind in the Age of Gladstone.* New York: Alfred A. Knopf, 1969. This comparative study provides insight into Democratic attitudes and programs during the Gilded Age.

**556.** Kent, Frank R. *The Democratic Party: A History*. New York: Century Company, 1928. Chs. 17–19. 220–73.

**557.** Kleppner, Paul. *The Cross of Culture: A Social Analysis of Midwestern Politics, 1850–1900*. New York: Free Press, 1970. Interpretation of politics in Michigan, Ohio, and Wisconsin.

**558.** _____. "The Greenback and Prohibition Parties." In **545**. 2:1549–1700. Claims that the Greenback party was reactionary.

**559.** _____. *The Third Electoral System 1853–1892: Parties, Voters, and Political Cultures*. Chapel Hill: University of North Carolina Press, 1979. This quantitative study characterizes the period as "an era of no decisions" on serious issues.

**560.** Marcus, Robert D. *Grand Old Party: Political Structure in the Gilded Age, 1880–1896*. New York: Oxford University Press, 1971. Chap. 2. Argues that the 1880 campaign reflected the parochial, decentralized nature of the Republican party.

**561.** Mayer, George H. *The Republican Party, 1854–1964*. New York: Oxford University Press, 1964. Chaps. 5, 6. Takes a critical view of the party in the Gilded Age and of the erudite Garfield, who was handicapped by his flexibility and Blaine's intrigues.

**562.** Merrill, Horace Samuel. *Bourbon Democracy of the Middle West, 1865–1896*. Baton Rouge: Louisiana State University Press, 1953. Portrays Garfield's opposition party as dominated by conservatives.

**563.** Minor, Henry. *The Story of the Democratic Party*. New York: Macmillan Company, 1928. Chap. 23. 325–38. Emphasizes role of tariff, currency, and Northern distrust as factors in the 1880 election.

**564.** Moos, Malcolm. *The Republicans: A History of Their Party*. New York: Random House, 1956. 155–62. Standard pro-Republican account.

**565.** Morgan, H. Wayne. "An Age in Need of Reassessment: A View Beforehand." In **542**. 1–13. Argues for a second look at the era.

**566.** _____. *From Hayes to McKinley: National Party Politics*. Syracuse: Syracuse University Press, 1969. A classic reinterpretation of the period finds bland presidents but significant issues and strong national parties.

**567.** _____. "The Republican Party, 1876–1893." In **545**. 2: 1411–1548. Garfield's nomination marked a turning point "away from wartime issues to industrial questions."

**568.** Myers, William S. *The Republican Party: A History*. New York: Century Company, 1928. Chap. 12. 249–79. The book authorized by Republican leadership discusses 1880 from an anti-Conkling and anti-Grant viewpoint.

**569.** Nevins, Allan. *The Emergence of Modern America, 1865–1878.* New York: Macmillan Company, 1927. Vol. 8 of *A History of American Life Series.* A chapter in this social history notes the moral collapse in government and business.

**570.** Ostrogorski, Moisei. *Democracy and the Organization of Political Parties.* 2 vols. 1902; rpt. New York: Doubleday, 1964. Classic study of American politics in the Gilded Age.

**571.** Parrington, Vernon Louis. *The Beginnings of Critical Realism in America, 1860–1920.* New York: Harcourt, Brace and Co., 1930. Dismisses Gilded Age politicians.

**572.** Peskin, Allan. "Who Were the Stalwarts? Who Were Their Rivals?: Republican Factions in the Gilded Age." *Political Science Quarterly* 99 (Winter 1984–85): 783–96. Argues that the party split was real and "not merely empty squabbles over patronage and personalities."

**573.** _____. "Why the Gilded Age?" *Hayes Historical Journal* 5 (Summer 1986): 5–6. Introduction argues for dispassionate look at the era.

**574.** Polakoff, Keith Ian. "The Disorganized Democracy: An Institutional Study of the Democratic Party, 1872–1880." Ph.D. dissertation, Northwestern University, 1968.

**575.** Rhodes, James Ford. *History of the United States from Hayes to McKinley: 1877–1896.* New York: Macmillan, 1919. Chap. 5. 111–38. Detailed but dated political history.

**576.** Salisbury, Robert S. "The Republican Party and Positive Government: 1860–1890." *Mid-America* 68 (January 1986): 15–34. Defends Republicans as more favorably inclined to action than the Democrats.

**577.** Shannon, Fred A. *The Centennial Years: A Political and Economic History of America from the Late 1870's to the Early 1890's.* New York: Doubleday, 1967. Chap. 4, 54–69. Downplays the "tame" election of 1880 and the Garfield administration.

**578.** Tarbell, Ida. *The Nationalizing of Business, 1878–1898.* History of American Life Series. New York: Macmillan Company, 1936. This social history is critical of business, "bigness," and government of the period.

**579.** Williams, R. Hal "'Dry Bones and Dead Language': The Democratic Party." In **542**. 129–48. Believes that Democrats lacked strong organization, vigorous leadership, and unifying issues.

**580.** Wilson, Woodrow. *Congressional Government: A Study in American Politics.* Boston: Houghton-Mifflin, 1885. Classic study by future president.

## B. Ohio Political Studies

**581.** Bonadio, Felice A. *North of Reconstruction: Ohio Politics, 1865–1870*. New York: New York University Press, 1970. Emphasizes Republican factionalism and rise of such new leaders as Garfield, who were concerned with tactics rather than principles.

**582.** _____. "Ohio—A 'Perfect Contempt for All Unity.'" in *Radical Republicans in the North: State Politics during Reconstruction*. Ed. James C. Mohr. 82–103. Baltimore: Johns Hopkins University Press, 1976. Notes the division within the party and the role of dissatisfied young leaders like Garfield.

**583.** Bradford, David H. "The Background and Formation of the Republican Party in Ohio, 1844–1861." Ph.D. dissertation, University of Chicago, 1947.

**584.** Flinn, Thomas A. "Continuity and Change in Ohio Politics." *Journal of Politics* 22 (August 1962): 521–44. Stresses the importance and persistence of traditional party loyalties after the Civil War.

**585.** Jordan, Philip D. *Ohio Comes of Age, 1873–1900*. Vol. 5 of *The History of the State of Ohio*. Ed. Carl Wittke. Columbus: Ohio Archaeological and Historical Society, 1943. 168–74.

**586.** Moore, Clifford H. "Ohio in National Politics, 1865–1896." *Ohio Archaeological and Historical Publications* 337 (1928): 220–427. Dated review of little value.

**587.** Noyes, Edward. "The Ohio G.A.R. and Politics from 1866 to 1900." *Ohio State Archeological and Historical Quarterly* 55 (1946): 79–105. Despite the article's title the article focuses on events after 1887.

**588.** Porter, George H. *Ohio Politics During the Civil War Period*. Studies in History, Economics and Public Law. 40, no. 2. New York: Longmans, Green & Co., 1911. 1–255. Dated work includes chapters on the Union party and the peace Democrats.

**589.** Roseboom, Eugene H. *The Civil War Era, 1850–1873*. Vol. 4. In *The History of the State of Ohio*. Ed. Carl Wittke. Columbus: Ohio Archaeological and Historical Society, 1944. Scattered references to Garfield's military experience.

**590.** Roseboom, Eugene H., and Francis P. Weisenburger. *A History of Ohio*. New York: Prentice Hall, 1934. Briefly mentions Garfield.

**591.** Smith, Joseph P. *History of the Republican Party of Ohio*. 2 vols. Chicago: Lewis Publishing Co., 1898. This valuable resource for 1854–1896 has a chapter on every year providing full reports on the state conventions as well as elections results. Second volume contains biographical sketches of Republican politicians.

**592.** Swift, Donald Charles. "The Ohio Republicans, 1866–1880." Ph.D. dissertation, University of Delaware, 1967.

**593.** Weisenburger, Francis P. *The Passing of the Frontier, 1825–1850.* vol. 3 of *The History of the State of Ohio*. Ed. Carl Wittke. Columbus: Ohio State Archaeological and Historical Society, 1941.

# 9
# Congressional Career, 1862–1880

## A. Congress

**594.** Beth, Loren P. *The Development of the American Constitution, 1877–1917.* This survey mentions Garfield's use in Congress of the riders to bills as well as his appointment controversy when president.

**595.** Boykin, Edward. *The Wit and Wisdom of Congress.* New York: Funk & Wagnalls, 1961. 208, 402. Two anecdotes.

**596.** Brooks, Noah. *Washington D.C. in Lincoln's Time.* Ed. Herbert Mitgang. Chicago: Quadrangle Books, 1971. Reprint of the reports by Lincoln's favorite reporter, the correspondent of the *Sacramento* (Calif.) *Union.* An interesting contemporary view of Washington.

**597.** Brown, Harry J. "Garfield's Congress." *Hayes Historical Journal* 3, no. 4 (Fall 1981): 57–77. Editor of the Garfield diaries provides an overview of the environment of Congress and the actions of Garfield in the nine congresses in which he served.

**598.** Carman, Harry J., and Reinhard H. Luthin. *Lincoln and the Patronage.* New York: Columbia University Press, 1954. Notes that Garfield was one of four future presidents who were appointed without any military training.

**599.** David, Paul T. *Party Strength in the United States, 1872–1920.* Charlottesville: University of Virginia, 1972. Statistics and charts on interparty competition over the last century, with an index by state and section.

**600.** Glaser, Donald Robert. "The Congressional Career of James A. Garfield during the Hayes Administration." M.A. thesis, Ohio State University, 1962.

**601.** Green, Constance McClaughin. *Washington Village and Capital, 1800–1878.* Princeton, N.J.: Princeton University Press, 1962. Chs. 11–16. Provides informative background view of the capital when Garfield was in Congress.

**602.** Haynes, George Henry. *The Senate of the United States: Its History and Practice . . .* 1938; rpt. New York: Russell & Russell, 1960. 745–47. This dated study mentions Garfield's quarrel with the Senate as a "contest of most momentous consequences."

**603.** Hendrick, Burton J. *Lincoln's War Cabinet.* Boston: Little, Brown, 1946. 365, 376, 384, 413, 421–26, 450. Although biased against the Radicals, this study provides a detailed discussion of Chase and notes Garfield's disillusionment with his mentor after 1862.

**604.** Holmes, Oliver W., ed. "Peregrinations of a Politician: James A. Garfield's Diary of a Trip to Montana in 1872." *Montana* 6, no.4 (October 1956): 34–45. Excerpts from Garfield's diary describing his mission to negotiate a treaty with the Flathead Indians. Includes parts of his official report. Reprinted from *Frontier and Midland: A Magazine of the Northwest* 15 no. 2 (Winter, 1934–1935).

**605.** Leech, Margaret. *Reveille in Washington, 1860–1865.* New York: Harper & Brothers, 1941. Description of the capital during the war, with biographies of prominent politicians.

**606.** McGerr, Michael E. "The Meaning of Liberal Republicanism: The Case of Ohio." *Civil War History* 28 (December 1982): 307–23. Asserts that the movement in Ohio was composed of former Democrats unhappy with the Whig economic doctrines of the party in the 1870s.

**607.** MacNeil, Neil. *Forge of Democracy: The House of Representatives.* New York: David McKay Co., 1963. This institutional perspective on the House has a few scattered references to Garfield.

**608.** Mallam, William D. "Lincoln and the Conservatives." *Journal of Southern History* 28 (1962): 31–45. Explores the declining strength of Republican conservatives in Congress.

**609.** Reynolds, Clifford P., comp. *Biographical Directory of the American Congress, 1774–1961.* Washington: Government Printing Office, 1961.

**610.** Ripley, Randall B. *Party Leaders in the House of Representatives.* Washington: Brookings Institution, 1967. This overview of the institution's operation has no direct references to Garfield.

**611.** Shade, William G., Stanley D. Hopper, and Stephen E. Moiles. "Partisanship in the United States Senate: 1869–1901." *Journal of Interdisciplinary History* 4 (1973): 185–205. Finds consistently high partisanship in roll-call voting in post-Reconstruction years.

**612.** Schlesinger, Arthur, Jr., and Roger Burns, eds. *Congress Investigates: A Documentary History, 1792–1974.* Vol. 3. New York: Chelsea House Publishers, 1972. Essays and documents on Johnson's impeachment, Credit Mobilier, and other key investigations during the period.

**613.** Williams, T. Harry. *Lincoln and the Radicals*. Madison: University of Wisconsin Press, 1941. Account of radical "Jacobins" like Garfield and Blaine who initially worked against his renomination.

**614.** Wilmerding, Lucius, Jr. *The Spending Power: A History of the Efforts of Congress to Control Expenditures*. New Haven: Yale University Press, 1943. 122, 134, 141–43, 229. This review of congressional spending from 1789 to 1921 contains several references to Garfield.

**615.** Zornow, William Frank. *Lincoln & the Party Divided*. 1954; rpt. Westport, Conn.: Greenwood Press, 1972. Places Garfield as one of young party members who distrusted Lincoln.

## B. Reconstruction and Johnson Impeachment

**616.** Beale, Howard K. *The Critical Year: A Study of Andrew Johnson and Reconstruction*. New York: Harcourt, Brace, 1930. This study of the 1866 election laments the Radical victory.

**617.** Benedict, Michael Les. *A Compromise of Principle: Congressional Republicans and Reconstruction, 1863–1869*. New York: Norton, 1974. Defends Radical Republicans who fought Johnson's plans to maintain white supremacy and political power in the South.

**618.** _____. *The Impeachment and Trial of Andrew Johnson*. New York: W. W. Norton, 1973. Major reinterpretation justifies the impeachment as an attempt to stop Johnson from destroying congressional Reconstruction.

**619.** _____. "Preserving the Constitution: The Conservative Basis of Radical Reconstruction." *Journal of American History* 61 (June 1974): 65–90. Argues that the limits of Reconstruction reflected the limits on congressional power set by the constitutional conservatism of Republican leaders.

**620.** _____. "The Rout of Radicalism: Republicans and the Election of 1867." *Civil War History* 18 (1972): 334–44.

**621.** Bowers, Claude E. *The Tragic Era: The Revolution After Lincoln*. Cambridge, Mass.: Houghton Mifflin Co., 1929. Anti-Republican view contains several hostile references to Garfield.

**622.** Brock, William Ranulf. *An American Crisis: Congress and Reconstruction, 1865–1867*. New York: St. Martin's Press, 1963. Anti-Republican attack.

**623.** Buck, Paul H. *The Road to Reunion: 1865–1900*. Boston: Little, Brown, 1937. Notes how the "bloody shirt" issue divided the nation in 1880 and how the grief surrounding Garfield's death united it.

**624.** Carter, Hodding. *The Angry Scar: The Story of Reconstruction*. Garden City, N.Y.: Doubleday, 1959. Southern perspective on Reconstruction and the Compromise of 1877.

**625.** Castel, Albert E. *The Presidency of Andrew Johnson*. American Presidency Series. Lawrence: University Press of Kansas, 1979. Reinterpretation suggests that his reelection plans undermined the potential of success for his Reconstruction plans.

**626.** Cox, Lawanda, and John Cox. *Politics, Principle, and Prejudice, 1865–1866*. New York: Free Press, 1963. An attack on Johnson's Reconstruction plan and the Radicals' role in thwarting his plan.

**627.** DeWitt, David Miller. *The Impeachment and Trial of Andrew Johnson*. New York: Macmillan, 1903. Dated but detailed account.

**628.** Donald, David. *The Politics of Reconstruction, 1863–1867*. 1965; rpt. Cambridge, Mass.: Harvard University Press, 1984. Finds a correlation between vote of the congressman and the political persuasion of the district. Garfield, who increasingly became a moderate in Congress, does not support the thesis.

**629.** DuBois, William E. B. *Black Reconstruction in America, 1860–1880*. New York: Harcourt, Brace, 1935. First full-length reinterpretation of Reconstruction.

**630.** Dunning, William A. *Reconstruction: Political and Economic, 1865–1877*. New York: Harper and Row, 1907. Classic criticism.

**631.** Fleming, Walter L. *Documentary History of Reconstruction*. 2 vols. Cleveland: Arthur H. Clark Co., 1906. This important collection provides an interesting backdrop on Reconstruction.

**632.** Foner, Eric. *Reconstruction: America's Unfinished Revolution, 1863–1877*. New York: Harper & Row, 1988. A recent study places Garfield with the young reform leaders in the House who backed off from federal intervention for political reasons.

**633.** Gillette, William. *Retreat from Reconstruction, 1869–1879*. Baton Rouge: Louisiana State University Press, 1979. This critical examination of the failed policies of Grant and Hayes provides a background for Garfield's Southern policy.

**634.** Kutler, Stanley I. "Reconstruction and the Supreme Court: The Numbers Game Reconsidered." *Journal of Southern History* 32 (February 1966): 42–56. Attempts to clear Radicals of "vindictive motives" in passing the Congressional Act of 1866.

**635.** Lynch, John R. *The Facts of Reconstruction*. 1913; rpt. Indianapolis: Bobbs-Merrill, 1970. Sympathetic defense of Reconstruction policies by a former black congressman from Mississippi.

**636.** McKitrick, Eric L. *Andrew Johnson and Reconstruction*. Chicago: University of Chicago Press, 1960. Revisionist at the time, this book attacks his rehabilitation.

**637.** McPherson, James M. "Some Thoughts on the Civil War as the Second Revolution." *Hayes Historical Journal* 3 (Spring 1982): 5–20. Contends that Reconstruction was an unfinished rather than a failed revolution.

**638.** Mantell, Martin E. *Johnson, Grant, and the Politics of Reconstruction*. New York: Columbia University Press, 1973. Portrays Grant as the dupe of Radical Republicans, who were economically motivated.

**639.** Milton, George Fort. *The Age of Hate: Andrew Johnson and the Radical Republicans*. New York: Coward-McCann, 1930. Hostile view of the Radicals.

**640.** Perman, Michael. *The Road to Redemption: Southern Politics,1869–1879*. This regional political history discusses how Garfield and others seriously misread the South.

**641.** Randall, James G., and David Donald. *The Civil War and Reconstruction*. 1939; rpt. Lexington, Mass.: D. C. Heath, 1969. Classic text has brief references to Garfield.

**642.** *Report of the Committee upon the Impeachment of the President*; No.7, 40th Cong. 1st Sess., 1867.

**643.** Sefton, James E. *Andrew Johnson and the Uses of Constitutional Power*. Boston: Little, Brown, 1980. Sympathetic study of Johnson's attacks on the Radicals.

**644.** Trefousse, Hans L. *Impeachment of a President: Andrew Johnson, the Blacks, and Reconstruction*. Knoxville: University of Tennessee Press, 1975. Sympathetic to the Radicals but believes that impeachment was counterproductive.

**645.** Wiecek, William M. "The Great Writ and Reconstruction: The Habeas Corpus Act of 1867." *Journal of Southern History* 36 (1970): 530–48. Challenges the "myth of judicial intimidation in Reconstruction." No mention of Garfield.

## C. Education Reform

**646.** Curti, Merle. *The Social Ideas of American Educators*. New York: Scribner's, 1935. 139–168. Discusses Barnard's career.

**647.** Harris, William T. "Establishment of the Office of the Commissioner of Education of the United States, and Henry Barnard's Relation to It." In *Report of the Commissioner of Education, 1902*. Washington: Government Printing Office, 1902. 905–16.

**648.** Mayo, A. D. "Henry Barnard as First United States Commissioner of Education." In *Report of the Commissioner of Education, 1902*. Washington: Government

Printing Office, 1902. Vol. 1:891–901. Examines his role as commissioner from 1867 to 1870.

**649.** _____. "Henry Barnard." In *Report of the Commissioner of Education (1896–1897)*. Washington: Government Printing Office, 1897. Vol. 1:769–810. Traces Barnard's life until 1860.

**650.** Peskin, Allan. "Short, Unhappy Life of the First Department of Education." *Public Administration Review* 33 (November/December 1973): 572–74. Reviews the history of the short-lived department which was undermined by careless legislation and poor administration.

**651.** Steiner, Bernard C. *Life of Henry Barnard: The First United States Commissioner of Education, 1867–1870*. Department of the Interior-Bureau of Education, Bulletin 1919, No. 8. Washington: Government Printing Office, 1919. Includes a chapter on his stint as Commissioner.

## D. Federal Army Reform

**652.** Andrews, Richard Allen. "Years of Frustration: William T. Sherman, The Army, and Reform, 1869–1883." Ph.D. dissertation, Northwestern University, 1968.

**653.** Langley, Lester D. "The Democratic Tradition and Military Reform, 1878–1885." *South West Social Science Quarterly* 48 (1967): 192–200.

**654.** Thomas, Donna Marie Eleanor. "Army Reform in America: The Crucial Years, 1876–1881." Ph.D. dissertation, University of Florida, 1980. Notes Garfield's prominent role as advocate of military reorganization and supporter of the subsequent Burnside Bill of 1878–1879.

**655.** Upton, Colonel Emory. *The Armies of Asia and Europe, Embracing Official Reports on the Armies of Japan, China, India, Persia, Italy, Russia, Austria, Germany, France, and England*. New York: D. Appleton and Company, 1878. Garfield endorsed Upton's proposed reform modelled on the German plan of a regular active force.

**656.** _____. *The Military Policy of the United States. By Brevet Maj. Gen. Emory Upton, United States Army*. Washington: Government Printing Office, 1904. Garfield was a strong supporter of the Upton Plan of army reform.

**657.** _____. *A New System of Infantry Tactics: Double and Single Rank; Adapted to American Topography and Improved Fire-arms*. New York: D. Appleton, 1868. Popular military textbook by prominent reform advocate.

**658.** _____. *The Prussian Company Column/by Brevet Major General Emory Upton, Read Before the Thayer Club of West Point, October 27, 1874*. New York: International Review, 1875.

**659.** Wood, Thomas J. "Military Organization." *United States Magazine* 4 (December 1865): 481–94. Advocates a plan of military reform for postwar America.

## E. Scandals

### 1. "Black Friday" Gold Panic Investigation

**660.** *House of Representatives Report #31.* 41st Cong. 2nd sess., 1870. "Gold Panic Investigation." Serial 1436; 131–68. Jay Gould testimony.

**661.** U.S. Congress, House Committee on Banking and Currency. 41st Cong., 2nd sess., 1870, HR. no.31 *Investigation into the Cause of the Gold Panic. Report of the Majority of the Committee on Banking and Currency. March 1, 1870.* Washington: Government Printing Office, 1870. Report, 1–23: committee investigation, 26–460, minority report, 461–83.

### 2. Credit Mobilier

**662.** *Henry S. McComb vs. the Credit Mobilier of America.* Pennsylvania Supreme Court, in Equity, Eastern District, January term, 1869, No. 19. The document on which the *Sun* based its revelations of September 4, 1872.

**663.** *House of Representatives Report #77.* 42 Cong., 3rd sess., 1873. "Report of the Poland Committee." The chief source for this scandal.

**664.** *Report of and Testimony Taken by the Poland Committee in 1873, House report No. 77, No. 78,* 42nd Cong., 3rd sess.,1873. These two reports contain the Credit Mobilier testimony, including Garfield's on page 130.

**665.** Thompson, Margaret Susan. *The "Spider Web": Congress and Lobbying in the Age of Grant.* Ithaca, N.Y.: Cornell University Press, 1985. This interesting look at Congressional behavior in the 1870s contains many citations to Garfield.

**666.** Trottman, Nelson. *History of the Union Pacific: A Financial and Economic Survey.* New York: A. M. Kelley, 1966. 30–54, 71–91. Notes favorably that Garfield vindicated himself with his district voters.

### 3. DeGolyer Incident

**667.** *Garfield and the DeGolyer Bribe: Testimony That Convicts.* Document, No. 18. n.p., 1880. Four-page pamphlet compiles testimony and other evidence that portrays Garfield as a "tool of Washington ring of the iniquitous robbers."

**668.** *Report of the Allison-Wilson Committee on the District of Columbia. Senate Reports,* No. 453, 43rd Cong. 1st sess., 1873. Chief source of the DeGolyer charges. Investigation of the DeGolyer McClelland Company and its street-paving contract for Washington, D.C.

# 10

# Compromise of 1877

## A. Articles and Monographs

**669.** Benedict, Michael L. "Southern Democrats in the Crisis of 1876–1877: A Reconsideration of Reunion and Reaction." *Journal of Southern History* 46 (November 1980): 489–524. Disputes Woodward's interpretation (**692**), arguing that the "bargain" was only an anticlimactic negotiation that served Hayes.

**670.** Black, J. S. "The Electoral Conspiracy." *North American Review* 125 (July 1877): 1–34. Vehement denunciation of the "Great Fraud" of 1876 committed by the Republican majority on the Electoral Commission.

**671.** Bone, Fanny Z. Lovell. "Louisiana in the Disputed Election of 1876." *Louisiana Historical Quarterly* 14 (July and October 1931): 408–40, 549–66; 15 (January and April 1932): 93–116, 234–67. Although biased, this account provides the best review of the subject and includes many public documents.

**672.** Clendenen, Clarence C. "President Hayes' 'Withdrawal' of the Troops—An Enduring Myth." *South Carolina Historical Magazine* 70 (October 1969): 240–50. Argues that there was no direct removal of troops from the South to end Reconstruction, just redeployment to meet military needs elsewhere.

**673.** DeSantis, Vincent P. "Rutherford B. Hayes and the Removal of the Troops and the End of Reconstruction." In *Region, Race and Reconstruction.* Ed. E. Morgan Kousser and James McPherson. New York: Oxford University Press, 1982. 417–50. Provides a more complex account of Hayes's decision.

**674.** Edmunds, George F. "Another View of 'The Hayes-Tilden Contest.'" *Century Magazine* 86 (May 1913): 103–7, 196–201. Former Vermont senator who was the "last surviving member of the Electoral Commission" defends his party from accusations of bribery leveled by a former Democratic congressman.

**675.** Flynn, James Joseph. "The Disputed Election of 1876." Ph.D. dissertation, Fordham University, 1953. Of limited value.

**676.** Haworth, Paul Leland. *The Hayes-Tilden Disputed Presidential Election of 1876.* Indianapolis: Bobbs-Merrill Company, 1906. Dated monograph existed until 1950 as the only extensive treatment of the incident.

**677.** Koenig, Louis "The Election That Got Away." *American Heritage* 11 (October 1960): 4–7, 99–104. General retelling of the crisis.

**678.** Kuntz, Norbert A. "Electoral Commission of 1877." Ph.D. dissertation, Michigan State University, 1969.

**679.** Marble, Manton. *A Secret Chapter of Political History* (N.p., 1878). Copy of privately printed 1878 pamphlet by a political lieutenant of Tilden who described his version of the events surrounding the 1876 election.

**680.** Northup, Milton Harlow. "A Grave Crisis in American History: The Inner History of the Origin and Formation of the Electoral Commission of 1877." *Century Magazine* 62 (October 1901): 923–34. Article by the secretary of the Special House Committee describes the creation of the commission.

**681.** Peskin, Allan. "Was There a Compromise of 1877?" *Journal of American History* 60 (June 1973): 63–75. Downplays the incident given the fluid political situation between 1877–1881 and the failure to implement the terms of agreement.

**682.** Polakoff, Keith Ian. *The Politics of Inertia: The Election of 1876 and the End of Reconstruction.* Baton Rouge: Louisiana State University Press, 1973. Sees the compromise reflecting a period of decentralized parties and weak national leaders.

**683.** Rable, George. "Republican Albatross: The Louisiana Question, National Politics, and the Failure of Reconstruction." *Louisiana History* 23 (Spring 1982): 109–30. Reviews the problems that undermined the Republican efforts in the 1870s.

**684.** Robinson, Lloyd. *The Stolen Election: Hayes versus Tilden—1876.* New York: Doubleday & Company, 1968. Popular account without footnotes.

**685.** Roske, Ralph J. "'Visiting Statesmen' in Louisiana, 1876." *Mid-America* 33 (April 1951): 89–102. Attacks the role of Republican "visiting statesmen."

**686.** Singletary, Otis A. "The Election of 1878 in Louisiana." *Louisiana Historical Quarterly* 40 (January 1957): 46–53. Describes the fraud-based Democratic triumph that marked the overthrow of the Republican party in the state.

**687.** Sternstein, Jerome L., ed. "The Sickles Memorandum: Another Look at the Hayes-Tilden Election-Night Conspiracy." *Journal of Southern History* 32 (August 1966): 342–57. Questions the accuracy of the election night conspiracy thesis outlined by Sickles, whose memo is included.

**688.** Tunnell, Ted. B., Jr. "The Negro, The Republican Party, and the Election of 1876 in Louisiana." *Louisiana History* 7 (Spring 1966): 101–6. Examination of the election in the state.

**689.** _____. *Crucible of Reconstruction: War, Radicalism, and Race in Louisiana, 1862–1877*. Baton Rouge: Louisiana State University Press, 1984. Traces the Republican party's decline, which prompted Garfield's criticism in 1875.

**690.** Watterson, Henry. "The Hayes-Tilden Contest for Presidency: Inside History of a Great Political Crisis." *Century Magazine* 86 (May 1913): 3–20. This Congressman, who was at the Wormley Hotel Conference, accuses the Republicans of bribery and describes their readiness to end Reconstruction.

**691.** Woodward, C. Vann. *Origins of the New South, 1877–1913*. Baton Rouge: Louisiana State University Press, 1951. Chapter 2. Notes Garfield's role in the 1877 Compromise.

**692.** _____. *Reunion and Reaction: The Compromise of 1877 and the End of Reconstruction*. Boston: Little, Brown, 1951. This important study sees the compromise as an economic alliance; it notes Garfield's role and his later failure to become Speaker. The lack of Southern Democratic support in that contest marked "the first breach in the Compromise of 1877."

**693.** _____. "Yes, There Was a Compromise of 1877." *Journal of American History* 60 (June 1973): 215–23. Reaffirms the compromise as a set of complicated negotiated arrangements, including speakership and cabinet posts. Concentrates on the process rather than the outcome.

## B. Government Reports on the 1876 Election

**694.** *Counting Electoral Votes*, 44th Cong., 2nd Sess., 1877. *Misc. Doc., #13.* House subcommittee compiled all important documents in a volume which ultimately contains more than 8,000 pages of testimony.

**695.** *Executive Document #2*, 44th Cong., 2nd sess., 1877. Reflects the Senate views and contains the "Sherman Report" by the so-called "visiting Republican statesmen" that Grant asked to go to Louisiana and check the vote.

**696.** *Hinds' Precedents of the House of Representatives* (5 vols), 59th Cong., 2nd sess., 1906–1907. Shorter account of 1876 election documents than the project compiled by the 44th Congress.

**697.** *House Report #261*. "Condition of the South." 43rd Cong., 2nd sess., 1875. Discusses the situation in Louisiana a year before Garfield went there as part of the Congressional investigation.

**698.** *House of Representatives Miscellaneous Document #31*. 45th Cong. 3rd sess., no. 140, 1879. "Presidential Election Investigations" [Potter Committee Report].

The report of the commission, which in 1878 investigated the 1876 election, is the chief source for the 1876 election.

**699.** *House of Representatives Report #156*, 44th Cong., 2nd sess. (1877). "The Recent Election in Louisiana."

**700.** *Proceedings of the Electoral Commission. Congressional Record.* Pt. 4, 44th Cong, 2nd sess. 1877. Official record of the commission gives the legal arguments of counsel members followed by brief written opinions.

## C. Samuel J. Tilden, Democratic Candidate in 1876

**701.** Bigelow, John. *The Life of Samuel J. Tilden.* 2 vols. New York: Harper & Brothers, 1895. 2:11–118. This spirited defense of Tilden includes chapters on the Louisiana vote controversy and on his testimony to Congress.

**702.** _____, ed. *Letters and Literary Memorials of Samuel J. Tilden.* 2 vols. New York: Harper and Brothers, 1908. These volumes provided for in his will bring together series of letters and documents.

**703.** _____. *The Writings and Speeches of Samuel J. Tilden.* 2 vols. New York: Harper & Brothers, 1885.

**704.** Flick, Alexander C. "Samuel Jones Tilden." *DAB* (1934) vol. 13:537–41.

**705.** _____. *Samuel Jones Tilden: A Study in Political Sagacity.* New York: Dodd, Mead & Co., 1939. Chaps. 25–30, 35. Favorable biography explores the 1876 election and his reluctance to enter the 1880 contest.

**706.** Gibson, A. M. *A Political Crime.* New York: W. S. Gottsberger, 1885. This account was financed by the defeated candidate.

**707.** Hirsch, Mark D. "Samuel J. Tilden: The Story of a Lost Opportunity." *American Historical Review* 56 (1951): 788–802. Critical of Tilden for his vacillation during the 1880 Democratic convention.

**708.** Tilden, Samuel. Papers. New York Public Library, New York. Tilden's will provided for publication of 4 volumes of papers and then instructed remaining documents be destroyed. His executors reduced 18 trunks to 13 small boxes, which are of little value.

**709.** _____. Papers. Columbia University Library, New York. Smaller collection of papers contains items from the 1876 campaign. For Rutherford B. Hayes, Republican candidate, see **1215–1240**.

# 11
# Legal Career and the Milligan Court Case

**710.** Fairman, Charles. *The Law and Martial Rule*. Chicago: Callaghan and Co., 1930. Critical review of the ruling.

**711.** Gambone, Joseph G. "Ex Parte Milligan: The Restoration of Judicial Prestige?" *Civil War History* 16 (1970): 246–59. Supports the view that congressional reaction to the Supreme Court attested to the "vigor not passivity of the Court."

**712.** Harmon, Joseph. *Garfield: The Lawyer*. Yonkers, N.Y.: Riverview Press, 1929. Pamphlet has brief review of 12 cases he was involved with between 1865 and 1877.

**713.** Hawkins, Seth Clayton. *Garfield at the Bar: An Aritectonic Rhetorical Criticism of Selected Speeches by James A. Garfield before the U.S. Supreme Court*. Ph.D. dissertation, Bowling Green University, 1975.

**714.** Klaus, Samuel, ed. *The Milligan Case: Milligan, Lambdin P., Defendant*. New York: A. Knopf, 1929.

**715.** Kutler, Stanley I. *Judicial Power and Reconstruction Politics*. Chicago: University of Chicago Press, 1968. Summary of the Milligan case notes that opinion was divided on its merits.

**716.** Rankin, Robert Stanley. *When Civil War Law Fails: Martial Law and Its Legal Basis in the United States*. Durham, N.C.: Duke University Press, 1939. Chap. 4. This monograph on martial law in America notes the public opinion outrage over the Milligan decision.

**717.** Robinson, Ira Ellsworth. *Three Great Protests Against Trial of Civilians by Military Commission: Arguments in Behalf of the Preservation of Constitutional Government and the Sacred Right of Trial by Jury*. Charleston, W.V.: Kanawha Citizen Print, 1917.

**718.** Todoroff, James. "James A. Garfield: The Lawyer" *Lake County Historical Quarterly* 22 (December 1980): 5. Short summary based on secondary sources.

**719.** Warren, Charles. *The Supreme Court in United States History*. 2: 1836–1918. Boston: Little, Brown & Co., 1926. Chap 29. Traditional view of the Radical attack on and intimidation of the Supreme Court.

# 12

# Presidential Election of 1880

## A. Republican Convention of 1880

**720.** Barker, Wharton. "The Secret History of Garfield's Nomination." *Pearson's Magazine* 35 (May 1916): 435–43. Claims credit for masterminding the nomination by recruiting support for Garfield without his assent or knowledge.

**721.** Bishop, Joseph B. *Presidential Nominations and Elections.* New York: Charles Scribner's Sons, 1916. 77–88.

**722.** Byrne, Gary C., and Paul Marx. *The Great American Conventions: A Political History of Presidential Elections.* Palo Alto, Calif.: Pacific Books, 1976. Chap. 12. Labels the 1880 conventions as "compromise models" that selected candidates who worked to draw party factions together.

**723.** Congressional Quarterly. *National Party Conventions, 1831–1980.* Washington: Congressional Quarterly, 1982. 46–48, 154–55. Ballot counts.

**724.** Cook, Sherwin Laurence. *Torchlight Parade: Our Presidential Pageant.* New York: Minton, Balch & Company, 1929. Chap. 11. General discussion of the convention and the campaign.

**725.** Eaton, Herbert. *Presidential Timber: A History of Nominating Conventions, 1868–1960.* New York: Free Press of Glencoe, 1964. 67–95. Popular account with bibliography but no notes.

**726.** Evans, Frank B. "Wharton Barker and the Republican National Convention of 1880." *Pennsylvania History* 27 (January 1960): 28–43. Reviews the claim that Barker played a key role in the convention.

**727.** Fitch, Charles E. "James A. Garfield." *International Review* 8 (1880): 447–58. Brief account by a Williams College graduate of the nomination and candidacy.

**728.** Hoar, George F. "Four National Conventions." *Scribner's* 25 (February 1899): 152–75. Memories of Republican conventions by the Massachusetts senator and Garfield friend includes long discussion of the 1880 convention.

**729.** Hughes, Sarah Forbes, ed. *Letters and Recollections of John Murray Forbes.* 2 vols. Boston: Houghton Mifflin, 1899. Vol. 2. 192–98. New England Republican provides an eyewitness account of the 1880 convention.

**730.** Jones, Charles A. "Ohio in the Republican National Conventions." *Ohio Archaeological and Historical Publications* 38 (January 1929): 1–46. Chatty "walk through" of little use.

**731.** Lupold, Harry Forrest, ed. "Garfield and the 1880 Election: Garfield-Beatty Exchange" *Lake County Historical Quarterly* 26 (2 & 3) (June/September 1984): 1–10. Quotes two letters referring to the opposition to Sherman's nomination by the Ravenna friend who was a Blaine delegate.

**732.** McClure, Alexander K. *Our Presidents and How We Make Them.* New York: Harper and Brothers, 1900. The famous publisher asserts that 1880 was the "greatest battle ever fought in a national convention."

**733.** McKee, Thomas Hudson. *The National Conventions and Platforms of All Political Parties, 1789–1905: Convention, Popular, and Electoral Vote. Also the Political Complexion of Both Houses of Congress at each Biennial Period.* 6th ed. Baltimore: Friedwald, 1906. 182–200.

**734.** Peskin, Allan. "The 'Put-up Job': Wisconsin and the Republican National Convention of 1880." *Wisconsin Magazine of History* 55 (1972): 263–74. Dismisses as "window dressing" the efforts of Wharton Barker to promote Garfield. Asserts that the nomination owed more to the logic of deadlock than to any underground machinations.

**735.** Porter, Kirk H., and Donald Bruce Johnson, comps. *National Party Platforms, 1840–1964.* Urbana: University of Illinois Press, 1972. 56–62.

**736.** *Proceedings of the Republican National Convention Held in Chicago, Illinois, June 2–8, 1880.* Chicago: John B. Jeffery Company, 1881.

**737.** Rhodes, James F. "The National Republican Conventions of 1880 and 1884." *Scribner's Magazine* 50 (September 1911): 297–306. Believes that 1880 was one of the most interesting gatherings.

**738.** Smith, Charles Emory. "How Conkling Missed Nominating Blaine." *Saturday Evening Post*, June 8, 1901: 2–3. The Postmaster General recollects how Conkling was advised to stop the Garfield stampede by having the New York delegation endorse Blaine.

**739.** Stein, Charles Emory. *Third Term Tradition: Its Rise and Collapse in American Politics.* New York: Columbia University Press, 1943. Chap. 6. Discussion of

Grant's efforts to seek a third term—the first such movement to defy the two-term tradition.

**740.** Stoddard, Henry Luther. *Presidential Sweepstakes: The Story of Political Conventions and Campaigns.* Ed. Francis W. Leary after Stoddard's death. New York: G. P. Putnam's Sons, 1948. 77–87. Interesting review of the 1880 convention and Garfield's presidency by a Republican activist and future New York editor.

**B. Campaign**

**741.** Boller, Paul F., Jr. *Presidential Campaigns.* New York: Oxford University Press, 1984. Chap. 24. Brief sketch of the "lackluster," "dull" campaign that resulted in the "triumph of 'boatman-Jim.'"

**742.** Burnham, Walter Dean. *Presidential Ballots, 1836–1892.* Baltimore: Johns Hopkins University Press, 1955. Statistics by county and state.

**743.** Clancy, Herbert J. *The Presidential Election of 1880.* Chicago: Loyola University Press, 1958. The only monograph on the election, this book utilizes existing manuscripts to provide a standard account of the contest.

**744.** Congressional Quarterly. *Presidential Candidates from 1788 to 1964, Including Third Parties, 1832–1964, and Popular Electoral Vote: Historical Review.* Washington: Congressional Quarterly, 1964. 37, 78, 104.

**745.** _____. *Presidential Elections Since 1789.* Washington: Congressional Quarterly Press, 1978. 37, 76, 101.

**746.** De Santis, Vincent. "Catholicism and Presidential Elections, 1865–1900." *Mid-America* 42 (April 1960): 67–79. Notes that the Catholic issue played no role in the 1880 election.

**747.** Dinnerstein, Leonard. "Election of 1880." In *History of American Presidential Elections, Vol. II; 1848–1896.* Ed. Arthur M. Schlesinger, Jr., Fred L. Israel, and William P. Hanson. New York: Chelsea House, 1971. 1491–1560. Describes it as an "insignificant" and issueless canvass. Entry includes party platforms and other documents.

**748.** Fischer, Roger A. *Tippecanoe and Trinkets Too: The Material Culture of American Presidential Campaigns, 1828–1984.* Urbana: University of Illinois Press, 1988. 114, 117, 119, 121. Suggests that the wide collection of campaign items (cologne bottles, badges, etc.) demonstrated the interest on the grassroots level.

**749.** Haynes, Frederick E. *Third Party Movements since the Civil War.* Iowa City: Iowa State Historical Society, 1916. 119–21, 145. Dated history of the Greenback party, with special emphasis on Iowa.

**750.** Hicks, John D. "The Third Party Tradition in American Politics." *Mississippi Valley Historical Review* 20 (June 1933): 3–28. This classic defense of the role of third parties notes that the return of prosperity undercut the hopes of the Greenback party.

**751.** House, Albert V. "The Democratic State Central Committee of Indiana in 1880: A Case Study in Party Tactics and Finance." *Indiana Magazine of History* 58 (September 1962): 178–210. Argues that Democratic disunity would have ensured a Republican victory even without large money contributions.

**752.** Kent, Frank R. *The Democratic Party: A History*. New York: Century Co., 1928. 263–73. Very general review of the election.

**753.** Lictman, Allan J. "Political Readjustment and Ethnocultural Voting in Late Nineteenth Century America." *Journal of Social History* 16 (Spring 1983): 55–82. Although the analysis starts with the 1888 campaign, this article provides insight into the political environment of Garfield.

**754.** Nash, Howard P., Jr. *Third Parties in American Politics*. Washington: Public Affairs Press, 1959. 134–39, 159–63. Brief account of the Greenback party.

**755.** North, Ira. L. "A Rhetorical Criticism of the Speaking of James Abram Garfield, 1876–1880." Ph.D. dissertation, Louisiana State University, 1954. Not available on microfilm.

**756.** Parker, Albert C. E. "Beating the Spread: Analyzing American Election Outcomes." *Journal of American History* 67 (June 1980): 61–87. Notes that 1880 witnessed an unusually large city vote, which the Republicans better mobilized.

**757.** Peskin, Allan. "The Election of 1880." *Wilson Quarterly* 4 (Spring 1980): 172–81. Overview of the contest notes that in late 19th-century politics filled "an entertainment gap."

**758.** Peterson, Svend. *A Statistical History of American Presidential Elections*. New York: Ungar Co., 1963. 48–50.

**759.** Pickens, Donald K. "The Historical Images in Republican Campaign Songs, 1860–1900." *Journal of Popular Culture* 15 (Winter 1981): 165–74. Insight into the party themes, such as the "bloody shirt" and nationalism. Uses songs from the Library of Congress music collection.

**760.** Reeves, Thomas C. "Chester A. Arthur and Campaign Assessments in the Election of 1880." *Historian* 31 (August 1969): 573–82. Uses the Arthur letter-books to show that he was "fully engaged" in assessments business.

**761.** _____. "Chester A. Arthur and the Campaign of 1880." *Political Science Quarterly* 84 (December 1969): 628–37. Letterbooks highlight Arthur's active role as state party chair in raising and distributing funds, arranging speakers and materials.

**762.** Roberts, William C. *The Leading Orators of Twenty-Five Campaigns, from the First Presidential Canvass to the Present Time*. New York: L. K. Strouse and

Co., 1884. 225–39. Brief biographies of Garfield, John Sherman, Leroy F. Youmans, and William Mahone.

**763.** Roseboom, Eugene H. *A History of Presidential Elections.* New York: Macmillan, 1964. Chap. 16. 253–62. Asserts that 1880 represented a party victory rather than a personal one.

**764.** Rosenstone, Steven J. et al. *Third Parties in America: Citizen Response to Major Party Failure.* Princeton: Princeton University Press, 1984. 63–67. Speculates that most Greenback party supporters voted Democrat in 1882.

**765.** Shea, John Gilmary. "The Anti-Catholic Issue in the Late Election: The Relation of Catholics to the Political Parties." *American Catholic Quarterly Review* 6 (1881): 36–50. Alleges that Republican leaders exploited anti-Catholic feeling.

**766.** Silber, Irwin. *Songs American Voted By.* Harrisburg, Pa.: Stackpole Books, 1971. Includes several songs of the 1880 campaign, which for the first time featured songs in a foreign language and versions of Gilbert and Sullivan tunes.

**767.** Van Deusen, John G. "Did the Republicans 'Colonize' Indiana in 1879?" *Indiana Magazine of History* 30 (1935): 335–46. Finds absurd the Democratic charge that blacks were imported to live in the state.

**768.** Williams, Frederick D. "Garfield's Front Porch Campaign: The Mentor Scene." *Lake County Historical Quarterly* 22 (September 1980) 1–8. Reprinted in *Ohio's Western Reserve: A Regional Reader.* Ed. Harry F. Lupold and Gladys Haddad. Kent: Kent State University Press, 1988. 185–191. Account of the events at "Lawnfield."

## C. Morey Letter and the Chinese Issue

**769.** Davenport, John I. *History of the Forged "Morey Letter": A Narrative of the Discovered Facts, Respecting this Great Political Forgery.* New York: J. I. Davenport, 1884. This partisan but important pamphlet was written by a New York election official who conducted at Garfield's request a two-year investigation. Includes a number of exhibits.

**770.** Hinckley, Ted C. "The Politics of Sinophobia: Garfield, The Morey Letter and the Presidential Election of 1880." *Ohio History* 89, no. 4 (Autumn 1980): 381–99. Reviews the role of the Morey letter that attempted to stigmatize Garfield as pro-Chinese labor.

**771.** Miller, Stuart Creighton. *The Unwelcome Immigrant: The American Image of the Chinese, 1785–1882.* Berkeley: University of California Press, 1969. This account of xenophobia points out that the numbers of Chinese immigrants did not approach the widespread public perception.

**772.** Pennanen, Gary. "Public Opinion and the Chinese Question, 1876–1879." *Ohio History* 77 (Winter, Spring, Summer 1968): 139–48. Notes the division of the

Republican party on the issue and Garfield's support for Hayes on the Exclusion Act.

**773.** Rodman, W. Paul. "The Origins of the Chinese Issue in California." *Mississippi Valley Historical Review* 25 (September 1938): 181–96. Shows how it had become the major issue in the state by the late 1870s.

**774.** Sandmeyer, Elmer Clarence. *The Anti-Chinese Movement in California.* Illinois Studies in the Social Sciences 24, no. 3. Urbana: University of Illinois, 1939. 5–127. Notes its importance at a time of political equilibrium in national politics.

**775.** Spoehr, Alexander. "Sambo and the Heathen Chinee: California's Racial Stereotypes in the Late 1870's." *Pacific Historical Review* 42 (May 1923): 185–205. Examines prejudice in the state before the 1880 election.

**776.** Wortman, Roy T. "Denver's Anti-Chinese Riot, 1880." *Colorado Magazine* 43 (Winter 1965): 275–91. Discusses the riot that newspapers blamed on the publicity given to the Morey letter.

## D. Election Literature

**777.** Austin, Harmon. *Garfield as a Candidate: A Broad, Comprehensive Refutation of Democratic Allegations. The Vote and Circumstances of Each Congressional Canvass Stated.* Warren, Ohio: n.p., 1880. The author was the Chairman of the Republican Central Committee for the 19th Ohio Congressional Committee.

**778.** *Bright Record of the Patriot Hancock. Black Record of the Politician Garfield . . .* Washington: Globe Printing and Publishing House, 1880.

**779.** *Campaign Speeches, 1880.* N.p., n.d. Twenty-three pamphlets in one volume. Includes speeches of Carl Schurz (July 20, 1880), Conkling (September 1880), and Blaine.

**780.** Democratic National Committee. *The (1880) Campaign Text Book—Why People Want a Change: The Republican Party Revisited . . . Life of Hancock and Frauds—Black Friday—Electoral Fraud of 1876. History of Carpetbag Governments . . . Democratic Economy and Republican Extravagance.* New York: National Democratic Committee, 1880.

**781.** _____. *Some Small Steals Helped along by Garfield, Landaulets and Liveries—Horses and Carriages Provided for an Official Aristocracy.* N.p., 1880.

**782.** *Documents Issued by the Union Republican Congressional Committee, 1880.* 2 vols. Washington: Collected by George C. Gorhan, 1880. 83 documents.

**783.** Edgar, George P., comp. *Gems of the Campaign of 1880 by Generals Grant and Garfield.* Jersey City, N.J.: Lincoln Association, 1881. Grant's brief remarks at eight places and excerpts from some of Garfield's earlier stump speeches.

**784.** Fisher, Roger. *American Political Ribbons and Ribbon Badges*. Lincoln, Mass.: Quarterman Publications, 1985. 171–91. Notes that the election inspired more than 60 known styles of ribbons, more than any campaign since 1860. Lists the ribbons as well as Garfield's inaugural and memorial ribbons.

**785.** _____. "Well I Should Smile: 1880 Presidential Put-Down Ribbons." *Keynoter* 90 (Fall 1990): 4–7. Discusses a collection of satirical ribbons that might be anti-Garfield items, Republican post-election gloats, or nonpartisan items mocking the political process.

**786.** Fuller, Frank. *The Moral Lesson of Gen. Garfield's Life: An Address. Delivered by Hon. Frank Fuller, Ex-governor of Utah: to the Young Men of New York, on Sunday Afternoon, October 31, 1880; at Cooper Institute*. 2nd ed. New York: Fowler & Wells, 1882.

**787.** Gwinn, C. J. M. (Vindex). *Reply to an Attack from ex-Gov. Seymour upon Gen. Garfield*. Philadelphia: n.p., 1880.

**788.** Hendricks, Thomas Andrew. *Hendricks' Great Speech on Garfield. Indianapolis, Ind., September 6th (1880)*. Chicago: G. S. Baldwin Publishers, 1880. Response to Garfield's protest of an attack on his involvement in the Louisiana election returns and the 1876 election.

**789.** Hinsdale, B. A. *The Life and Character of James A. Garfield*. N.p., 1880. This four-page pamphlet emphasizes Garfield's moral and religious character and includes testimonials from evangelistic newspapers and ministers.

**790.** _____. *The Republican Text-book for the Campaign of 1880: A Full History of General James A. Garfield's Public Life, With Other Political Information*. New York: D. Appleton, 1880. Includes Republican platform, an examination of the corruption, and a short biographical sketch of the candidate by the Hiram president and close friend.

**791.** Hutchins, Stilson. *Democratic Political Manual for 1880*. Washington: Washington Post Publishing Co., 1880. This party handbook reflects the lack of issue orientation in the 1880 canvass. It ridicules Garfield's war record and his congressional activities.

**792.** *The Republican Campaign Song Book for 1880*. Washington: n.p., 1880. Collection of partisan songs.

**793.** Republican Congressional Committee. *The Garfield and Arthur Campaign Songbook*. Washington: Republican Congressional Committee, 1880. A collection of forty songs from the campaign.

**794.** Republican National Committee. *Abuse of Garfield: A Democratic Necessity*. New York: David H. Gildersleeve, 1880.

**795.** Republican Party (Ohio State Executive Committee). *Garfield and Arthur Campaign Tracts. July 1880.* Columbus: n.p., 1880. Excerpts from speeches made by Republican leaders in July 1880 and Garfield's letter of acceptance.

**796.** Schurz, Carl. *Speech of Hon. Carl Schurz, of Missouri, at Indianapolis, Indiana, July 20,1880.* N.p, n.d. Campaign speech by political reformer and member of the Hayes cabinet.

**797.** Smalley, Eugene Virgil. "Biographical Sketches of James A. Garfield." In Republican Party National Committee, *The Republican Leaders: Biographical Sketches of James A. Garfield, Republican Candidate for President and Chester A. Arthur, Republican Candidate for Vice-president.* New York: National Republican Committee, 1880. Pamphlet includes nineteen-page biography by Garfield's personal friend who recounts the "romantic events" of his childhood and political life. Vol. 6 of **270**.

**798.** _____. *The Republican Manual: History, Principles, Early Leaders, Achievements of the Republican Party; with Biographical Sketches of James A. Garfield and Chester A. Arthur.* New York: American Book Exchange, 1880. 6 volumes.

**799.** Trumball, Lyman. *Speech of Hon. Lyman Trumball at Belleville, Illinois. August 30, 1880. Republican Party as a Party of False Pretenses and the Democratic Party as the Only National Party.* Washington: Rufus H. Darby, 1880. Cites the Democratic party as the party of reform.

**800.** Western Reserve Historical Society. *If Elected . . . Presidential Memorabilia.* Cleveland: Western Reserve Historical Society, 1988. 9. Picture of the display case of the 1880 campaign from the Society's collection.

### E. Presidential Candidates in 1880

*1. Dow, Neal       Maine     Prohibition party candidate*

**801.** Byrne, Frank L. "Neal Dow and the Prohibition Movement." Ph.D. dissertation, University of Wisconsin, 1957.

**802.** Dow, Neal. Scrapbooks. Library, Drew University, Madison, N.J. 21 scrapbooks with newspaper clippings and few letters relating to the career of this perennial presidential candidate and the prohibition movement.

**803.** _____. Letters. Maine Historical Society, Portland. Diary, a few letters and 2 volumes of typed copies of letters. Originals destroyed.

**804.** _____. *The Reminiscences of Neal Dow.* Portland: Evening Express Publishing Company, 1898. Covers only the years before 1866.

**805.** Minor, Alonzo A. "Neal Dow and His Life Work." *New England Magazine* 10 (June, 1894): 397–412.

**806.** Organ, T. W. *Biographical Sketch of Gen. Neal Dow*. New York: National Executive Committee of the Prohibition Reform Party, 1880. Campaign biography.

**807.** Waterman, W. Randall. "Neal Dow." *DAB* (1930) vol. 6:411–12.

### 2. Hancock, Winfield Scott    Pennsylvania    Democratic candidate

**808.** Brisbin, James S. *A Soldier's Story of a Soldier's Life: Winfield Scott Hancock, the Constitutional Soldier*. Philadelphia: L. Lum Smith, 1880. Campaign biography emphasizing his military career.

**809.** Cole, J. R. *The Life and Public Services of W. S. Hancock*. Cincinnati: Douglass Brothers, 1880. Flattering campaign biography.

**810.** Denison, Charles Wheeler, and G. B. Herbert. *Hancock "the Superb": The Early Life and Public Career of Winfield S. Hancock*. Cincinnati: Forshee & McMakin, 1880. Campaign biography written by Union Army veteran.

**811.** Forney, John W. *Life and Military Career of Winfield Scott Hancock*. Philadelphia: Hubbard Bros., 1880. This campaign biography by a friend includes several letters.

**812.** Freed, A. T. *Hancock: The Life and Public Service of Winfield Scott Hancock*. 1880. Seventy-page campaign biography pamphlet.

**813.** Goodrich, F. E. *Life of W. S. Hancock*. N.p.: A. T. Hubbard, 1886.

**814.** Hancock, Almira Russell (Mrs. Winfield), ed. *Reminiscences of Winfield Scott Hancock*. New York: Charles L. Webster and Co., 1887. Chap. 18, 170–176. Little mention of her husband's campaign except that he was disillusioned with political leaders.

**815.** Hancock, Winfield Scott. Collection. Library of Congress. 1864–1868. 6 items relating to military affairs.

**816.** _____. Scrapbook on the Hancock-Garfield Campaign and scrapbooks about General Hancock. Montgomery County Historical Society, Norristown, Pa.

**817.** *Hancock Military Record*. Summary Prepared for Adjutant General, 1864. Library of Congress.

**818.** Hill, Henry. "Life of General W. S. Hancock." In *Our Presidential Candidates and Political Compendium . . .* Newark, N.J.: F.C. Bliss & Company, 1880. Chap. 4.

**819.** Jenkins, Howard M. "Genealogical Sketch of General W. S. Hancock." *Pennsylvania Magazine of History and Biography* 10 (1886): 100–6. Traces Hancock genealogy from his grandparents, who came to America in 1730.

**820.** Junkin, David Xavier, and F. H. Norton. *Life of Winfield Scott Hancock: Personal, Military and Political*. New York: D. Appleton & Co., 1880. Campaign biography.

**821.** *Letters and Addresses Contributed at a General Meeting of the Military Service Institution, Held at Governor's Island, N.Y., February 25, 1886 in Memory of Winfield Scott Hancock*. New York: G. P. Putnam's Sons, 1886.

**822.** Rhodes, Charles Dudley. "Winfield Scott Hancock." *DAB* (1932) vol. 8:221–22.

**823.** Southwick, Leslie H., comp. *Presidential Also-Rans and Running Mates, 1788–1980*. Jefferson, N.C.: McFarland & Co., 1984. 347–55. Speculates that Hancock may have been a "superb president."

**824.** Southworth, Alvan Scott. *Life of Gen. Winfield Scott Hancock*. New York: American News Company, 1880. Campaign biography.

**825.** Stone, Irving. *They Also Ran: The Story of the Men Who Were Defeated for the Presidency*. 1943; rpt. Garden City, N.Y.: Doubleday, 1966. 174–90. Asserts that Hancock combined the best qualities of Fremont and McClelland.

**826.** Taylor, John M. "General Hancock: Bullets to Ballots." Unpublished type-script, written in 1954. George Washington University Library, Washington, D.C.

**827.** _____. "General Hancock: Soldier of the Gilded Age." *Pennsylvania History* 126 (April 1965): 187–96. Sympathetic account acknowledges his flaws as a candidate.

**828.** Tucker, Glenn. *Hancock, the Superb*. Indianapolis: Bobbs-Merrill, 1960. Contains only brief discussion of 1880 election.

**829.** Walker, Francis A. *General Hancock*. New York: D. Appleton and Co., 1895. Chap. 20. 305–08. This sympathetic biography by a member of Hancock's military has only brief comments on the election.

**830.** _____. Papers. Pennsylvania State Archives, Harrisburg. 15 items related to the Civil War.

### 3. Weaver, James Baird      Iowa   Greenback Labor candidate

**831.** Allen, E. A. *The Life and Public Services of James Baird Weaver*. N.p.: People's Party Publishing Company, 1892. Campaign biography.

**832.** Dillaye, Stephen. "Life and Services of General J. B. Weaver." In *Our Presidential Candidates and Political Compendium . . . .* Newark, N. J.: F. C. Bliss & Company, 1880. 95–143.

**833.** Haynes, Frederick E. *James Baird Weaver*. Iowa City: State Historical Society of Iowa, 1919. Chap. 9, 155–78. Makes use of Weaver's scrapbook and newspaper clippings, but offers little on the 1880 campaign.

**834.** Hicks, John D. "James Baird Weaver." *DAB* (1936) vol. 19:568–70.

**835.** Weaver, James Baird. *Call to Action*. Des Moines: Iowa Printing Company, 1892. Campaign document published during the 1892 campaign summarizes his "political principles."

**836.** _____. Papers. State Historical Society of Iowa, Des Moines. Papers. 4 boxes.

**837.** _____. Papers. University of Iowa Libraries, Iowa City. Family correspondence and papers.

**838.** Weller, Luman Hamlin. Correspondence. State Historical Society of Wisconsin, Madison. 11 boxes. Material on Weaver's career.

# 13
# The Garfield Administration

## A. Inauguration

**839.** Allderdice, Elizabeth Winslow. "Over the Hill to the White House." New York: Denison & Company, 1881. Poem written for the inauguration.

**840.** Chapin, Elizabeth (Moore). *American Court Gossip: Or, Life at the National Capitol*. Marshalltown, Iowa: Chapin & Hartwell Bros., 1887. 44–56. Eyewitness account of the inauguration and comments on his administration published in the *Iowa State Register*.

**841.** Chester, Edward W. "Beyond the Rhetoric: A New Look at Presidential Inaugural Addresses." *Presidential Studies Quarterly* 10 (Fall 1980): 571–82. Notes the mixed reviews of his speech as well as its common themes employed by all Gilded Age presidents.

**842.** Durbin, Louise. *Inaugural Cavalcade*. New York: Dodd, Mead, 1971. 34–41. Describes the ceremonies drawing on contemporary sources.

**843.** Ferrell, Robert H., ed. "Young Charley Dawes Goes to the Garfield Inauguration: A Diary." *Ohio Historical Quarterly* 70 (October 1961): 332–42. Observations of the future Vice-President when, at the age of fifteen, he accompanied his father to Washington.

**844.** *[Invitation to] Inaugural Reception & Promenade Concert . . . at the National Museum, Washington, D.C. March 4th, 1881*. New York: H. Lee Bank Note Co., 1881. Five copies of the invitation are in Garfield's folder in Library of Congress.

**845.** "The Inauguration." *Harper's Weekly* 25 (March 19, 1881): 180.

**846.** *Inauguration Ball, March 4th, 1881*. Washington: Inaugural Committee, 1881. Program.

**847.** Kittler, Glenn D. *Hail to the Chief! The Inauguration Days of Our Presidents.* Philadelphia: Chilton Books, 1965. Chap. 20, 108–13. Good account of the event.

**848.** Lott, Davis *The Inaugural Addresses of the American Presidents: From Washington to Kennedy.* New York: Holt, Rinehart & Winston, 1961. 143–48.

**849.** Marchman, Watt P., ed. "The Washington Visits of Jenny Halstead, 1879–1881, From Her Letters." *Historical and Philosophical Society of Ohio Bulletin* 12 (July 1954): 179–93. Describes the inauguration ceremonies and the ball she attended with President and Mrs. Hayes.

**850.** "President Garfield's Inauguration: A Vast Crowd and Unusually Brilliant Spectacle." *Frank Leslie's Illustrated Newspaper* 52 (March 19, 1881): 38–39. Contains several illustrations.

**851.** U.S. Congress. Senate. *Committee of Arrangements for the Inauguration, 1881. Arrangements for the Inauguration of the President of the United States on the Fourth of March, 1881.* Washington: Government Printing Office, 1881.

**852.** _____. "Inauguration Ceremonies." *Congressional Record, 47th Cong., Special Session of the Senate*, 12 (March 4, 1881): 2–3.

**853.** Washington, D.C. Inaugural Committee, 1881. *Inaugural Programme, Published by Permission of the Executive Committee.* Washington: Gibson Bros., 1881.

**854.** Wheeler, E. J. "Inaugural Ode, March 4th, 1881." *Independent* 33 (March 10, 1881): 4.

## B. Cabinet: Formation and Administration

**855.** Fowler, Dorothy G. *The Cabinet Politician: The Postmasters General, 1829–1909.* New York: Columbia University Press, 1943. 174–79. Heralded by reformers, James had little opportunity to promote change.

**856.** Fuller, Wayne E. *The American Mail: Enlarger of the Common Life.* Chicago: University of Chicago Press, 1972. Contains a few direct references to Garfield.

**857.** Getchell, George H. *Our Nation's Executive and Their Administrations. . . 1775–1885.* New York: Getchell & Fuller, 1885. Informative but dated account. Includes names of cabinet and congressional members.

**858.** Godkin, E. L. "Cabinet Officers in Congress." *The Nation* 32 (Feb. 17, 1881): 107–9. Discusses the Senate debate over whether cabinet members should be allowed in the chamber.

**859.** Horn, Stephen. *The Cabinet and Congress.* New York: Columbia University Press, 1960. 66–71. Notes the debate on the procedual reform regarding appearance of cabinet members before Congress.

**860.** Klotsche, J. Martin. "The Star Route Cases." *Mississippi Valley Historical Review* 22 (September 1935): 407–18. Only study of the post office scandal involving ex-Senator Stephen W. Dorsey of Arkansas, secretary of the Republican National Committee.

**861.** Leland, Earl J. "The Post Office and Politics, 1876–1884: The Star Route Frauds." Ph.D. dissertation, University of Chicago, 1964.

**862.** *Star Route Frauds*. Reports in House Misc. Doc. No. 38, 48th Cong. 1st sess., Pt.2, 1882. Chief source for this mail fraud scandal discovered in the Garfield administration.

**863.** Waltmann, Henry G. "The Interior Department, War Department and Indian Policy, 1865–1887." Ph.D. dissertation, University of Nebraska, 1962.

## C. Congress and the Conkling Crisis

**864.** Binkley, Wilfred E. *President and Congress*. New York: Alfred A. Knopf, 1947. 158–59, 174–75. Asserts that Garfield had a plan to duel "to the finish with the most militant champion of senatorial courtesy."

**865.** Brigham, Johnson. *Blaine, Conkling and Garfield: A Reminiscence and Character Study*. New York: G. E. Strechert & Co., 1919. Published paper read at Prairie Club of Des Moines, April, 1919. Anecdotal look at the personality and difficulties of Conkling.

**866.** Connery, Thomas B. "Secret History of the Garfield-Conkling Tragedy" *Cosmopolitan* 23 (June 1897): 145–62. Good inside view by a New York editor who was asked by Conkling to be a press ally during the incident.

**867.** Dawes, H. L. "Conkling and Garfield." *Century Magazine* 143 (January 1894): 341–44. At the time of the dispute this Republican attempted to mediate.

**868.** Goldsmith, William M. *The Growth of Presidential Power: A Documented History*. Vol. 2. New York: Chelsea House, 1974. 1005–6. Includes documents relating to Garfield's confrontation with Conkling.

**869.** Harris, Joseph P. *The Advice and Consent of the Senate: A Study on the Confirmation of Appointment by the U.S. Senate*. Berkeley: University of California Press, 1953. 84–87. Believes that the claims of Conkling represented the "high water mark" in senatorial presumption.

**870.** Hartman, William J. "Politics and Patronage: The New York Customs House, 1852–1902." Ph.D. dissertation, Columbia University, 1952. Surveys the importance of this patronage plum.

**871.** Kimmitt, J. S., comp. *Presidential Vetoes, 1789–1976*. Washington: U.S. Government Printing Office, 1978. 59. Notes that Garfield vetoed no bills during his truncated administration during the 47th Congress, first session.

**872.** Merritt, Ewin A. *Recollections, 1828–1911*. Albany: J. B. Lyon, 1911. Chap. 11. 123–40. The dismissed Collector of New York City Port gives his reaction and provides relevant correspondence.

**873.** Rothman, David J. *Politics and Power: The United States Senate, 1869–1901*. Cambridge: Harvard University Press, 1966. 32–35. Recounts the Conkling feud.

### D. Patronage, the Spoils System, and Civil Service Reform

**874.** Blodgett, Geoffrey. *The Gentle Reformers: Massachusetts Democrats in the Cleveland Era*. Cambridge: Harvard University Press, 1966. Examination of the Democratic supporters of civil service.

**875.** _____. "The Mind of the Boston Mugwumps." *Mississippi Valley Historical Review* 48 (March 1962): 614–34. Concentrates on 1884 election, describing the reformers as political amateurs.

**876.** _____. "The Mugwump Reputation, 1870 to the Present." *Journal of American History* 66 (March 1980): 867–88. Reviews the poor reputation of the Mugwumps.

**877.** _____. "Reform Thought and the Genteel Tradition." In **542**. 55–76. Critical of the elite reformers.

**878.** Dobson, John M. *Politics in the Gilded Age: A New Perspective on Reform*. New York: Praeger Publishers, 1972. Notes the disappointment of many Independents with Garfield and their efforts to use his death to promote reform.

**879.** Fish, Carl R. *The Civil Service and the Patronage*. 1904; rpt. Cambridge: Harvard University Press, 1920. This classic observes that Garfield served during the "high water mark of Senate claims" on appointments.

**880.** Foulke, William Dudley. *Fighting the Spoilsmen: Reminiscences of the Civil Service Reform Movement*. 1919; rpt. New York: Arno Press, 1974. The reformer makes a few references to Garfield.

**881.** Hoogenboom, Ari. "An Analysis of Civil Service Reformers." *Historian* 23 (1960): 54–78. Emphasizes the "essentially conservative" nature of the reformers.

**882.** _____. *Outlawing the Spoils: A History of the Civil Service Reform Movement, 1865–1883*. Urbana: University of Illinois Press, 1961. Chs. 10–11. Negative portrayal of the reformers as unsuccessful businessmen who exaggerated the corruption.

**883.** _____. "The Pendleton Act and the Civil Service." *American Historical Review* 64 (1959): 301–18. Notes the impact of the act on both the social origins and social positions of civil servants.

**884.** _____. "Spoilsmen and Reformers: Civil Service Reform and Public Morality." In **542**. 69–90.

**885.** _____. "Thomas A. Jenckes and Civil Service Reform." *Mississippi Valley Historical Review* 42 (March 1961): 636–58. Discusses the role of this reform spokesman and future commission chair.

**886.** Lambert, Henry. *The Progress of the Civil Service Reform in the United States.* Boston: Newton Civil Service Reform Association, 1885. Pamphlet mentions impact of the assassination on reform.

**887.** Peskin, Allan. "The Unwilling Martyr: President Garfield and Civil Service Reform." *Hayes Historical Journal* 4, no.3 (Fall 1984): 28–37. This examination of his views notes that the Pendleton Act was more radical than anything he proposed.

**888.** Ross, Earle D. *The Liberal Republican Movement.* New York: Henry Holt and Co., 1919. Early study of the Republican reformers.

**889.** Skowronek, Stephan. *Building a New American State: An Expansion of National Administrative Capacities, 1877–1920.* Cambridge, Eng.: Cambridge University Press, 1982. Scattered references to Garfield in this analysis of American reform.

**890.** Sproat, John G. *"The Best Men": Liberal Reformers in the Gilded Age.* New York: Oxford University Press, 1968. 107–10. Notes Garfield's ambiguity on the reform movement.

**891.** Stewart, Frank M. *The National Civil Service Reform League: History, Activities and Problems.* Austin: University of Texas Press, 1929. 31–32. This dated history notes that reformers were quick to see the propaganda significance of Guiteau's crime.

**892.** Thatcher, John Howard. "Public Discussion of Civil Service Reform, 1864–1883." Ph.D. dissertation, Cornell University, 1943.

**893.** Van Riper, Paul. *History of the United States Civil Service.* Evanston, Ill.: Row, Peterson and Company, 1958. Chap. 4. Mentions impact of the assassination on promotion of reform.

**894.** White, Leonard. *The Republican Era: A Study in Administrative History, 1869–1901.* New York: Macmillan, 1965. 34–35, 61–65. This landmark study praises Garfield's work on appropriations and recounts his later conflict with Congress.

## E. Congressional Documents

**895.** U.S. Congress. *Congressional Record.* Washington: Government Printing Office, 1874– . Transcript of debates, often edited by the speakers before publication.

**896.** _____. *House Journal.* Washington: Government Printing Office, 1789– . Outline of daily business.

**897.** _____. *Journal of the Executive Proceedings of the Senate of the United States of America*. Washington: Government Printing Office, 1789– . Outline of daily business.

**898.** _____. *Senate Journal*. Washington: Government Printing Office, 1789– . Outline of daily business.

**899.** U.S. National Archives. *Papers of the United States Senate Relating to Presidential Nominations, 1789–1901*. Record group 46. Washington: Government Printing Office, 1964.

**900.** *United States Statutes-at-Large*. Washington: Government Printing Office, 1789– .

**901.** U.S. Supreme Court. *United States Reports*. Washington: Government Printing Office, 1790– . Opinions and decisions.

### F. Race and Sectional Tensions

**902.** Beatty, Bess. *A Revolution Gone Backward: The Black Response to National Politics, 1876–1896*. Westport, Conn.: Greenwood Press, 1987. Chap. 2, 31–44. Critical of Garfield efforts.

**903.** De Santis, Vincent P. "President Garfield and the Solid South." *North Carolina Historical Review* 36 (October 1959): 442–65. Recounts Garfield's efforts to recruit William Mahone, leader of the Virginia Readjusters.

**904.** _____. "Republican Efforts to 'Crack the Democratic South.'" *Review of Politics* 14 (1952): 244–64. Notes Garfield's limitations in promoting civil rights and in cementing an alliance with the Readjusters.

**905.** _____. *Republicans Face the Southern Question: The New Departure Years, 1877–1897*. Baltimore: Johns Hopkins University Press, 1959. Chap. 4. Reviews Garfield's efforts to abandon the conciliatory policy of Hayes and to initiate limited cooperation with Independents in the South.

**906.** Garrett, Romeo B. *The Presidents and the Negro*. Peoria, Ill.: Bradley University Press, 1982. 172–75. Discusses Garfield's appointments of blacks, such as Blanche K. Bruce and Henry Highland Garnet.

**907.** _____. "Republican Party and the Southern Negro, 1877–1897." *Journal of Negro History* 45 (April 1960): 71–87. Tracing black dissatisfaction with the Republican party, notes that Garfield received little negative reaction because of his short term.

**908.** Grossman, Lawrence. *The Democratic Party and the Negro: Northern and National Politics, 1868–92*. Urbana: University of Illinois Press, 1976. 55–57. Notes that the inaction of Garfield and Arthur set "the stage for Negro rebellion against Republican neglect."

**909.** Hirshon, Stanley P. *Farewell to the Bloody Shirt: Northern Republicans and the Southern Negro, 1877–1893*. Bloomington: Indiana University Press, 1962. Chap. 4, 78–98. Notes that his policies to break up the Solid South included "bloody shirt," education aid, and political alliance in Virginia.

**910.** Logan, Rayford W. *The Negro in American Life and Thought: The Nadir, 1877–1901*. New York: Dial, 1954. Reprinted as *The Betrayal of the Negro, From Rutherford B. Hayes to Woodrow Wilson*. New York: Collier Books, 1965. Contains only a few citations to Garfield.

**911.** Patton, James W. "The Republican Party in South Carolina, 1876–1895." *Essays in Southern History Presented to Joseph Gregoire de Roulhac Hamilton*. Ed. Fletcher M. Green. Chapel Hill: University of North Carolina Press, 1949.

**912.** Peskin, Allan. "President Garfield and the Southern Question: The Making of a Policy That Never Was." *Southern Quarterly* 16, no. 4 (1978): 375–86. Acknowledges that he had no defined Southern policy in 1881 and speculates on what it might have been.

**913.** Sinkler, George. *The Racial Attitudes of American Presidents, from Abraham Lincoln to Theodore Roosevelt*. Garden City: Doubleday, 1971. 199–212.

## G. Tariff

**914.** *Garfield and the Tariff, His Record in Congress on the Subject of Free Trade and Protection*. N.p., 1880.

**915.** Gignilliat, John L. "Pigs, Politics, and Protection: The European Boycott of American Pork, 1879–1891." *Agricultural History* 35 (1961): 3–12. Discusses the reaction during Garfield's administration to a misleading British report.

**916.** Hinton, John W. *Garfield, The American Protectionist and True Friend of American Labor: Lecture, Delivered at Beaver Dam, Wisconsin, March 9th, 1882*. [Wisconsin: s.n., 1882].

**917.** Hunsberger, George E. "Garfield and the Tariff." M.A. thesis, Oberlin College, 1931.

**918.** Miller, Clarence L. *The States of the Old Northwest and the Tariff, 1865–1888*. Emporia, Kan.: Emporia Gazette Press, 1929.

**919.** Snyder, L. L. "The American-German Pork Dispute, 1879–1891." *Journal of Modern History* 17 (1945): 16–28. Traces the diplomatic implications of the decade-long economic battle.

**920.** Stanwood, Edward. *American Tariff Controversies in the Nineteenth Century*. 2 vols. Boston: Houghton Mifflin, 1903. 2: Chap. 15. This pro-tariff monograph provides a thorough examination of its impact on party politics.

**921.**  Tarbell, Ida M. *The Tariff in Our Time*. New York: Macmillan, 1906. Chapter 4. This anti-tariff attack by a noted journalist asserts that by "instinct and training" Garfield was a free trader.

**922.**  Taussig, Frank W. *The Tariff History of the United States*. New York: G. P. Putnam's Sons, 1909. Classic account.

**923.**  Terrill, Tom E. *The Tariff, Politics, and American Foreign Policy, 1874–1901*. Westport, Conn.: Greenwood Press, 1973. Thorough study of the topic.


## H. Trust and Monopoly Questions

**924.**  Hacker, Louis M. *The World of Andrew Carnegie, 1865–1901*. Philadelphia: J. B. Lippincott, 1967. Comprehesive and sympathetic account of the most successful businessman in the age of Garfield.

**925.**  Kirkland, Edward C. *Business in the Gilded Age: The Conservatives' Balance Sheet*. Madison: University of Wisconsin Press, 1952. Sympathetic view of the conservative world view that Garfield often reflected.

**926.**  _____. *Dream and Thought in the Business Community, 1860–1900*. Ithaca, N.Y.: Cornell University Press, 1956. Examines the views and motivations of businessmen in the Gilded Age.

**927.**  _____. *Industry Comes of Age: Business, Labor, and Public Policy, 1860–1897*. New York: Holt, Rinehart, and Winston, 1961. Important revision of the "robber baron" thesis.

**928.**  Thorelli, Hans B. *The Federal Anti-Trust Policy: Organization of an American Tradition*. Baltimore: Johns Hopkins University Press, 1955. Chaps. 1–3. Traces early anti-monopoly precedents and policies.

**929.**  Tipple, John. "Robber Baron in the Gilded Age: Entrepreneur or Iconoclast?" In **542**. 13–37. Defense of the industrial vanguard.


## I. Currency Questions

**930.**  Dewey, Davis R. *Financial History of the United States*. 10th ed. New York: Longmans, Green and Co., 1912.

**931.**  Friedman, Milton, and A. J. Schwartz. *A Monetary History of the United States, 1867–1920*. Princeton: Princeton University Press, 1963.

**932.**  Hepburn, Alonzo Barton. *A History of Currency in the United States*. New York: Augustus M. Kelley, 1967.

**933.**  Knox, John Jay. *A History of Banking in the United States Since the Civil War*. 5 vols. New York: A. M. Kelley, 1917–1939.

**934.** Laughlin, James Laurence. *History of Bimetallism in the United States.* 4th ed. New York: D. Appleton, 1897.

**935.** Myers, Margaret G. *A Financial History of the United States.* New York: Columbia University Press, 1970.

**936.** Nichols, Jeannette P. "John Sherman and the Silver Drive of 1877–1878: The Origins of the Gigantic Subsidy." *Ohio State Archeological and History Quarterly* 46, no.2 (1936): 148–64. Lauds Sherman's promotion of resumption in 1879 and his efforts to defeat cheap money.

**937.** Noyes, Alexander D. *Forty Years of American Finance, 1865–1907.* New York: G. P. Putnam's Sons, 1909.

**938.** Nugent, Walter T. K. *Money and American Society, 1865–1880.* New York: Free Press, 1968. Examines the acceptance of conservative money doctrines advocated by Garfield.

**939.** _____. "Money, Politics, and Society: The Currency Question." In **542.** 109–128. Critical of the "compulsive preoccupation of Americans with the money issue" during the Gilded Age.

**940.** Redlich, Fritz. *The Molding of American Banking: Men and Ideas.* Part II, 1840–1910. 1951; rpt. New York: Johnson Reprint Co., 1968.

**941.** Shultz, William J., and M. R. Caine. *Financial Development of the United States.* New York: Prentice-Hall, Inc., 1937.

**942.** Studenski, Paul, and Herman E. Kroos. *Financial History of the United States.* New York: McGraw Hill, 1943.

**943.** Taus, Esther R. *Central Banking Functions of the United States Treasury, 1789–1941.* New York: Columbia University Press, 1943.

**944.** Taussig, Frank W. "The Silver Situation in the United States." *Publication of the American Economic Association* 7 (1892): 1–118.

**945.** Unger, Irwin. *The Greenback Era: A Social and Political History of American Finance, 1865–1879.* Princeton: Princeton University Press, 1964. This comprehensive study of the issue suggests that politicians were more sophisticated in their motivations on the issue.

**946.** Usher, Ellis B. *The Greenback Movement of 1875–1884 and Wisconsin's Part in It.* Milwaukee: E. B. Usher, 1911.

**947.** Weinstein, Allen. "Origins of the Silver Question: Myths, Policies and Politics of a Monetary issue, 1867–1878." Ph.D. dissertation, Yale University, 1967.

**948.** _____. *Prelude to Populism: Origins of the Silver Issue, 1867–1878.* New Haven: Yale University Press, 1970. Good overview of the issue.

## J. Foreign Relations

### 1. General

**949.** Barnes, William, Morgan Barnes, and John Heath. *The Foreign Service of the United States: Origins, Development, and Function.* Washington: Department of State, 1961.

**950.** Bemis, Samuel Flagg, and Grace Gardner Griffin. *Guide to the Diplomatic History of the United States, 1775–1921.* Washington: Government Printing Office, 1935.

**951.** Bevans, Charles I., ed. *Treaties and Other International Agreements of the United States of America, 1776–1949.* Washington: Government Printing Office, 1968–1974. Vol. 6. 68–87. Angell Treaty of 1880, which restricted Chinese immigration.

**952.** Campbell, Charles S. *The Transformation of American Foreign Relations, 1865–1900.* New York: Harper and Row, 1976.

**953.** DeConde, Alexander, ed. *Encyclopedia of American Foreign Policy: Studies of the Principal Movements and Ideas.* 3 vols. New York: Charles Scribner's Sons, 1978.

**954.** Dennett, Tyler. *Americans in Eastern Asia.* 1922; rpt. New York: Barnes & Noble, 1963. Chap. 28. Discusses the Sino-American Immigration Treaties of 1876 and 1880.

**955.** Dulles, Foster Rhea. *China and America: The Story of Their Relations Since 1784.* Princeton: Princeton University Press, 1946.

**956.** _____. *Prelude to World Power: American Diplomatic History, 1860–1900.* New York: Macmillan, 1965. General introduction to the period.

**957.** Grenville, John A. S., and George Berkeley Young. *Politics, Strategy, and American Diplomacy: Studies in Foreign Policy, 1873–1917.* New Haven: Yale University, 1966.

**958.** Hasse, A. R., ed. *Index to Documents Relating to United States Foreign Affairs.* 3 vols. Washington: Government Printing Office, 1921.

**959.** LaFeber, Walter. *The New Empire: An Interpretation of American Expansion, 1860–1898.* Ithaca, N.Y.: Cornell University Press, 1963. Stresses economic thesis to explain expansion.

**960.** Logan, Rayford W. *The Diplomatic Relations of the United States and Haiti, 1776–1891.* Chapel Hill: University of North Carolina Press, 1941.

**961.** Montague, Ludwell L. *Haiti and the United States, 1714–1938.* New York: Russell and Russell, 1940.

**962.** Moore, John Basset. *History and Digest of the International Arbitrations to Which the United States Has Been a Party.* Vols. 1–3. Washington: Government Printing Office, 1898.

**963.** Nahm, Andrew C. "Reaction and Response to the Opening of Korea, 1876–1884." In *Studies on Asia.* Ed. Robert K. Sakai. Lincoln: University of Nebraska Press, 1965.

**964.** Robertson, William Spence. *Hispanic-American Relations with the United States.* New York: Oxford University Press, 1923.

**965.** Tansill, Charles Callan. *Canadian-American Relations, 1875–1911.* New York: P. Smith, 1964.

**966.** Terrill, Tom E. *The Tariff, Politics, and American Foreign Policy, 1860–1900.* Westport, Conn.: Greenwood Press, 1973.

**967.** Treat, Payson J. *Diplomatic Relations Between the United States and Japan, 1853–1905.* 3 vols. Stanford, Calif.: Stanford University Press, 1928.

**968.** U.S. State Department. *Treaties, Conventions, International Acts, Protocols, and Agreements between the U.S.A. and Other Powers, 1776–1937.* Washington: Government Printing Office, 1910–1938.

**969.** White, Elizabeth Brett. *American Opinion of France from Lafayette to Poincare.* 67–70, 94–109. New York: Alfred A. Knopf, 1927. Reviews samples of American press opinion during the claims crisis.

**970.** Williams, William Appleman. *The Tragedy of American Diplomacy.* New York: Delta Books, 1961. An important economic interpretation of the promotion of trade expansion and "informal imperialism."

**971.** Wilson, Beckles. *America's Ambassadors to France (1777–1924): A Narrative of Franco-American Diplomatic Relations.* 317–27. New York: Frederick A. Stakes Company, 1928. Discusses the tenure of Levi P. Morton, New York banker and ally of Conkling's.

## 2. Garfield Administration

**972.** Anderson, David L. "The Diplomacy of Discrimination: Chinese Exclusion, 1876–1882." *California History* 52 (Spring 1978): 320–45. Discusses how domestic political considerations complicated diplomacy.

**973.** _____. "Diplomatic Reversal: Frelinghuysen's Opposition to Blaine's Pan-American Policy in 1882." *Mississippi Valley Historical Review* 42 (March 1956): 653–71. Examines the repudiation of Blaine's conference proposal.

**974.** _____. "A New Approach to the Origins of Blaine's Pan-American Policy." *Hispanic American Historical Review* 39 (August 1959): 375–412. Notes that Garfield left control of foreign affairs almost entirely in Blaine's hands.

**975.** Blaine, James G. *Foreign Policy of the Garfield Administration: Peace Congress of the Two Americas.* Chicago?: s.n., 1882. This pamphlet was first published as an article in the *Chicago Weekly Magazine*, Sept. 16, 1882.

**976.** Burnette, Ollen Lawrence, Jr. "The Senate Foreign Relations Committee and the Diplomacy of Garfield, Arthur, and Cleveland." Ph.D. dissertation, University of Virginia, 1952.

**977.** Campbell, Charles S. *The Transformation of American Foreign Relations, 1865–1900.* New York: Harper & Row, 1976.

**978.** Carroll, Edward J. "The Foreign Relations of the United States with Tsarist Russia, 1867–1900." Ph.D. dissertation, Georgetown University, 1953.

**979.** "Chile-Peru Investigation." *House of Representatives Report #1790*, 47th Cong. 2nd sess. 1883.

**980.** Dobson, John. *America's Ascent: The United States Becomes a Great Power, 1880–1914.* DeKalb: Northern Illinois University Press, 1978.

**981.** Dozer, Donald. M. "The Opposition to Hawaiian Reciprocity, 1876–1888." *Pacific Historical Review* 14 (1945): 157–83. Details the fight led by Henry Alvin Brown, the champion of domestic sugar.

**982.** Edwards, Owen Dudley. "American Diplomats and Irish Coercion, 1880–1883." *Journal of American Studies* 1 (October 1967): 213–32. Describes Blaine's response on the issue of imprisoned Irish-Americans.

**983.** Hagan, Kenneth J. *American Gunboat Diplomacy and the Old Navy, 1877–1889.* Westport, Conn.: Greenwood Press, 1973. Provides some insight into the policies of Garfield and Arthur.

**984.** Holbo, Paul S. "Economics, Emotion, and Expansion: An Emerging Foreign Policy." In **542**. 199–222. Review concentrates on policy after Garfield.

**985.** Lash, Jeffery Norman. "Stephen Augustus Hurlbut: A Military and Diplomatic Politician, 1815–1882." Ph.D. dissertation, Kent State University, 1980. Illinois congressman who served as ambassador to Peru.

**986.** Millington, Herbert. *American Diplomacy and the War of the Pacific.* New York: Columbia University Press, 1948. Examines American efforts to stop the war initiated by Chile.

**987.** Perkins, Dexter. *The Monroe Doctrine, 1867–1907.* Baltimore: Johns Hopkins University Press, 1937.

**988.** Peskin, Allan. "Blaine, Garfield and Latin America." *Americas (Academy of American Franciscan History)* 36, no. 1 (1979): 79–89. Argues that Garfield played a key role in foreign policy of his administration.

**989.** Pike, Frederick B. *Chile and the United States, 1880–1962*. Notre Dame, Ind.: University of Notre Dame, 1963.

**990.** Plesur, Milton. "America Looking Outward: The Years from Hayes to Harrison." *Historian* 22 (May 1960): 280–95. This general review of American diplomacy finds stirrings of expansionism.

**991.** _____. *America's Outward Thrust: Approaches to Foreign Affairs, 1865–1890*. De Kalb: Northern Illinois University Press, 1971. Places the Garfield administration in the context of a survey of policy in the entire Gilded Age.

**992.** _____. *The Awkward Years: American Foreign Relations Under Garfield and Arthur*. Columbia: University of Missouri, 1961. This major work on the period argues that Blaine had a "free rein" during this time of transition.

**993.** _____. "Rumblings Beneath the Surface: America's Outward Thrust, 1865–1890." In [*Gilded Age*-Morgan]. 140–68. Makes no direct reference to Garfield, but supports the argument that the period was the start of expansionism.

**994.** Romero, Matias. "Settlement of the Mexico-Guatemala Boundary Question, 1882." *Bulletin of the American Geographical Society* 29, no.2 (1897): 123–59. Recollections by the Mexican representative in the 1881 negotiations that ended a sixty-year dispute.

**995.** _____. "Mr. Blaine and the Boundary Question between Mexico and Guatemala." *Bulletin of the American Geographical Society* 29, no.3 (1897): 281–330. The Mexican ambassador defends Blaine's role from the charge that he was unfriendly to Mexico.

**996.** Smith, Theodore C. "The Garfield-Blaine Tradition." *Massachusetts Historical Society Proceedings* 57 (March 1924): 291–307. Asserts that Blaine did not have a strong influence over the President.

**997.** Snyder, Louis L. "The American-German Pork Dispute, 1879–1891." *Journal of Modern History* 42 (1945): 16–28. Traces the ten-year dispute that began with the German decree in 1880 prohibiting importation.

**998.** Stevens, Sylvester K. *American Expansion in Hawaii, 1842–1898*. 1945; rpt. New York: Russell & Russell, 1968. Traces American efforts at economic expansion (which Garfield approved) and the political annexation (which he consistently opposed).

**999.** Wilgus, A. C. "Blaine and the Pan-American Movement." *Hispanic American Historical Review* 5 (1922): 622–708.

**1000.** Winchester, Richard C. "James G. Blaine and the Ideology of American Expansionism." Ph.D. dissertation, University of Rochester, 1966.

# 14
# Administration Personalities

## A. Members of the Cabinet

### 1. Arthur, Chester A.        Vice-President

**1001.** Chandler, William E. *Address on the Occasion of the Completion . . . of a Monument . . . Birthplace of Pres. Chester A. Arthur*. Concord, N.H.: Rumford Printing Company,1903. Eulogy.

**1002.** Goldstein, Joel K. *The Modern American Vice-Presidency*. Princeton: Princeton University Press, 1982. Few references to Arthur.

**1003.** Howe, George Frederick. *Chester Arthur: A Quarter-Century of Machine Politics*. New York: Dodd, Mead and Co., 1934. Well-written, though dated, biography of a politician who made only minor contributions to history.

**1004.** Kocher, Douglas J. "Temporary Vilification: The Chicago Press and Chester Arthur: 1881." *Journalism History* 9 (Summer 1982): 53–55, 60. Finds press hostility to Arthur.

**1005.** Levin, Peter R. *Seven By Chance: The Accidental President*. New York: Farrar, Straus & Co., 1948. Chap. 7, 147–76.

**1006.** Newcomer, Lee. "Arthur's Removal from the Customs House." *New York History* 18 (October 1937): 401–10. Hayes's removal of Arthur was motivated by a desire for reform and not hostility to Conkling.

**1007.** Paxson, Frederic Logan. "Chester Alan Arthur." *DAB.* (1928) vol. 1:373–76.

**1008.** Poole, Susan D. *Chester A. Arthur: The President Who Reformed*. Roseda, Calif.: M. Bloomfield & Co., 1977. Of little value.

**1009.** Reeves, Thomas C. *Gentleman Boss: The Life of Chester Alan Arthur.* New York: Knopf, 1975. Most recent biography views Arthur as a respectable and admirable chief executive.

### 2. Blaine, James G.        Secretary of State

**1010.** Beale, Harriet Blaine, ed. *Letters of Mrs. James Blaine.* 2 vols. New York, 1908. Includes her account of the assassination.

**1011.** Blaine, James G. *Political Discussions: Legislative, Diplomatic, and Popular, 1865-1886.* Norwich, Conn.: Henry Bill Publishing Co., 1887. Fifty-five speeches, including foreign policy of Garfield administration.

**1012.** _____. *Twenty Years of Congress: From Lincoln to Garfield With a Review of the Events which Led to the Political Revolution of 1860.* 2 vols. Norwich, Conn.: Henry Bill Publishing Co., 1884–1886. Vol. 2. Observations on Congress and the 1876 election. Last chapter makes brief comments on the 1880 election and has praise for Garfield.

**1013.** Conwell, Russel H. *The Life and Public Services of James G. Blaine.* Augusta, Maine: E. C. Allen & Co., 1884. Campaign biography.

**1014.** Crawford, Theon Clark. *James G. Blaine: A Study of His Life and Career.* New York: Franklin Press, 1893. A journalist wrote this general account of little value.

**1015.** Fish, Carl Russell. "James Gillespie Blaine." *DAB* (1929) vol. 2: 322–29.

**1016.** Hurlbert, William Henry. *Atrocious Foreign Policy of Secretary Blaine.* N.p., 1884. Campaign attack pamphlet.

**1017.** _____. *Meddling and Muddling, Mr. Blaine's Foreign Policy.* N.p., Privately printed, 1884.

**1018.** Johnson, Willis Fletcher. *Life of James G. Blaine: The Plumed Knight.* Philadelphia: Atlantic Publishers, 1893. Very general account without notes.

**1019.** Langley, Lester D. "James Gillespie Blaine: The Ideologue as Diplomatist." In *Makers of American Diplomacy: From Benjamin Franklin to Henry Kissinger.* Ed. Frank J. Merli and Theodore A. Wilson. New York: Scribner's, 1974. 253–78.

**1020.** Liberal Statesmanship (psued.). *Jews in Russia. Mr. Blaine's Interposition in Their Behalf.* N.p., 1884.

**1021.** Lockey, James B. "James G. Blaine." In *The American Secretaries of State and Their Diplomacy.* Ed. Samuel Flagg Bemis. Vol 7. New York: Alfred A. Knopf, 1928. 261–97. Short biographical sketch includes correspondence on the American question and with Great Britain.

**1022.** Muzzey, David Saville. *James G. Blaine: A Political Idol of Other Days.* New York: Dodd, Meade & Co., 1934. Portrays Blaine as a prime minister responsible for decision-making in the Garfield administration.

**1023.** Poore, Ben Perley. *Life and Public Services of Hon. James G. Blaine . . . and Gen. John A. Logan.* Des Moines, Iowa: O. C. Haskell, 1884. Campaign biography.

**1024.** Ridpath, John Clark. *Life and Work of Jas. G. Blaine.* Philadelphia: Standard Pub. Co., 1893. Campaign biography by a popular Garfield biographer.

**1025.** Russell, Charles E. *Blaine of Maine: His Life and Times.* New York: Cosmopolitan Book Corporation, 1931. This critical biography by a former reporter disparages Garfield as a weak politician.

**1026.** Sherman, Thomas H. *Twenty Years with James G. Blaine: Reminiscences by His Private Secretary.* New York: Grafton Press, 1928. Contains a few anecdotes as well as Blaine's memorandum recollecting the events on July 2, 1881.

**1027.** Stanwood, Edward. *James Gillespie Blaine.* Boston: Houghton Mifflin, 1905. Chap. 7. 216–57. Dated look at Blaine's role as co-equal with Garfield.

**1028.** Strobel, Edward H. *Mr. Blaine and His Foreign Policy: An Examination of His Most Important Dispatches while Secretary of State.* Boston: H. W. Hall, 1884. Campaign pamphlet.

**1029.** Talbot, Thomas. H. *The Proudest Chapter in His Life: Mr. Blaine's Administrtion of the State Department. His Conduct of South American Affairs.* Boston: Cupples, Upham & Co., 1884. Defense of Blaine used in the 1884 campaign.

**1030.** Tyler, Alice Felt. *The Foreign Policy of James G. Blaine.* Minneapolis: University of Minnesota Press, 1927. 1–79. Contends that Blaine, like William Seward, championed an aggressive policy.

### 3. Hunt, William Henry      Secretary of the Navy

**1031.** Hunt, Thomas. *The Life of William H. Hunt.* Brattleboro, Vt.: Private printing for the author by E. L. Hilldreth and Company, 1922. Chapter 18, 216–52. Chapter reviews his father's cabinet service and effort to build the "new Navy."

**1032.** Long, John Davis. *The New American Navy.* Vol. 1. New York: Outlook Company, 1903. 15–20. Mentions Hunt's support for naval expansion.

**1033.** Maclay, Edgar S. *A History of the United States Navy from 1775–1893.* New York: D. Appleton and Company, 1901. Vol. 3: 22–23. Brief reference.

**1034.** Pauline, Charles O. "A Half Century of Naval Administration." *Proceedings of the United States Naval Institute* 39 (September 1915): 1217–67.

**1035.** Seager, Robert II. "Ten Years before Mahan: The Unofficial Case for the New Navy, 1880–1890." *Mississippi Valley Historical Review* 40 (December 1953): 491–512. Reviews the arguments that fueled agitation for naval expansion.

**1036.** Sprout, Harold, and Margaret Sprout. *The Rise of American Naval Power, 1776–1918.* Princeton: Princeton University Press, 1939. Chapter covering the years 1881–1889 notes that 1881 marked the milestone in the start of building a new navy.

**1037.** White, Melvin J. "William Henry Hunt." *DAB* (1932) vol. 9:396–97.

### 4. James, Thomas Lemuel      Postmaster-General

**1038.** James, Thomas Lemuel. "The Postal Service in Commerce." In *1795-1895: One Hundred Years of American Commerce.* Ed. Chauncey M. Depew. New York: D. O. Haynes & Co., 1895. rpt. New York: Greenwood Press, 1968. 33–37. This brief essay on history is of limited value.

**1039.** Schulze, Paul. "Thomas Lemuel James." *DAB* (1932) vol 9:589.

### 5. Kirkwood, Samuel Jordan      Secretary of the Interior

**1040.** Clark, Dan Elbert. *Samuel Jordan Kirkwood.* Iowa City: State Historical Society of Iowa, 1917. Chap. 30, 359–70. This biography of the "War Governor" notes his lack of notable constructive activity during his cabinet service.

**1041.** Horack, Frank E. "Samuel Jordan Kirkwood." *DAB* (1933) vol. 10:436–37.

**1042.** Lathrop, Henry W. *The Life and Times of Samuel J. Kirkwood.* Iowa City: The Author (Chicago: Press of Regan Printing House), 1893. A sympathetic biography by a journalist friend relies mostly on eyewitness anecdotes. Notes his role in the 1880 campaign, but contains little discussion of his abbreviated cabinet service.

### 6. Lincoln, Robert Todd      Illinois Secretary of War

**1043.** Goff, John S. *Robert Todd Lincoln: A Man in His Own Right.* Norman: University of Oklahoma Press, 1968. Only biography of this son of a famous father. Chapter on his service as Secretary of War is of limited value.

**1044.** Paxson, Frederic Logan. "Robert Todd Lincoln." *DAB* (1933) vol. 11: 266–67.

### 7. MacVeagh, Wayne      Pennsylvania Attorney General

**1045.** Fuller, Joseph V. "Wayne MacVeagh." *DAB* (1933) vol. 12:446–51.

### 8. Windom, William       Minnesota Secretary of the Treasury

**1046.** Folwell, W. W. *A History of Minnesota.* 4 vols. St. Paul: Minnesota Historical Society, 1924–1926. Vol. 2:246, 341; Vol. 33:115–16. Brief references to the senator who served in the Garfield and Harrison administrations.

**1047.** Herrick, Robert P. *Windom: The Man and the School.* Minneapolis: Press of Byron and Willard, 1903. Short biographical sketch of little value is followed by a history of the Windom Institute in Montevideo, Minnesota (formerly Western Minnesota Seminary).

**1048.** Shippee, Lester B. "William Windom." *DAB* (1933) vol. 20:383–84.

## B. Supreme Court Justices

### 1. Chase, Salmon P.       Chief Justice

**1049.** Bullard, F. Lauriston. "Garfield and Chase: Their Ideas of Lincoln." *Lincoln Herald* 51 (December 1949): 2–5, 36. Uses Garfield letters to trace the changing views.

**1050.** Friedman, Leon. "Salmon P. Chase." In *The Justices of the United States Supreme Court, 1789–1969: Their Lives and Major Opinions*, eds. Leon Friedman and Fred L. Israel. New York: Chelsea House Publishers, 1969. Vol. 2: 1113–51.

**1051.** Gertis, Louis S. "Salmon P. Chase: Radicalism and the Politics of Emancipation, 1861–1864." *Journal of American History* 60 (June 1973): 42–62. Discusses the Radical measures promoted during the war by Garfield's political mentor.

**1052.** Hart, Albert Bushnell. *Salmon Portland Chase.* Boston: Houghton Mifflin, 1899. Dated biography of the man who befriended Garfield.

**1053.** Randall, James G. "Salmon Porter Chase." *DAB* (1930) vol. 4:27–34.

**1054.** Smith, D. V. *Chase and Civil War Politics.* Columbus: F. J. Heer Printing Co., 1931. Monograph on his presidential ambitions.

**1055.** Warden, Robert B. *An Account of the Private Life and Public Service of Salmon Portland Chase.* Cincinnati: Wilstach, Baldwin & Co., 1874. Biased account includes excerpts of Chase's letters.

**1056.** Wilson, Charles R. "The Original Chase Organization Meeting and the 'Next Presidential Election.'" *Mississippi Valley Historical Review* 23 (1936–1937): 61–79. Two documents relating to Chase's efforts to replace Lincoln in 1864.

### 2. Matthews, Stanley       Associate Justice appointed by Garfield

**1057.** Filler, Louis. "Stanley Matthews." In **1050**: 1351–75.

**1058.** Greve, Charles T. "Stanley Matthews 1824–89." In *Great American Lawyers*. Ed. William D. Lewis. Philadelphia: John Watson Co., 1907. 7:395.

**1059.** Lowne, Seldon Gage. "Stanley Matthews." *DAB* (1933) vol. 12:418–20.

**1060.** Magrath, C. Peter. *Morrison R. Waite: The Triumph of Character.* New York: Macmillan Co., 1963. Chap. 12. This biography of the Chief Justice discusses Matthews's as well as Garfield's views on judicial appointments.

## C. Members of Congress

### 1. Allison, William Boyd      Iowa Republican representative

**1061.** Nichols, Jeannette P. "William Boyd Allison." *DAB* (1928) vol. 1: 220–22.

**1062.** Sage, Leland L. *Willam Boyd Allison*. Iowa City: State Historical Society, 1956.

### 2. Bayard, Thomas Francis      Delaware Democratic senator

**1063.** Robinson, William Alexander. "Thomas Francis Bayard." *DAB* (1928) vol. 2:70–72.

**1064.** Tansill, Charles C. *The Congressional Career of Thomas Francis Bayard, 1868–1885*. Washington: Georgetown University Press, 1946. Careful account.

**1065.** _____. *The Foreign Policy of Thomas Bayard, 1885-97*. Washington: Georgetown University Press, 1941. Covers only his years as Secretary of State in the Cleveland administration.

### 3. Cameron, James Donald      Pennsylvania Republican senator

**1066.** McClure, Alexander K. *Old Times, Notes of Pennsylvania: A Connected and Chronological Record . . . of Pennsylvania . . .* Philadelphia: John Winston, 1905. Written by a political opponent.

**1067.** Meneely, A. Howard. "James Donald Cameron." *DAB* (1929) vol. 3:435-36.

### 4. Chandler, William Eaton      New Hampshire Republican senator

**1068.** Paxson, Frederic Logan. "William Eaton Chandler." *DAB* (1929) vol. 3:616–18.

**1069.** Richardson, Leon B. *William E. Chandler, Republican*. New York: Dodd, Mead and Company, 1940. This dated biography is the only one available.

### 5. Conkling, Roscoe    New York Republican senator

**1070.** Chidsey, Donald Barr. *The Gentleman from New York: A Life of Roscoe Conkling.* New Haven, Conn.: Yale University Press, 1935. 296–312. This first full-length biography is critical of Conkling and has praise for Garfield's patronage fight.

**1071.** Conkling, Alfred R. *The Life and Letters of Roscoe Conkling, Orator, Statesman, Advocate.* New York: C. L. Webster & Co., 1889. Published shortly after the senator's death, this brief review by his nephew contains little information.

**1072.** Gorham, Geo. C. *Roscoe Conkling Vindicated.* New York: N.p., 1888. Written by a friend of Conkling, this book presents Conkling's side of his dispute with Garfield.

**1073.** Jordan, David M. *Roscoe Conkling: Voice in the Senate.* Ithaca, N.Y.: Cornell University Press, 1971. This pro-Conkling biography attacks Garfield's "shabby treatment" of him.

**1074.** Paxson, Frederic Logan. "Roscoe Conkling." *DAB* (1930) vol. 4:346.

**1075.** Shores, Venila L. *The Hayes-Conkling Controversy.* New York: Northampton, Mass.: Department of History of Smith College, [1919]. Dated account of the controversy of another President's fight with Conkling.

**1076.** Young, May D. Russell. *Men and Memories: Personal Reminiscences.* New York: F. Tennyson Neely, 1961. Vol. 1: 214. Claims that Conkling was scornful toward Garfield.

### 6. Cox, Jacob Dolson    Ohio Republican representative

**1077.** Cochran, Henry. "Political Experiences of Major General Jacob Dolson Cox." 2 vols. 1940. Typed copy of unfinished biography deposited in Oberlin College Library.

**1078.** Cox, Jacob Dolson. "Oration on the Youth and Early Manhood of General James A. Garfield. Speech Delivered at the Society of the Army of the Cumberland: Fourteenth Reunion, 1882." Cincinnati: n.p., 1883.

**1079.** Ewing, J. R. *Public Services of J. D. Cox.* Washington: Neale Pub. Co., 1902. Twenty-page pamphlet.

**1080.** Hockett, Homer Carey. "Jacob Dolson Cox." *DAB* (1930) vol. 4:476–78.

### 7. Cox, Samuel Sullivan        Democratic representative from Ohio and New York

**1081.** Cox, S. S. *Free Land and Free Trade*. New York: Putnam, 1880. This strong advocate of free trade who often criticized Garfield argues for enlarged foreign markets for American crops.

**1082.** _____. *Three Decades of Federal Legislation, 1855–1885: Personal and Historical Memories*. Providence, R.I.: J. A. & R. A. Reid, 1885. Recollections of service on the electoral commission.

**1083.** Cox, William Van Zandt, and M. Harlow Northrup. *Life of Samuel Sullivan Cox*. Syracuse: M. H. Northrup, 1899. Dated account.

**1084.** Hockett, Homer Carey. "Samuel Sullivan Cox." *DAB* (1930) vol. 4: 482–83.

### 8. Dorsey, Stephen W.        Campaign manager and Arkansas Republican senator

**1085.** Herndon, D. T. *Centennial History of Arkansas*. Little Rock: S. J. Clarke Publishing Co., 1922. Brief reference to this senator who left no collection of papers despite his service in the Senate and in 1880 as secretary to the Republican National Committee.

**1086.** *Proceedings in the Second Trial of the Case of the United States vs. J. W. Dorsey . . . For Conspiracy*. Washington: Government Printing Office, 1883. 4 vols. Major source for second trial in the Star Route mail scandal.

**1087.** Thomas, David Y. "Stephen W. Dorsey." *DAB* (1931) vol. 5:387.

### 9. Edmunds, George Franklin        Vermont Republican senator

**1088.** Adler, Selig. "The Senatorial Career of George Franklin Edmunds, 1866–1891." Ph.D. dissertation, University of Illinois, 1934. Based mostly on his speeches.

**1089.** Kuntz, Norbert. "Edmunds' Contrivance: Senator George Edmunds of Vermont and the Electoral Compromise of 1877." *Vermont History* 38 (Autumn 1970): 305–15.

**1090.** Robinson, William Alexander. "George Franklin Edmunds." *DAB* (1931) vol. 6:24–27.

**1091.** Welch, Richard E. "George Edmunds of Vermont: Republican Half Breed." *Vermont History* 36 (1968): 64–73. Argues that his strategy helped stop Grant's bandwagon at the 1880 convention.

### 10. Hewitt, Abram Stevens       New York Democratic representative

**1092.** Nevins, Allan. *Abram S. Hewitt, with Some Account of Peter Cooper.* New York: Harper and Brothers, 1935. 364–88, 435–37. Served on the Electoral Commission and in 1880 lent his name to the infamous Morey letter.

**1093.** Parker, William B. "Abram Stevens Hewitt." *DAB* (1932) vol. 8:604–6.

### 11. Hoar, George Frisbie       Massachusetts Republican senator

**1094.** Gillet, Frederick. *George Frisbie Hoar.* Boston: Houghton Mifflin Co., 1934. Laudatory biography dedicated to relatives of the senator.

**1095.** Haynes, George H. "George Frisbie Hoar." *DAB* (1932) vol. 9:87–88.

**1096.** Hess, James William. "George F. Hoar, 1826–1884." Ph.D. dissertation, Harvard University, 1964.

**1097.** Hoar, George F. *Autobiography of Seventy Years.* 2 vols. New York: Charles Scribner's Sons, 1903. 1:384–404. Friend of Garfield's discusses the 1880 convention where he presided.

**1098.** Welch, Richard E., Jr. *George Frisbie Hoar and the Half Breed Republicans.* Cambridge: Harvard University Press, 1971. Chap. 6.

### 12. Ingalls, John James       Kansas Republican senator

**1099.** Ingalls, John James. *A Collection of the Writings of John James Ingalls: Essays, Addresses, and Orations.* Kansas City, Mo.: Hudson-Kimberly Publishing Co., 1902.

**1100.** McGrane, Reginald C. "John James Ingalls." *DAB* (1932) vol. 9:462–63.

### 13. Kelley, William D.       Pennsylvania Republican representative

**1101.** Brown, Ira V. "William D. Kelley and Radical Reconstruction." *Pennsylvania Magazine of History and Biography* 85 (July 1961): 316–29. Attacks the stereotype of "Pig-Iron" Kelley by noting his role in promoting civil rights.

**1102.** Kelley, William D. *A Personal Explanation by Hon. William D. Kelley of Pennsylvania, Elicited by the Remarks of Hon. James A. Garfield, of March 6, 1878, in the House of Representatives, March 9, 1878.* Washington: N.p., 1878. Speech attacks Garfield's address advocating specie resumption.

### 14. Logan, John A.       Illinois Republican senator

**1103.** Edget, Edwin Francis. "John Alexander Logan." *DAB* (1932) vol. 8: 363–65.

**1104.** Jones, James Pickett. *Black Jack: John A. Logan and Southern Illinois in the Civil War Era.* 1967; rpt. Carbondale: Southern Illinois University Press, 1995.

**1105.** Logan, Mary S. *Reminiscences of a Soldier's Wife: An Autobiography*. New York: Charles Scribner's Sons, 1913. Inside look at Republican politics by the senator's wife, who viewed Garfield with suspicion as the "consummate politician."

### 15. Mahone, William        Virginia Independent senator

**1106.** Blake, Nelson Morehouse. *William Mahone of Virginia: Soldier and Political Insurgent*. Richmond: Garrett & Massie, 1935. Chap. 8, 196–234. Most complete study of this leader who was one of the "most maligned characters in Virginia history."

**1107.** Degler, Carl N. *The Other South: Southern Dissenters in the Nineteenth Century*. New York: Harper & Row, 1974. 271–304. Discusses Mahone's movement as part of a dissenting tradition.

**1108.** Moore, James T. "Black Militancy in Readjuster Virginia, 1879–1883." *Journal of Southern History* 41 (May 1975): 167–86. Notes the role of the racial strategy in the movement's collapse.

**1109.** Morton, Richard L. *Virginia Since 1861*. Vol. 3 of *History of Virginia*. Chicago: American Historical Society, 1924. Chap. 9. Dated chapter on Readjuster movement.

**1110.** Pearson, Charles C. *The Readjuster Movement in Virginia*. New Haven: Yale University Press, 1917. Chap. 11. This early account includes chapter on the 1880–1881 alliance with the Republicans.

**1111.** Pulley, Raymond H. *Old Virginia Restored: An Interpretation of the Progressive Impulse, 1870–1930*. Charlottesville: University Press of Virginia, 1968. Chap. 2. 24–47. Discusses Garfield's encouragement of Mahone alliance and his hope for a Republican victory in the state.

**1112.** Wynes, Charles E. *Race Relations in Virginia 1870–1902*. Totowa, N.J.: Rowman & Littlefield, 1971. Chap. 2. Discusses the impact of political revolution lead by the "liberal, but dictatorial" Mahone.

### 16. Platt, Thomas Collier        New York Republican senator

**1113.** Gosnell, Harold. *Boss Platt and His New York Machine: A Study of Political Leadership*. Chicago: University of Chicago Press, 1924. Studies his later career when he built a powerful machine in the Empire State.

**1114.** Platt, Thomas Collier. *The Autobiography of Thomas Collier Platt*. Ed. Louis J. Lang. New York: B. W. Dodge and Co., 1910. This Conkling associate provides an unsympathetic view of Garfield's role in the 1880 election and the subsequent patronage battles.

### 17. Plumb, Preston    Kansas Republican senator

**1115.** Connelley, William Elsey. *The Life of Preston Plumb, 1837–1891: U.S. Senator from Kansas for Fourteen Years from 1877 to 1891.* Chicago: Browne & Howell Co., 1913. Chap. 39, 245–48. This eulogistic biography includes anecdotes of the 1880 convention.

### 18. Schenck, Robert Cumming    Ohio Republican representative

**1116.** Schenck, Alexander DuBois. *The Rev. Wm. Schenck, His Ancestry and His Descendants.* Washington: Rufus H. Darby, 1883. Relative of the Congressman traces the family history.

**1117.** Spaudling, E. Wilder. "Robert C. Schenck." *DAB* (1932) vol. 17:427–28.

**1118.** Peskin, Allan. "An Ohio Yankee at Dom Pedro's Court: Notes on Brazilian Life in the 1850's by an American Diplomat, Robert C. Schenck [with Donald Ramos]." *The Americas* 38 (April 1982): 497–514.

### 19. Sherman, John    Ohio Republican senator

**1119.** Bronson, S. A. *John Sherman: What He Has Said and Done: Being a History of the Life and Public Services of the Hon. John Sherman, Secretary of the Treasury of the United States.* New York: H. W. Derby, 1880.

**1120.** Bridges, Roger D. "The Constitutional World of Senator John Sherman, 1861–1869." Ph.D. dissertation, University of Illinois, 1970.

**1121.** Burton, Theodore E. *John Sherman.* Boston: Houghton Mifflin Co., 1906. Scattered references to Garfield.

**1122.** Kerr, Winfield S. *John Sherman: His Life and Public Service.* 2 vols. Boston: Sherman, French & Co., 1908. Dated sympathetic biography.

**1123.** Nichols, Jeannette P. "John Sherman." *DAB* (1935) vol. 17:84–88.

**1124.** _____. "John Sherman: A Study in Inflation." *Mississippi Valley Historical Review* 21 (September 1934): 181–94. Includes a discussion of why the "Icicle of the Treasury" never received the presidential nomination.

**1125.** _____. "John Sherman and the Silver Drive of 1877–78." *Ohio State Archaeological and Historical Quarterly* 46 (April 1937): 148–65. Traces his pragmatic efforts to check the development of the currency question and the Greeenback party.

**1126.** Sherman, John. *Recollections of Forty Years in the House, Senate and Cabinet, An Autobiography.* 2 vols. New York: Werner Co., 1895. 2: 774–83. In this important source Sherman is bitter toward Garfield, whom he blames for the failure to win the 1880 nomination.

**1127.** _____. *Selected Speeches and Reports on Finance and Taxation from 1859 to 1878*. New York: D. Appleton and Company, 1879.

### 20. Vallandigham, Clement L.        Ohio Democratic representative

**1128.** Gray, Wood. *The Hidden Civil War: The Story of the Copperheads*. New York: Viking Press, 1942. Strong attack in this negative survey of Midwestern Copperheads.

**1129.** Klement, Frank L. *The Limits of Dissent: Clement L. Vallandigham & the Civil War*. Lexington: University Press of Kentucky, 1970. The only historical biography of Lincoln's strongest critic.

**1130.** Smith, Thomas H. "Crawford County 'Ez Trooly Dimecratic.' " *Ohio History* 76 (1967): 33–53. This local study of the Peace Democrats provides insight into the movement statewide.

**1131.** Smith, William E. "Clement Laird Vallandigham." *DAB* (1935) vol. 19:143–45.

**1132.** Vallandigham, Clement L. *The Record of Hon. C. L. Vallandigham on Abolition, the Union, and the Civil War*. Columbus: J. Walter & Co., 1863. Autobiographical account.

**1133.** Vallandigham, James L. *Biographical Memoir of Clement L. Vallandigham by His Brother*. New York: J. Walter & Co., 1864. Sixty-four-page booklet published soon after his brother's return from Canada.

**1134.** _____. *A Life of Clement Vallandigham*. Baltimore: Turnbull Brothers, 1872. This defense by his brother has some questionable stories but also some valuable letters that have since been lost.

**1135.** Zornow, William F. "Clement L. Vallandigham and the Democratic Party in 1864." *Bulletin of the Historical and Philosophical Society of Cincinnati* 19 (January 1961): 21–37.

### 21. Wade, Benjamin Franklin        Ohio Republican senator

**1136.** Meneely, A. Howard. "Benjamin Franklin Wade." *DAB* (1936) vol. 19: 303–5.

**1137.** Riddle, A. G. *The Life of Benjamin Wade*. Cleveland: W. W. Williams, 1886. A close friend wrote this brief and sympathetic biography of the Ohio Radical, about whom Garfield had qualms regarding his possible succession to the presidency.

**1138.** Trefousse, Hans L. *Benjamin Franklin Wade: Radical Republican from Ohio*. New York: Twayne Publishing Inc., 1961. This first historical biography defends him as a "fighter for freedom."

## D. Associates

### *1. Black, Jeremiah Sullivan*     *Pennsylvania lawyer involved in the Milligan case and the Electoral Commission dispute*

**1139.** Black, Chauncey F. *Essays and Speeches of Jeremiah S. Black: With a Biographical Sketch.* New York: Appleton and Co., 1885. Son compiled these speeches and added a biographical memoir.

**1140.** Brigance, William Norwood. *Jeremiah Sullivan Black: A Defender of the Constitution and the Ten Commandments.* Philadelphia: University of Pennsylvania, 1934.

**1141.** Clayton, Mary (Black), ed. *Reminiscences of Jeremiah S. Black.* St. Louis: Christian Publishing Co., 1887. Contains a few anecdotes.

**1142.** Nichols, Roy F. "Jeremiah Sullivan Black." *DAB* (1933) vol. 11:310–13.

### *2. Depew, Chauncey M.*     *New York Republican leader*

**1143.** Chapin, J. D., ed. *Orations, Addresses and Speeches.* New York: Private printing, 1910. Collection of Depew's speeches.

**1144.** Clemens, Will M., ed. *The Depew Story Book.* London: F. T. Neely, 1891. 11–18. This collection of stories contains a short biographical sketch of little value.

**1145.** Depew, Chauncey M. "Leaves from My Autobiography." *Scribner's* 70 (November/December 1921): 515–30, 664–76. Little on Garfield but very critical of Conkling.

**1146.** _____. *My Memoirs of Eighty Years.* New York: Charles Scribners, 1924. Chap. 8, 107–15. Includes anecdotes on 1880 race and his visit to Mentor.

**1147.** Seitz, Don C. "Chauncey Mitchell Depew." *DAB* (1930) vol. 5:244–47.

**1148.** Yeager, Willard Hayes. *Chauncey Mitchell DePew—The Orator: Includes Many Speeches Including One to the Young Men's Republican Club on June 12, 1880.* Washington: George Washington University Press, 1934.

### *3. Gould, Jay*     *New York   Infamous speculator involved in Gold Panic*

**1149.** U.S. Congress. Committee on Banking and Currency. *Gold Panic Investigation.* New York: Arno Press, 1974. Reprint of the 1870 edition, which was issued as no. 31 of the House of Representatives Report. Chap. 8. Most valuable source on the Gold Corner attempt of 1869.

**1150.** Grodinsky, Julius. *Jay Gould: His Business Career, 1867–1892.* Philadelphia: University of Pennsylvania, 1957. This biography stresses Gould's transformation after his later losses and notes that the controversial figure left behind no collection of papers.

**1151.** Halstead, Murat, and J. Frank Beale, Jr. *Life of Jay Gould: How He Made His Millions.* Philadelphia: Edgewood Pub. Co., 1892. Unsympathetic contemporary account of the New York businessman who tried to corner the gold market.

**1152.** Klein, Maury. *The Life and Legend of Jay Gould.* Baltimore: Johns Hopkins University Press, 1986. Chap. 10. A major revision of one of history's most vilified businessmen.

**1153.** _____. "In Search of Jay Gould." *Business History Review* 52, no. 2 (Summer 1978): 166–99. Author's search is a spirited defense of the controversial person.

**1154.** O'Connor, Richard. *Gould's Millions.* New York: Doubleday, 1962. 90–110. Written for a popular audience, the biography has a brief discussion of "Black Friday."

**1155.** Warshow, Robert I. *Jay Gould: The Story of a Fortune.* New York: Greenberg, 1928. Chap. 12. This unsympathetic account has a dated account of "Black Friday."

### *4. Hay, John　　　Lincoln's secretary and later Garfield acquaintance*

**1156.** Clymer, Kenton. *John Hay: The Gentleman as Diplomat.* Ann Arbor: University of Michigan Press, 1975. Well-researched book focuses on Hay's foreign policy views and actions.

**1157.** Dennett, Tyler. *John Hay: From Poetry to Politics.* New York: Dodd, Mead & Co., 1933. Notes that Hay was closer to Garfield than to either McKinley or Roosevelt. He assumed the role of "candid friend" in the 1880 campaign, but declined the offer to be Garfield's private secretary.

**1158.** Dennis, Alfred L. P. "John Hay." In *The American Secretaries of State and Their Diplomacy.* Ed. Samuel F. Bemis. New York: Alfred A. Knopf, 1927–1929. vol. 9:115–89.

**1159.** Thayer, William R. *The Life and Letters of John Hay.* 2 vols. Boston: Houghton Mifflin Co., 1915. 1: 441–50.

### *5. Hinsdale, Burke Aaron　　　Ohio educator and president of Hiram College*

**1160.** Benton, Elbert J. "Burke Aaron Hinsdale." *DAB* (1932) vol. 9:66–67.

**1161.** Sussels, Ida. "Burke Hinsdale as Educator." Ph.D. dissertation (Education), New York University, 1939. See entries **23**, **410**, **789**, **1389**, and **1429**.

### 6. Hopkins, Mark        *Massachusetts educator and president of Williams College*

**1162.** Carter, Franklin. *Mark Hopkins*. Boston: Houghton, Mifflin and Company, 1893. 219, 292–94, 303–6. Written by a former Williams student shortly after Hopkins's death.

**1163.** Denison, John Hopkins. *Mark Hopkins: A Biography*. New York: Charles Scribner's Sons, 1935. Written by his grandson, this flattering biography describes Garfield's attachment to Williams.

**1164.** Hopkins, Mark. *The Law of Love and Love as a Law: or Christian Ethics*. New York: Armstrong and Co., 1868. Philosophical lectures by Garfield's mentor on political and economic questions.

**1165.** _____. *Lectures on the Evidence of Christianity*. Boston: T. R. Marvin and Son, 1846. Discusses origins of Christianity.

**1166.** _____. *Lectures on Moral Science*. Boston: Gould and Lincoln, 1862. Twelve lectures delivered while Garfield attended Williams College.

**1167.** _____. *An Outline Study of Man: Or, The Body and Mind in One System*. New York: Charles Scribner's Sons, 1883. Lectures given at Johns Hopkins.

**1168.** _____. *The Scriptural Idea of Man*. 1883. Lectures given at various theological seminaries.

**1169.** _____. *Teachings and Counsels: 20 Baccalaureate Sermons with a Discourse on President Garfield*. New York: Charles Scribner's Sons, 1884. 375–95. Includes the memorial discourse on Garfield delivered at Williams College on July 4, 1882.

**1170.** Howe, M. A. DeWolfe. *Classic Shades: Five Leaders of Learning and Their College*. 1899; rpt. Boston: Little, Brown and Company, 1928. 81–120.

**1171.** Spring, L. W. *Mark Hopkins, Teacher*. New York: Industrial Education Association, 1888.

**1172.** Starr, Harris Elwood. "Mark Hopkins." *DAB* (1932) vol. 9:215–17.

### 7. Ingersoll, Robert G.        *Illinois lawyer and Republican orator*

**1173.** Cramer, Clarence H. *Royal Bob, The Life of Robert G. Ingersoll*. Indianapolis: Bobbs-Merrill Co., 1952. Chaps. 12–13.

**1174.** Ingersoll, Robert G. *Great Speeches of Col. R. G. Ingersoll*. Ed. J. B. McClure. Chicago: Rhodes & McClure, 1897.

**1175.** Kittredge, H. E. *Ingersoll: A Biographical Appreciation*. New York: Dresden Publishers, 1910. Laudatory and of little value.

**1176.** Larson, Orvin. *American Infidel: Robert G. Ingersoll: A Biography*. New York: Citadel Press, 1962. 153–81. Covers 1880 election and his role as defense counsel in the Star Route trials.

**1177.** Paxson, Frederic Logan. "Robert Green Ingersoll." *DAB* (1932) vol. 9:469–70.

**1178.** Rogers, Cameron. *Colonel Bob Ingersoll: Biographical Narrative of the Great American Orator and Agnostic*. New York: Doubleday, 1927. Popular narrative with notes.

### *8. Kelly, John*      *New York leader of Tammany Hall*

**1179.** Fiske, Stephen. *Off-Hand Portraits of Prominent New Yorkers*. 1884; rpt. New York: Charles Scribner's Sons, 1932. Notes his unceasing opposition to Tilden.

**1180.** Holt, Lucius H. "John Kelly." *DAB* (1932) vol. 10:308–9.

**1181.** McLaughlin, J. Fairfax. *The Life and Times of John Kelly: Tribune of the People*. New York: American News Company, 1885. Flattering biography makes no mention of his role in the 1880 election.

**1182.** Werner, M. R. *Tammany Hall*. Garden City, N.Y.: Doran and Co., 1928. Chap. 5, 276–303. The chapter on John Kelly in this critical review of the organization does not refer to 1880 election.

### *9. Morton, Levi P.*      *New York political leader*

**1183.** Leach, J. G. *Memoranda Relating to the Ancestry and Family of Hon. Levi Parsons Morton, Vice-President of the U.S., 1889–93*. Cambridge: Riverside Press, 1894. Genealogical information.

**1184.** McElroy, Robert. *Levi Parsons Morton: Banker, Diplomat and Statesman*. New York: G. P. Putnam's Sons, 1930. Dated, sympathetic biography dedicated to Morton's grandchildren.

**1185.** Paxson, Frederic Logan. "Levi Parsons Morton." *DAB* (1934) vol. 13:258–59.

### *10. Reid, Whitelaw*      *Garfield advisor and editor of* **New York Tribune**

**1186.** Cortissoz, Royal. *The Life of Whitelaw Reid*. 2 vols. New York: Charles Scribner's Sons, 1921. Undocumented biography by a Reid associate is important for letters not otherwise available.

**1187.** Duncan, Bingham. *Whitelaw Reid: Journalist, Politician, Diplomat.* Athens: University of Georgia Press, 1975. Chaps. 6, 7. Recent biography discusses his role in undermining Tilden in 1876 and advising Garfield in 1880–1881.

**1188.** Jones, Robert H. "Whitelaw Reid." In **455**. 10. Account of Reid's days as a reporter.

**1189.** Reid, Whitelaw. *Abraham Lincoln.* London: University of Birmingham, Harrison and Sons, 1910. Pamphlet.

**1190.** _____. *After the War: A Southern Tour.* Cincinnati: Moore, Wilstach and Baldwin, 1866.

**1191.** Smart, James G. "Whitelaw Reid: A Biographical Study." Ph.D. dissertation, University of Maryland, 1964.

### *11. Wells, David A.*       *Connecticut free trade advocate and Garfield acquaintance*

**1192.** Ferleger, Herbert Ronald. *David A. Wells and the American Revenue System, 1865–1870.* Philadelphia: Porcupine Press, 1977. Limited in time and scope.

**1193.** Joyner, Fred Bunyan. *David Ames Wells: Champion of Free Trade.* Cedar Rapids, Iowa: Torch Press, 1939. Dated look at Gilded Age tariff reformer.

**1194.** Mitchell, Broadus. "David Ames Wells." *DAB* (1936) vol. 19:637–38.

**1195.** Terrill, Tom E. "David A. Wells, the Democracy, and Tariff Reductions, 1877–1894." *Journal of American History* 56 (December 1969): 540–55. Explores the ideas and influence of this Garfield friend who hoped that his sound money belief would get him an appointment.

**1196.** Wells, David A. "Evils of the Tariff System." *North American Review* 139 (September 1884): 273–82. Typical of Wells's many articles in the popular press.

**1197.** _____. *Freer Trade Essential to Future National Prosperity and Development.* New York: W. C. Martin's Steam Print House, 1882.

**1198.** _____. *Recent Economic Changes: And Their Effect on the Production and Distribution of Wealth and the Well-Being of Society.* New York: N.p., 1889. Statement on the relationship between overproduction and the need for trade expansion.

**1199.** _____. *Report of the Special Commissioner of Revenue for the Year 1868.* House Exec. Docs. 40th Cong., 3 sess., 1868.

**1200.** _____. *Why We Trade and How We Trade.* New York: G. P. Putnam's sons, 1878. Promoted internationalism based on free trade.

## E. Former Presidents

### 1. Grant, Ulysses S.

**1201.** Badeau, Adam. *Grant in Peace*. Hartford: S. S. Scranton and Co., 1887. This close friend of Grant's provides a personal perspective on his views on a third-term run and on Garfield.

**1202.** _____. *Military History of Ulysses S. Grant from April 1861 to April 1865*. 3 vols. New York: D. Appleton, 1868–1881. Contemporary account.

**1203.** Carpenter, John A. *Ulysses S. Grant*. New York: Twayne, 1970. This revisionist biography finds much to be admired in his support for freedmen.

**1204.** Catton, Bruce. *U.S. Grant and the Military Tradition*. Boston: Little, Brown, 1954. Popular biography discusses Grant's presidency in one chapter.

**1205.** Church, William Conant. *Ulysses S. Grant and the Period of National Preservation and Reconstruction*. New York: Garden City Pub. Co., 1926. Flattering and dated biography concentrates on military activity.

**1206.** Fuller, John F. C. *The Generalship of Ulysses S. Grant*. New York: Dodd, Mead and Company, 1929.

**1207.** Grant, Ulysses S. *Personal Memoirs of U. S. Grant*. 2 vols. New York: J. J. Little, 1886. Rev. ed. by E. B. Long. 1 vol. New York: Grosset, 1952. This exceptional, well-written autobiography ends with the conclusion of the Civil War.

**1208.** Grant, Ulysses S. III. *Ulysses S. Grant: Warrior and Statesman*. New York: William Morrow, 1969. Admiring biography by his grandson attempts to answer numerous critics.

**1209.** Hesseltine, William T. *Ulysses S. Grant, Politician*. New York: Dodd, Mead and Co., 1935. Standard biography finds him unequal to the political task required of the times.

**1210.** McFeely, William S. *Grant: A Biography*. New York: W. W. Norton, 1981. Definitive biography praises Grant as military leader and criticizes him as president who lacked programs and goals.

**1211.** McPherson, James M. "Grant or Greeley? The Abolitionist Dilemma in the Election of 1872." *American Historical Review* 71 (October 1965): 43–62. Gives perspective on the dilemma Garfield faced when he was upset with Grant's reelection.

**1212.** Moran, P. R., ed. *Ulysses S. Grant, 1822–1885: Chronology, Documents, Bibliographical Aids*. Dobbs Ferry, N.Y.: Oceana, 1968. Prepared for high school and undergraduate students, contains chronology, collection of edited documents, and brief annotated bibliography.

**1213.** Paxson, Frederic Logan. "Ulysses Simpson Grant." *DAB* (1931) vol. 7: 492–501.

**1214.** Peskin, Allan. "The 'Little Man on Horseback' and the 'Literary Fellow': Garfield's Opinions of Grant." *Mid-America* 55, no. 4 (1973): 271–83. Discusses how Garfield's initial disdain changed to "grudging admiration" at the end of Grant's term.

### 2. Hayes, Rutherford B.

**1215.** Barnard, Harry. *Rutherford B. Hayes and His America.* Indianapolis: Bobbs-Merrill Co., 1954. Biography examines in detail the 1876 election and also provides psychological perspective on the Ohio president.

**1216.** Bishop, Arthur, ed. *Rutherford B. Hayes, 1822–1893: Chronology, Documents, Bibliographical Aids.* Dobbs Ferry, N.Y.: Oceana Press, 1971. Of limited value.

**1217.** Davison, Kenneth E. *The Presidency of Rutherford B. Hayes.* Westport, Conn.: Greenwood Press, 1972. This sympathetic biography is the most comprehensive examination of Hayes as president.

**1218.** _____. "Rutherford B. Hayes Special Edition." *Ohio History* 77 (Winter-Spring-Summer 1968): 1–208. Entire issue devoted to Hayes.

**1219.** Davison, Kenneth E., and Helen M. Thurston, eds. "Contemporary Estimates of President Hayes." *Hayes Historical Journal* 2 (Fall 1978): 132–38. Reprint of January 28, 1893 *Literary Digest* article that surveyed favorable comments on Hayes by twenty prominent newspapermen.

**1220.** DeSantis, Vincent P. "President Hayes' Southern Policy." *Journal of Southern History* 21 (November 1955): 476–94. Discusses his failure in strategy to lure Southern Democrats.

**1221.** Eckenrode, Hamilton J. *Rutherford B. Hayes: Statesman of Reunion.* New York: Dodd, Mead and Co., 1930. Dated standard biography.

**1222.** Garrison, Curtis W. "Conversations with Hayes: A Biographer's Notes." *Mississippi Valley Historical Review* 25 (December 1938): 368–80. Notes include Hayes's opinions on Garfield's speeches and on the Democratic contenders.

**1223.** Gladden, Washington. *Great Commoner of Ohio . . . Rutherford Birchard Hayes . . . Jan. 22, 1893.* Columbus, Ohio: Nitschke Press, 1893. Eulogy by a prominent minister.

**1224.** _____. "Rutherford Birchard Hayes." *Ohio Archaeological and Historical Quarterly* 4 (1895): 338–61. Eulogistic account of Hayes contains some comparison of him with Garfield.

**1225.** Hoogenboom, Ari. *The Presidency of Rutherford B. Hayes*. American Presidency Series. Lawrence: University Press of Kansas, 1988. Balanced account portrays Hayes as moderately successful and well-intentioned but naive on racial issues.

**1226.** _____. *Rutherford B. Hayes: Warrior and President*. Lawrence: University Press of Kansas, 1995. Most recent biography.

**1227.** House, Albert V. "President Hayes' Selection of David M. Key for Postmaster General." *Journal of Southern History* 4 (February 1938): 87–93. Cites letters from the Henrick B. Wright collection discussing Hayes's appointments as part of the Compromise agreement.

**1228.** Howells, William Dean. *Sketch of the Life and Character of Rutherford B. Hayes: Also a Biographical Sketch of William A. Wheeler*. New York: Hurd & Houghton, 1876. The author also wrote a campaign biography for Garfield.

**1229.** McPherson, James M. "Coercion or Conciliation? Abolitionists Debate President Hayes's Southern Policy." *New England Quarterly* 39 (1966): 474–97. Notes that the majority of abolitionists criticized Hayes's policy.

**1230.** Nevins, Allan. "Rutherford Birchard Hayes." *DAB* (1932) vol. 8:446–51.

**1231.** Nichols, Jeannette P. "Rutherford B. Hayes and John Sherman." *Ohio History* 77 (1968): 125–38. Informative examination of the two politicians who shared a surprisingly close relationship.

**1232.** Peskin, Allan. "Garfield and Hayes: Political Leaders of the Gilded Age." *Ohio History* 77 (1968): 111–24. Garfield's biographer compares the two presidents who, despite similarities in background and ideology, never fully sympathized with each other.

**1233.** Porter, Daniel R. "Governor Rutherford B. Hayes." *Ohio History* 77 (1968): 58–72. Notes that Hayes earned the sobriquet "the good governor."

**1234.** Ransom, Frederick D. "The Great Unknown: Governor Rutherford B. Hayes of Ohio." Ph.D. dissertation, West Virginia University, 1978. Examination of his gubernatorial administration.

**1235.** Sinkler, George. "Race: Principles and Policy of Rutherford B. Hayes." *Ohio History* 77 (1968): 149–67. This examination of Hayes's Southern strategy provides a background to Garfield's actions.

**1236.** Swift, Donald C. "Ohio Republicans and the Hayes Administration Reforms: Part I. The Assault on the Spoils System." *Northwest Quarterly* 42 (Fall 1970): 99–106; "Part II: Ohio Republicans and the Hayes Administration Reforms" 43 (Winter 1971): 11–22. Brief review of the two policies and their impact on Ohio politics.

**1237.** Thelen, David P. "Rutherford B. Hayes and the Reform Tradition in the Gilded Age." *American Quarterly* 22 (Summer 1970): 150–65. Acknowledges that the ideology of Hayes and the reformers undermined any effective action.

**1238.** Vazzano, Frank P. "Hayes, Congress, and the Resurrection of Presidential Authority." Ph.D. dissertation, Kent State University, 1972.

**1239.** Williams, Charles Richard. *The Life of Rutherford Birchard Hayes.* 2 vols. Boston: Houghton Mifflin, 1914. This sympathetic, dated biography provides details but not interpretations.

**1240.** Williams, T. Harry. *Hayes of the Twenty-third: The Civil War Volunteer Officer.* New York: Alfred A. Knopf, 1965. Military historian studies how Hayes, a volunteer officer like Garfield, became a successful soldier.

### 3. Lincoln, Abraham

**1241.** Donald, David. *Lincoln.* New York: Simon and Schuster, 1995. Winner of the Pulitzer Prize.

**1242.** _____. *Lincoln Reconsidered: Essays on the Civil War Era.* New York: Alfred A. Knopf, 1961. Classic set of revisionist essays.

**1243.** Nicolay, John G., and John Hay. *Abraham Lincoln: A History.* 10 vols. New York: Century, 1890. Lincoln's secretaries wrote this "insider" biography of their famous employer.

**1244.** Oates, Stephen B. *Abraham Lincoln: The Man Behind the Myths.* New York: Harper & Row, 1984. Admiring second look.

**1245.** _____. *With Malice Toward None: The Life of Abraham Lincoln.* New York: Harper & Row, 1977. Well-written, one-volume biography.

**1246.** Quarles, Benjamin. *Lincoln and the Negro.* New York: Oxford University Press, 1962. Discusses how blacks responded to Lincoln.

**1247.** Randall, James G. "Abraham Lincoln." *DAB* (1933) vol. 11:242–58.

**1248.** _____. *Lincoln, the President.* 4 vols. New York: Dodd, Mead, 1945–1955. Standard biography completed by Richard N. Current upon Randall's death. Sixty-page bibliography at end of volume two.

**1249.** _____. *Mr. Lincoln,* ed. Richard N. Current. New York: Dodd, Mead, 1957. One-volume edition concentrates on his personal life.

**1250.** Sandburg, Carl. *Abraham Lincoln: The Prairie Years and the War Years.* 6 vols. New York: Harcourt, Brace and World, 1926–1939.

**1251.** Strozier, Charles B. *Lincoln's Quest for Union: Public and Private Meanings.* New York: Basic Books, 1982. Attempts to use psychohistory approach to the famous president.

**1252.** Thomas, Benjamin P. *Abraham Lincoln: A Biography.* New York: Alfred A. Knopf, 1952. Well-written narrative that until's Donald's book was the best one-volume biography.

**1253.** Thomas, John L., ed. *Abraham Lincoln and the American Tradition.* Amherst: University of Massachusetts Press, 1986. Collection of political essays.

**1254.** Thurow, Glen E. *Abraham Lincoln and the American Political Religion.* Albany: State University of New York Press, 1976. Describes the development of political creed as a civic religion.

# 15

# Assassination

## A. Assassination and Medical Treatment

**1255.** Adams, J. Howe. *A History of the Life of D. Hayes Agnew, M.D., LD.* Philadelphia: n.p., 1892. 220–49. Biography of the most famous of Garfield's doctors.

**1256.** Agnew, D. H. *The Principles and Practice of Surgery.* Philadelphia: J. B. Lippincott and Co., 1878. 3 vols. Vol 1: 186, 331. The prominent surgeon makes brief reference to the Garfield case.

**1257.** "An Autograph of President Garfield." *Century Magazine* 23 (1881): 82. Notes the failure to discover an earlier use of the Latin phrase that Garfield penned on his deathbed.

**1258.** Baker, F. "President Garfield's Case: A Diagnosis Made July 4th." *Walsh's Retrospect* 2 (1881): 617–22. A future medical professor gave a correct diagnosis when he was an anatomy assistant.

**1259.** Bell, Alexander Graham. *Upon the Electrical Experiments to Determine the Location of the Bullet in the Body of the Late President Garfield; And upon A Successful Form of Induction Balance for Painless Detection of Metallic Masses...* Washington: Gibson Brothers, 1882. 58p. Despite the incorrect conclusion about the location of the bullet, Bell finds the method encouraging.

**1260.** Bliss, D. W. *Feeding Per Rectum: As Illustrated in the Case of the Late President Garfield and Others.* Washington: N.p., n.d. Rpt. from the *Medical Record*, July 15, 1882. Asserts that his efforts to provide nutrient enemata prolonged the life of the President.

**1261.** _____. "Record of the Post-Mortem Examination on the President's Body." *American Journal of Medical Science* 82 (October 1881): 583–90. Autopsy report by the five attending physicians.

**1262.** _____. "Report of the Case of President Garfield." *Medical Record* 20 (October 8, 1881): 393–402. Defense by the surgeon in charge of the case. Accompanied by detailed account of the autopsy.

**1263.** _____. "The Story of President Garfield's Illness." *Century Magazine* 23 (December 1881): 299–305. Defends self as a doctor and praises Garfield as a patient.

**1264.** Brooks, Stewart M. *Our Murdered Presidents: The Medical Story*. New York: F. Fell, 1966. 55-125. Detailed discussion of the event and treatment.

**1265.** Cardinal, Eric J. "Assassination of James A. Garfield." *Lake County Historical Quarterly* 23, no.2 (June 1981): 1–6. Notes the similarities to the attacks on Lincoln and Reagan.

**1266.** *Complete Medical Record of President Garfield's Case Containing All the Official Bulletins from the Date of the Shooting to the Day of His Death Together with the Official Autopsy . . . Compiled From the Records of the Executive Mansion.* Washington: Chas. A. Wimer, 1881.

**1267.** Cunningham, Homer F. *The Presidents' Last Years: George Washington to Lyndon Baines Johnson*. Jefferson, N.C.: McFarland & Co., 1989. 150–55. Recounting of "Eighty-Day Struggle for Life."

**1268.** Day, Richard H. *Review of the Surgical Treatment of President Garfield*. New Orleans: Graham and Sons, 1882. Reprint from the *New Orleans Medical and Surgical Journal* 10 (August 1882): 81–95. Contends that the surgical treatment was faulty and erroneous. Argues that the death was not inevitable.

**1269.** *Excerpts from Opinions of the Distinguished Medical Men and Other Countries Justify the Treatment of the Late President Garfield Together with a Letter in Reply to the Resolution of the Special Committee of the House of Representatives Referring to the Expense Consequent Upon His Illness and Death.* Washington: Gibson Brothers, 1882. Compilation of journal excerpts in the United States and overseas justifying Garfield's treatment. Response to concerns over the expenses of the treatment.

**1270.** *Expenses of the Last Illness and Burial of President Garfield: April 19, 1882, Committed to the Committee of the Whole House on the State of the Union and Ordered To Be Printed: Mr. Taylor, From the Select Committee to Audit the Expense . . . to Accompany Bill H.R. 5889.* Washington: House of Representatives, 1882.

**1271.** Ferrick, John D. *From Falling Hands: The Story of Presidential Succession*. New York: Fordham University Press, 1965. 117–39. Good discussion.

**1272.** Fish, Stewart A. "The Death of President Garfield." *Bulletin of the History of Medicine* 24 (July-August 1950): 378–92. Concludes that better procedures could have saved the President.

**1273.** Friedman, Robert. "The Air-Conditioned Century." *American Heritage* 35, no. 5 (August/September, 1984): 20–33. History of air-conditioning notes the engineers' efforts to cool Garfield's bedroom.

**1274.** Hamilton, F. H. "The Case of President Garfield." *Medical Gazette* 8 (1881): 333–34. Replies to criticisms of the treatment.

**1275.** Hammond, William A., J. Marion Sims, John T. Hodgen, and John Ashurst, Jr. "The Surgical Treatment of President Garfield." *North American Review* 133 (1881): 578–610. Spirited defense of the treatment notes that even if the bullet had been located, surgery could not have removed it.

**1276.** Harper, S. B. "Gunshot Wounds of Three Presidents of the United States." *Proceedings of the Staff Meetings of the Mayo Clinic* 19 (January 12, 1944): 13–19. Concludes that the treatment for Garfield, Lincoln, and McKinley was consistent with the best medical opinions of the time.

**1277.** Kerwood, John R. "Assassination of President Garfield." *American History Illustrated* 5 (January 1969): 12–25. Very general account that includes many contemporary illustrations.

**1278.** "The Late President Garfield's Case." *Medical Record* 20 (October 8, 1881): 410–11. Mistake in diagnosis, though deplorable, was understandable.

**1279.** Lawrence, W., W. W. Upton, and J. Gilfillan. *Miscellaneous Documents, no. 14, series 2–2115, 47th Congress, House of Representatives, 2d session, Jan. 2, 1883.* A board of House members after deliberations cut by almost two-thirds the fees given to the team of doctors.

**1280.** Marti, Jose. *Muerte Del Presidente Garfield.* Buenos Aires: Azul, 1930.

**1281.** Marx, Rudolph. *The Health of the Presidents.* New York: G. P. Putnam, 1960. 235-46. This review of the efforts notes how modern conditions could have saved Garfield.

**1282.** Miller, Joseph M. "The Death of James Abram Garfield." *Surgery, Gynecology, and Obstetrics* 107 (July 1958): 113–18.

**1283.** Monteiro, George. "John Hay on Garfield's Deathbed Latin." *Western Illinois Regional Studies* 6, no.1 (January 1983): 38–41. Reprint of letter explaining words—"Stangulatus pro republica"—written by the wounded President.

**1284.** Moses, John B., and Wilbur Cross. *Presidential Courage.* New York: W. W. Norton & Co., 1980. 107–21. Account based on secondary sources of medical efforts after the assassination.

**1285.** Navy Department. *Reports of Officers of the Navy on Ventilating and Cooling the Executive Mansion During the Illness of President Garfield.* Washington: Government Printing Office, 1882. Discusses attempts to set up a primitive form of air conditioning. Includes record of room temperature.

**1286.** Parker, Owen W. "The Assassination and Gunshot Wound of President James A. Garfield." *Minnesota Medicine* 34 (March 1954): 227–33, 258. Very general account.

**1287.** Reyburn, Robert. *Clinical History of the Case of President James Abram Garfield . . . by . . . One of the Attending Surgeons in the Case of President Garfield.* Chicago: Office of the Journal of the Association, 1894.

**1288.** Shrady, George F. "The Question of Malpractice in the Case of the Late President Garfield." *Medical Record* 20 (November 26, 1881): 600–1. Asserts that the diagnosis error was unavoidable and that the wound was fatal.

**1289.** _____. "Surgical and Pathological Reflections on President Garfield's Wounds." *Medical Record* 20 (October 8, 1881): 404–6. At the invitation of Bliss, surgeons Weisse and Shrady examined evidence and defended the treatment.

**1290.** Smith, A. H. "President Garfield at Elberon." *American Medicine* 9 (January 21, 1905): 118–19. A doctor reports on the events, including the autopsy.

**1291.** Temkin, Owsei, and Janet Koudelka. "Simon Newcomb and the Location of President Garfield's Bullet." *Bulletin of the History of Medicine* 24 (July/August 1950): 393–97. Newcomb suggested using a rotating magnet to locate the bullet—a method Alexander Bell used on July 14.

**1292.** Tindall, Dr. William. "Echoes of a Surgical Tragedy." *Proceedings of the Columbia Historical Society* 23 (1920): 147–66. Eyewitness defends the actions of Bliss.

**1293.** Turnipseed, E. B. "A Dissenting Voice . . . in Regard to Diagnosis, Prognosis, and Treatment of the Case of President Garfield." *Medical Record* 20 (1881): 620–24. Suggests that a bullet forceps of his design would have helped.

**1294.** Vincent, Esther H. "Presidential Gunshot Wounds." *Surgery, Gynecology and Obstetrics* 91 (July/September 1950): 117–18. Concludes that the treatment could hardly be praised in light of modern knowledge of proper hygiene.

**1295.** Wadsworth, H. N. "Location of Lead in the Living Human Subject by Electricity." *Boston Medical and Surgical Journal* 105 (September 15, 1881): 259–60. Recounts author's successful efforts in 1875 to locate lead bullets in four patients in Washington.

**1296.** Walker, Kenneth R. *The Days the Presidents Died: Leading Men, Issues and Ideas.* Little Rock, Ark.: Pioneer Press, 1966. Discusses the issues and ideas in America on September 19, 1881.

**1297.** Weisse, Faneuil D. "Surgico-Anatomical Study of the Gunshot Wound of President Garfield." *Medical Record* 20 (October 8, 1881): 402–3. Believes that the incorrect diagnosis was unavoidable.

**1298.** White, J. W. *A Review of Some of the More Important Surgical Problems of President Garfield's Case*. Philadelphia: n.p., 1882. Rpt. from *Medical News* 40 (June 24, 1882): 677. His research suggests that there was no instance of recovery from such a wound.

**1299.** Wimer, Charles A., comp. *Complete Medical Record of President Garfield's Case, Containing All the Official Bulletins from the Date of the Shooting to the Day of His Death, Together with the Official Autopsy, Made September 20, 1881, and a Diagram Showing the Course Taken by the Ball*. Washington: C. A. Wimer, 1881.

**1300.** Wold, Karl C. *Mr. President, How Is Your Health?* St. Paul: Bruce Publishing Co., 1948. 133–39. Brief review of the assassination.

## B. Assassin and Trial

**1301.** Alexander, Henry H. *The Life of Guiteau, and the Official History of the Most Exciting Case on Record: Being the Trial of Guiteau for Assassinating Pres. Garfield*. Cincinnati, Ohio: Jones Brothers, 1882. This long narrative of the crime and trial asserts that Guiteau was feigning insanity.

**1302.** Beard, George M. "The Case of Guiteau: A Psychological Study." *Journal of Nervous and Mental Disease* 9 (January 1882): 90–125. Although he never testified, Beard was a strong advocate that the prisoner was insane since the age of eighteen.

**1303.** _____. *The Psychology of the Salem Witchcraft Excitement of 1692 and Its Practical Application to Our Time*. New York: G. P. Putnam's Sons, 1882. Believes that Guiteau was misdiagnosed and that the future would equate his trial with the Salem trials.

**1304.** Buckham, T. R. *Insanity Considered in Its Medico-Legal Relations*. London: J. B. Lippincott & Co., 1883. Provides insight into contemporary beliefs and expert opinions on insanity in 1882.

**1305.** Buckley, J. M. "A Study of Guiteau." *New York Christian Advocate* 57 (January 12, 1882): 17–18. The editor supplies an analysis during the middle of the trial.

**1306.** Cassity, John H. *The Quality of Murder: A Psychiatric and Legal Evaluation of Motives and Responsibilities in the Plea of Insanity as Revealed in Outstanding Murder Cases of this Century*. New York: Julian Press, Inc., 1958. 19–30. Convinced that Guiteau was insane before and at the time of the crime.

**1307.** Channing, W. *The Mental Status of Guiteau, the Assassin of President Garfield*. Cambridge: Riverside Press, 1882. Argues that Guiteau was insane.

**1308.** Clark, Thomas D. "My Name is Charles Guiteau." *American Heritage* (Summer 1951): 14–17, 69. General description of the trial and the public attention and uproar.

**1309.** Clarke, James W. *American Assassins: The Darker Side of Politics.* Princeton: Princeton University Press, 1982. 198–213. Describes Guiteau as one of the most deranged of the American assassins.

**1310.** Clemmer, Mary. "A Woman's Letter from Washington. The Assassination." *Independent* 33 (July 21, 1881): 1–3. Interesting observations by a correspondent on July 13, 1881.

**1311.** *The Crime Avenged; Or Guiteau on the Gallows . . . with Complete Secret History of Career, Crime . . . of Guiteau.* Police Gazette series of Famous Criminals, no. 8 New York: R. K. Fox [1882]. Sequel to *Guiteau's Crime and the Assassin.* Demonstrates the popular interest and press exploitation of the trial.

**1312.** Crotty, William J. "Presidential Assassinations." *Society* 9 (May 1972): 18–29. Classification of assassinations.

**1313.** Donovon, Robert J. *The Assassins.* New York: Harper & Brothers, 1952. 14–62.

**1314.** Edmunds, George F. "The Conduct of Guiteau." *North American Review* 134 (March 1882): 221–81. Discusses the lack of decorum at the trial.

**1315.** Elwell, J. J. "Guiteau: A Case of Alleged Moral Insanity." *Alienist and Neurologist* 4 (April 1883): 193–201. Lawyer defends the verdict.

**1316.** _____. "Guiteau—A Case of Alleged Moral Insanity: A Rejoinder to the Reply of E. C. Spitzka, M.D." *Alienist and Neurologist* 4 (October 1883): 621–45. This defense of the prosecution attacks the defense witnesses.

**1317.** Fenning, Frederick. "The Trial of Guiteau." *American Journal of Psychiatry* 13 (1933): 127–39. This review of thirty-six medical witnesses notes that the two top authorities—Spitzka and Gray—took opposite sides.

**1318.** Fisher, T. W. *Was Guiteau Sane and Responsible for the Assassination of President Garfield?* Cambridge: Riverside Press, 1882. Rpt. from *Boston Medical Surgical Journal* 106 (June 29, 1882): 601–5. Believes Guiteau was insane but responsible.

**1319.** Folsom, Charles F. "The Case of Guiteau, Assassin of the President of the United States." *Boston Medical and Surgical Journal* 106 (February 16, 1882): 145–53. Concise contemporary account by a Boston doctor who examined Guiteau in jail and concluded that he was insane.

**1320.** _____. "The Responsibility of Guiteau." *American Law Review* 16 (February 1882): 85–100. Concedes that Guiteau was medically insane but argues that he committed a deliberate murder.

**1321.** _____. *Studies of Criminal Responsibility and Limited Responsibility.* Boston: Privately printed, 1909.

**1322.** Freedman, Laurence Z. "Psychopathology of Assassination." *Assassinations and the Political Order.* Ed. William J. Crotty. New York: Harper & Row, 1971. 143–60. This discussion includes comparison of Guiteau with Oswald.

**1323.** Godding, William W. "The Last Chapter in the Life of Guiteau." *Alienist and Neurologist* 3 (October 1882): 550–57. This description of the execution and the autopsy concludes that future historians would not pronounce the verdict a "happy ending."

**1324.** _____. *Two Hard Cases: Sketches from a Physician's Portfolio.* New York: Houghton Mifflin, 1882. 34–357. Discussion by a key defense witness who was superintendent of the government asylum in Washington, D.C.

**1325.** Gray, John P. *The U.S. v. Charles J. Guiteau . . . Opinion of John P. Gray, MD, Superintendent of the Utica Insane Asylum on the Question of the Sanity of the Prisoner.* Washington: N.p., 1882. Important prosecution witness quotes extensively from Guiteau's November 7, 1881 interview. Includes trial transcript.

**1326.** _____. "The United States vs. Charles J. Guiteau, Review of the Guiteau Trial." *American Journal of Insanity* 38 (January 1882): 303–448. Gray was editor of this journal.

**1327.** *The Great Guiteau Trial: With Life of the Cowardly Assassin: A Full Account; A Complete History; The Judge's Charge to the Jury; Speeches of Counsel on Both Sides . . . Guiteau as a "Theologian," a Politician . . . a Member of the Oneida Community.* Philadelphia: Barclay & Co., 1881.

**1328.** Grinnell, Charles E. "Concerning Some Criticisms upon the Trial of Guiteau." *American Law Review* 16 (January 1882): 50–55. Defends the trial as fair.

**1329.** _____, ed. *Points of Law for Lawyers and General Readers, Suggested by Garfield's Case.* Boston: Little, Brown, 1881.

**1330.** Guiteau, Charles J. "Autobiography." *New York Herald*, Oct. 6, 1881.

**1331.** _____. *Garfield against Hancock: A Speech by Charles J. Guiteau of Illinois.* New York: Republican National Committee, 1881. Guiteau hounded the state party in New York to permit him to speak, then published his speech. Rambling attack on Democrats.

**1332.** _____. Letters of Charles J. Guiteau. File No. 14056, National Archives. Contains many of Guiteau's prison letters and prospectus—"The New York Theocrat." Also contains depositions and other materials collected by the prosecution.

**1333.** _____. Letters. Chicago Historical Society. Includes letters from Guiteau's youth.

**1334.** _____. *A Reply to Recent Attacks on the Bible, Together with some Valuable Ideas on Christ's Second Coming and on Hades, or the Resting Place of the Dead.* Syracuse: Masters & Stone, 1878. 28 p.

**1335.** _____. *The Truth: A Companion to the Bible. By Charles J. Guiteau, Theologian.* Boston: Lathrop and Co., 1879. Rambling record of biblical observations.

**1336.** _____. *The Truth and The Removal.* Washington: n.p., 1882. Part I-*The Truth.* Part II-*The Removal: "A Synopsis of My Trial for Removing Garfield and Letters of Commendation."* Guiteau's record of the trial. He intended to sell the book from his cell through the mail for two dollars.

**1337.** Guiteau, John W. *Letters and Facts, not Heretofore Published, Touching on the Mental Condition of C. J. Guiteau, since 1865.* Washington: N.p., c.1882. This collection of letters assembled by the assassin's brother for an appeal for a stay of execution was often cited by doctors who supported the defense.

**1338.** "Guiteau-Finis." *Medical News* 41 (July 1882): 12. The postautopsy editorial concedes that "the neurologists' diagnosis" was correct.

**1339.** Hamilton, Allan McLane. "The Case of Guiteau." *Boston Medical and Surgical Journal* 106 (March 9, 1882): 235–38. Opinion of a prosecution witness.

**1340.** _____. *Recollections of an Alienist, Personal and Professional.* New York: George H. Doran, 1916. 350–60. This witness never changed his opinion that Guiteau was insane.

**1341.** Hammond, William. *Reasoning Mania: Its Medical and Medico-Legal Relations, with Special Reference to the Case of Charles J. Guiteau.* New York: G.P. Putman, 1882. Rpt. of article in the *Journal of Nervous and Mental Disorders.* Endorses the conviction in the belief that it would serve as an example to other maniacs.

**1342.** Hastings, Donald W. "The Psychiatry of Presidential Assassination, Part II: Garfield and McKinley." *Lancet* 85 (April 1965): 157–62. Discusses Guiteau's record of emotional instability and psychopathic behavior.

**1343.** Hayes, H. G., and C. J. Hayes. *A Complete History of the Trial of Guiteau. Philadelphia, 1882. Includes the "Autobiography of Charles Julius Guiteau, Assassin of President Garfield" and "Married Life of Charles Julius Guiteau, by His Former Wife, Mrs. Annie J. Dunmire."* New York: Hubbard Brothers. 1883. This publication of the detailed trial notes compiled by stenographic press reporters includes as appendixes the "Autobiography" dictated by Guiteau to Edmund A. Bailey (405–52) and the statement by Guiteau's wife, who recounted numerous incidents of his dishonesty and her belief of his alleged insanity (455–523).

**1344.** Hicks, William W. Reverend William W. Hicks Diary and Letters. Francis A. Countway Library of Medicine, Harvard Medical Library, Cambridge, Mass.

Collection of material of the Washington minister includes his diary detailing his interviews with the prisoner and letters relating to the efforts to obtain a stay of execution. Also includes Guiteau's account of the trial, *The Removal.*

**1345.** _____. "The True Story of Guiteau." *New York Sunday World* (Nov. 12, 19, 26, and Dec. 3, 1893). This Washington clergyman was an important source who shared many conversations with Guiteau and championed a stay of execution.

**1346.** Hughes, Charles H. "A Physical Analysis of a Legally Sane Character: The Mental Status of Guiteau as Gleaned from His Speech and Conduct." *Alienist and Neurologist* 3 (October 1882): 588–617. St. Louis doctor argues for the insanity defense.

**1347.** Ireland, William W. *Through the Ivory Gate: Studies in Psychology and History.* Edinburgh: Bell & Bradfute, 1889. 160–228. Prominent English alienist provides a contemporary reaction.

**1348.** Jackson, E. Hilton. "The Trial of Guiteau." *Virginia Law Register* 9 (1904): 1023–35. Dated review of little value.

**1349.** Kiernan, James G. "The Case of Guiteau." *Chicago Medical Review* 4 (December 1881): 544–45. Defense witness believes that Guiteau's type of insanity was supported by family history.

**1350.** Kirkham, James F., Sheldon G. Levy, and William J. Crotty. *Assassination and Political Violence: A Report to the National Commission on the Causes and Prevention of Violence.* Washington: Government Printing Office, 1969. Makes reference to the assassination of Garfield.

**1351.** Lamb, D. S. "The Autopsy of Guiteau: The Official Report." *Alienist and Neurologist* 3 (July 1882): 468.

**1352.** Lawson, John D., ed. "The Trial of Charles J. Guiteau for the Murder of President Garfield." In *American State Trials: A Collection of the Important and Interesting Criminal Trials.* 14: 1–158. St. Louis: Thomas Law Book Co., 1923. Narrative with excerpts from the trial.

**1353.** *"List of Cincinnati Citizens Giving One Cent Each to Pay for the Fine of the Old Soldier Capt. C. A. Cook Who Slapped the Mouth of One George Morrison Who Said He Hoped that Wounded President Would Die."* N.p., n.d. Copy in Western Reserve Historical Society. This supplement in a Cincinnati newspaper lists the donors from across the nation who helped pay the fine of a Captain Cook.

**1354.** McBride, James H. "The Mental Status of Guiteau: A Review." *Alienist and Neurologist* 4 (October 1883): 543–65. Superintendent of the Hospital for the Insane in Milwaukee gives a rebuttal to **1315**.

**1355.** Madigan, M. J. "Was Guiteau Sane? A Reply to Dr. Elwell's Rejoinder." *Alienist and Neurologist* 5 (April 1884): 227–59 and 5 (July 1884): 386–430. Defense advocate reviews the case from a two-year perspective.

**1356.** Mitchell, Stewart. "The Man Who Murdered Garfield." *Proceedings of the Massachusetts Historical Society* 67 (1941–1944): 452–89. This dated but useful biographical sketch traces the family and provides a two-page bibliography.

**1357.** "The Moral Responsibility of the Insane." *North American Review* 134 (January 1882): 1–39. Contributors to this symposium included George M. Beard, J. S. Jewell, Charles Folsom, and J. J. Elwell.

**1358.** Norton, Frances Marie [Frances Guiteau Scoville]. *The Stalwarts, or Who Were to Blame: A Novel, Portraying Fifty Years of American History, Showing These Political Complications which Culminated in Civil War and Even in the Assassination of Two Good Presidents. By the Only Sister of Charles J. Guiteau.* Chicago: Frances Marie Norton, 1888. A rambling novel by his sister suggests a connection between the assassination and the acquittals in the Star Route mail fraud trials.

**1359.** Ogilvie, J. *History of the Attempted Assassination of James A. Garfield, Together with Complete History of Charles J. Guiteau.* Cincinnati: Cincinnati Publishing Co., 1881. Compiled and written while Garfield was still struggling to stay alive, this rushed book reflects the public interest and provides a sampling of press reports and sermons on his illness.

**1360.** Packard, Jerrold M. *American Monarchy: A Social Guide to the Presidency.* New York: Delacrite Press, 1983. 114, 142. Chatty book mentions the two bills introduced in Congress to make it a federal crime to kill a President.

**1361.** Paine, Lauran. *The Assassins' World.* New York: Taplinger Publishing Co., 1975. 124–27. Short account of little value.

**1362.** Peskin, Allan. "Charles Guiteau of Illinois." *Journal of the Illinois State Historical Society* 70 (May 1977): 130–39. This review of Guiteau's life challenges the often-applied but misleading tag of "disappointed office-seeker."

**1363.** Porter, John Kilhan. *Guiteau Trial. Closing Speech to the Jury of John K. Porter, of New York, in the Case of Charles J. Guiteau, the Assassin of President Garfield, Washington, January 23, 1882.* New York: John Polhemus, 1882.

**1364.** Ridpath, John Clark. *The Life and Trial of Guiteau, the Assassin Embracing a Sketch of His Early Career, His Dastardly Act . . .* Cincinnati: Jones Brothers & Co., 1881. Daily summaries of the fifty-day trial.

**1365.** Ring, Nancy McN. "The Religious Affiliations of Our Presidential Assassins." *Mid-America* 16 (October 1933): 89–104; 16 (January 1934): 147–56. Notes that Guiteau affiliated himself with many religious groups.

**1366.** Robinson, G. Wilse. "A Study of Political Assassinations." *American Journal of Psychiatry* 121 (May 1965): 1060–64. Labels Guiteau a schizophrenic.

**1367.** Rosenberg, Charles E. "The Place of George M. Beard in Nineteenth-Century Psychiatry." *Bulletin of the History of Medicine* 36 (1962): 245–59. This pominent doctor argued the defense position.

**1368.** _____. *The Trial of the Assassin Guiteau: Psychiatry and Law in the Gilded Age.* Chicago: University of Chicago Press, 1968. Well-written analysis.

**1369.** *Six Lies Nailed: The Assassin of President Lincoln Lie. The Assassin of President Garfield Lie. The Assassin of President McKinley Lie. The Lincoln Prophecy Lie. The Lafayette Prophecy Lie. The Pope Pius IX and the Confederacy Lie.* Brooklyn: International Catholic Truth Society, 1914. This pamphlet gives a rambling review of the Garfield and the other assassinations.

**1370.** Spitzka, Edward C. "The Case of Guiteau." *Boston Medical and Surgical Journal* 106 (March 23, 1882): 285–86. Chief expert on the defense side would testify twenty years later that Leon Czolgosz was insane.

**1371.** _____. "A Contribution to the Question of the Medical Status of Guiteau and the History of His Trial." *Alienist and Neurologist* 4 (April 1883): 201–20. Quotes from transcripts to defend his conclusion on insanity.

**1372.** _____. "Editorial Notes and Comments. The Guiteau Autopsy." *American Journal of Neurology and Psychiatry* 1 (August 1882): 381–92; 1 (November 1882): 522–40.

**1373.** _____. "A Reply to J. J. Elwell, M.D., in re Guiteau." *Alienist and Neurologist* 4 (July 1883): 417–38.

**1374.** Stearns, Henry P. *Expert Testimony in the Case of United States v. Guiteau.* Hartford, Conn.: Case, Lockwood & Braunard Co., 1882. Rpt. of *Archives of Medicine* 7 (June 1882): 286–307. Argues that Guiteau's love of notoriety is evidence that he was not insane.

**1375.** Trumble, Alfred. *Guiteau's Crime. The Full History of the Murder of President James A. Garfield With Complete Secret Biography of the Assassin.* New York: R. K. Fox, 1881. Police Gazette series of famous criminals.

**1376.** U.S. Supreme Court. *Report of the Proceedings in the Case of the United States vs. Charles J. Guiteau, Tried in the Supreme Court of the District of Columbia, Holding a Criminal Term, and Beginning November 14, 1881. H. H. Alexander and Edward D. Easton, official stenographers.* Washington: Government Printing Office, 1882. 3 vols. 2,681-page trial transcript is the chief source of the trial, which lasted from November 14, 1881 to January 25, 1882.

**1377.** _____. *In the Supreme Court of the District of Columbia, Holding a Criminal Term of June Term, AD 1881. The U.S. versus Charles J. Guiteau. no. 14, 056. Bill of Exception.* n.p. (1881). Reprint of the document submitted to the President of the United States by John W. Guiteau in the Matter of Application for a Commission De Lunatico Inquirendo, June 23, 1882. File No. 14056, National Archives.

**1378.** _____. *The United States vs. Charles J. Guiteau* . New York: Arno Press, 1973. Reprint of the 1882 edition.

**1379.** Weinstein, Allen, and R. Jackson Wilson. *Freedom and Crisis: An American History*. New York: Random House Inc., 1974. Chap. 27. A chapter in this textbook treats the President and Guiteau as personifications of the shallow politics of the 1880's.

**1380.** _____. *Instructor's Manual for Freedom and Crisis: An American History*. New York: Random House Inc., 1974. 89–95. Views the assassination as a paradigm of the political period and suggests that students speculate on Guiteau's perception of politics.

**1381.** Weisz, Alfred E., and Robert L. Taylor. "American Presidential Assassinations." *Diseases of the Nervous System* 30 (October 1969): 659–68. General review emphasizes the mental disorder of all the assassins.

## C. Obituaries

### 1. Eulogies

**1382.** Blaine, James Gillespie. *Eulogy of James Abram Garfield, by James G. Blaine, Delivered before the Senate and House of Representatives of the United States, Feb. 27, 1882*. Boston: New England News Co., 1882. This eulogy became an oratorical classic.

**1383.** *Garfield Memorial: Sorrow of the People of Buenos Ayres for the Death of General James A. Garfield, President of the United States of America*. Buenos Ayres: Lowe, Anderson & Co., 1881. Meeting of Americans living in the city.

**1384.** Hoar, George F. *James Abram Garfield*. Worcester, Mass.: Charles Hamilton Press, 1881. Eulogy delivered by a close political acquaintance on December 30, 1881.

**1385.** *James A. Garfield: Tributes from Over Seas: being Selections from Foreign Testimonials to the Late President Garfield*. Boston: J. Q. Adams & Co., 1881.

**1386.** LeRoy, William. *Sermon Preached at the Memorial Services on Occasion of the Funeral of the Late President Garfield at the Pro-Cathedral of St. Peters, Liverpool . . . on September 26, 1881*. Liverpool: James Cornish & Sons, 1881.

**1387.** *Literary Society of Washington, D.C. A Tribute of Respect from the Literary Society of Washington to Its Late President, James Abram Garfield*. Washington: N.p., 1881. Tribute on November 9, 1881 by an association of which Garfield was a member.

**1388.** Lowell, James Russell. "Speech at Memorial Meeting in London. 24-September-1881 at Exeter Hall." In James Russell Lowell, *Democracy and Other*

*Addresses.* Boston: Houghton, Mifflin and Company, 1887. 43–56. Cites the analogy of Joseph.

**1389.** *Remarks of President B. A. Hinsdale at Hiram College Memorial Service Held at First Presbyterian Church, Cleveland . . . September 25, 1881.* N.p., 1881.

### 2. Published Eulogies

A sampling of the more than 200 eulogies that appeared after Garfield's death.

**1390.** Beach, Seth Curtis. *Our Martyred President: A Tribute to the Memory of James Abram Garfield. Late President . . . Preached in the First Church in Dedham, Mass., Sept. 11 and Sept. 25, 1881.* Dedham, Mass.: Hugh McQuillen, 1881.

**1391.** Beard, I. W. *A Sermon on the Death of President Garfield, Preached in St. Thomas Church, Dover, N.H., Sunday, A.M., September 25th, 1881.* Dover: State Press, 1881.

**1392.** Behrends, Adolphus Julius Frederick. *The National Calamity: A Sermon Preached Before His Own Congregation, Sunday Morning, July 10th, 1881 . . . .* Providence: Providence Press, 1881.

**1393.** Boardman, George Dana. *An Address in Commemoration of James Abram . . . Delivered . . . First Baptist Church of Philadelphia, on the Day of His Funeral, at Cleveland, Ohio, Sept. 26, 1881.* N.p., 1881.

**1394.** Howe, William Beth White. *Address on the Death of President Garfield by Rev. W.B.W. Howe, Bishop of the Diocese of South Carolina.* Charleston, S.C.: News and Courier Book Presses, 1881.

**1395.** *Memorial Addresses Delivered before the Two Houses of Congress on the Life and Character of Abraham Lincoln, James A. Garfield, (and) William McKinley.* Washington: Government Printing Office, 1903.

**1396.** Nickerson, A. C. *Eulogy on President James A. Garfield, . . . Before the Citizens of Templeton, Mass., Sept. 26, 1881.* Gardner, Mass.: A. G. Bushnell & Co., 1881.

**1397.** Osborne, C. P. *General James A. Garfield: Memorial Address . . . Branford, Conn., Sept. 25, 1881 . . .* New Haven: Hoggson & Robinson, 1881.

**1398.** Palmer, Edwin Beaman. *Sermon . . . [on] the Death of President . . . in the First Parish Meeting House, Ipswich, Mass., Sept. 25, 1881.* Boston: Lyman Rhodes & Co., 1881.

**1399.** Towmbly, Alexander S. *Sermon on . . . President Garfield . . . in Winthrop Church, Charleston, Mass . . . Sept. 25, 1881.* Boston: D. F. Jones & Co., 1881.

**1400.** Woodbury, Augustus. *Our Dead President: A Sermon . . . in the Westminster Congregational Church, Providence, R.I. . . . Sept. 25, 1881.* Providence: S. S. Rider, 1881.

### 3. Poems

**1401.** Allderdice, Elizabeth Winslow. "From High to Higher: Over the Hill to the White House and Our President: A Sequel to Over the Hill." New York: Denison & Company, 1881. 28-page poem dated September 20, 1881.

**1402.** *In Memoriam: Gems of Poetry and Song on James A. Garfield.* Columbus, Ohio: J.C. McClenahan & Co., 1881. Besides 120 poems from various American newspapers, this collection contains 14 poems from the *Boston Globe,* including one by Oliver Wendell Holmes ("After the Burial"), and Henry W. Longfellow ("President Garfield: 'E Venni Dal Marario A Questa Pace' ").

**1403.** *The Poets' Tribute to Garfield: A Collection of Memorial Poems.* Cambridge: Moses King, 1882. Contains more than 150 poems gathered from newspapers across the nation.

### 4. Other Presidential Obituaries

**1404.** Peckham, Howard H. "Tears for Old Tippecanoe: Religious Interpretations of President Harrison's Death." *Proceedings of the American Antiquarian Society* 69 (1959): 17–36. Discussion of the reaction of 1841 provides a context to understanding the reaction to Garfield's demise.

**1405.** Stewart, Charles J. "Lincoln's Assassination and Protestant Clergy of the North." *Journal of the Illinois State Historical Society* 54 (1961): 268–93. Gives a framework for understanding eulogies on Garfield.

## D. Memorials and Memorabilia

**1406.** Adelman, Edward Henry. "Ohio Presidential Sites: The Establishment, Operation and Preservation of Memorials to United States Presidents in Ohio." M.A. thesis (Architecture), Bowling Green University, 1989. 88–94, 115–31, 224–37, and bibliography, 307–9. Description of Lawnfield and of the Memorial.

**1407.** Cox, Jacob D. *Garfield Memorial Association, Cleveland, Ohio; Dedication of the Memorial, May 30, 1890*; *Address.* Cleveland: The Association, 1890. Address by a close political friend of Garfield's.

**1408.** Fairmont Park Art Association. *Unveiling of the Memorial to General James A. Garfield, Fairmont Park, Philadelphia . . . May 30th, 1896.* Philadelphia: Allen, Lane & Scott, 1896.

**1409.** *The Garfield Memorial Program of the National Exposition for the Benefit of the Garfield Monument Fund, November 25 to December 3rd, 1882.* New York: American Bank Note Co., [1882]. Event held in Washington, D.C.

**1410.** Garfield Monument Association of the Pacific Coast. *History of the Monument with the Address at the Unveiling.* San Francisco: Association, 1883.

**1411.** *The James A. Garfield Monument at Lake View Cemetery, Including a Brief Outline of Garfield's Career*. Cleveland: Lake View Cemetery Association, 1930.

**1412.** Garfield National Memorial Association. *Historic and Descriptive Sketch of the Garfield Memorial at Lake View Cemetery*. Cleveland: Garfield National Memorial Association, 1889. History of the Memorial and the details of its planning and construction.

**1413.** _____. *The Man and the Mausoleum: Dedication of the Memorial Structure in Cleveland, Ohio, May 30, 1890. Published under the Direction of the Garfield Memorial Committee*. Reprinted 1924. Brooklyn: Albertype Co., 1889. Description of dedication ceremonies including the address by Jacob D. Cox and the parade. Has detailed pictures of the mosaic works and memorial windows.

**1414.** Keifer, J. W. *Oration at the Unveiling of the Statue of James A. Garfield. Washington, May 12, 1887 by J. W. Keifer*. Springfield, Ohio: Globe Co., [1887]. Remarks made at the dedication of the statue near the capitol.

**1415.** Kochmann, Rachel M., and Helen Swenson. *Presidential Burial Sites*. Park Rapids, Minn.: Haas Printing, 1976. Picture of the memorial and contemporary visitation information.

**1416.** Laird, Archibald. *Monuments Marking the Graves of the Presidents*. North Quincy, Mass.: Christopher Publishing House, 1971. 139–46. Pictures of the mausoleum and the doorway inscription.

**1417.** Lord, Clifford L., ed. *Presidential Executive Orders, 1862–1938*. New York: Hastings House, 1944. Sole order of the administration was in 1881, #21 (9–22), on "Mourning Formalities for President Garfield."

**1418.** *Official Catalogue of the National Bazaar, Industrial and Art Exposition, Held at the U.S. Capitol, and Other Buildings. November 25th to December 3, 1882 in Aid of the Garfield Monument Funding Under the Auspices of the Society of the Army of the Cumberland*. Washington: F. T. Wilson, 1882. Listing of donated items to be sold in the Capitol rotunda with each state having a booth selling items.

**1419.** Peskin, Allan. "The Funeral of the Century." *Lake County Historical Quarterly* 23 (September, 1981) 1–4. Reprinted in **768**. Account of services at Cleveland.

**1420.** _____. "If You Seek His Monument: Reflections on the Meaning of the Garfield Tomb." 9 *Timeline* (August/September, 1992): 40–51. Detailed discussion includes many pictures of the panels and decoration.

**1421.** _____. "Sermon in Stone: Symbols and Iconography in the Garfield Memorial." In *Proceedings of the Western Reserve Studies Symposium* 5 (1990): 1–11.

**1422.** *Report of the Participation of the Republican Invincibles of Philadelphia in the Funeral Obsequies of James A. Garfield Held at Cleveland, Ohio, September 26, 1881*. Philadelphia: N.p., 1881. Report of veterans who belong to Republican party club in Philadelphia. Provides information on participants' view of the ceremonies held at Lakeview Cemetery.

**1423.** Sibert, Russell D. "Monument to a President: Garfield's Tomb Preserves Echoes of a Bygone Era and Man." *Hiram Magazine* 62 (Winter 1990): 12–17. Well-written review of the monument and the historic cemetery where it is located.

**1424.** U.S. Congress, 49th Cong., 1st ses., 1885–1886. *Addresses on the Acceptance by Congress of the Statue of James A. Garfield, Presented by the State of Ohio*. Washington: Government Printing Office, 1886.

**1425.** Van Loon, W. H. *Lawnfield Memorial to James A. Garfield, 20th President of the United States*. Mentor, Ohio: Lake County Chapter of the Western Reserve Historical Society, 1962.

# 16
# Personal Life of James A. Garfield

## A. Family

### 1. Garfield, Eliza Ballou        1801–1887    Mother

**1426.** Farber, Doris. *The Mothers of American Presidents*. New York: New American Library, 1968. 123–34. Discusses her difficult life and life story, which she wrote at the age of 67 for the "gratification of my children."

**1427.** Garfield, Eliza Ballou, 1801–1887. Western Reserve Historical Society, Cleveland. 1 vol. Diary, Jan. 1–July 2, 1881. Comments on incidents at Lawnfield and at the White House, where she resided from March until June, 1881.

**1428.** Hampton, William Judson. *Our Presidents and Their Mothers*. New York: Cornhill Publishing Co., 1922. 155–63. Cites Garfield's close relationship with his mother and his letter to her when he was wounded.

**1429.** Hinsdale, B. A. *Eliza Ballou Garfield: Mother of President James A. Garfield: Addresses Made at Her Burial*. Cleveland: Leader Printing Co., 1888. Pamphlet contains address by Hinsdale and her pastor, H. R. Cooley.

### 2. Garfield, Lucretia Rudolph        1832–1917    Wife

**1430.** Bassett, Margaret. *Profiles and Portraits of American Presidents and Their Wives*. Freeport, Maine: Bond-Wheelwright Co., 1969. 193–98.

**1431.** Garfield, Lucretia R. Papers. Library of Congress. 1807–1958. 155 containers. Includes the typed copy of her diary, family papers, correspondence, biographical material, photographs, scrapbooks, and other material relating to family matters and President Garfield's assassination.

**1432.** Gordon, Lydia L. *From Lady Washington to Mrs. Cleveland*. Boston: Lee & Shepard Publishers, 1889. 408–31.

**1433.** Klapthor, Margaret Brown. *The First Ladies*. Washington: White House Historical Association, 1981. 48–49. Biographical sketch accompanied by Brady photo.

**1434.** Peskin, Allan. "Lucretia Garfield." In *American First Ladies: Their Lives and Legacy*. Ed. Lewis L. Gould. New York: Garland Publishing Co., 1996.

**1435.** Smith, Bessie White. *The Romances of the Presidents*. Boston: Lothrop, Lee & Shepard & Co., 1932. 270–83. Sentimental account.

### 3. Garfield, Abram        1872–1958   Son

**1436.** Brown, Harry James. "As the Twig Is Bent: The Education of the Garfield Children." *Lake County Historical Quarterly* 23 (March 1981): 1–8. Discusses the education and careers of the Garfield children.

**1437.** Garfield, Abram. Papers. Western Reserve Historical Society, Cleveland. 1886–1972. 2 boxes (1.25 linear feet). Includes 12 student sketchbooks as well as 5 diaries from 1881–1942 written by this architect.

**1438.** "Obituary-Abram Garfield." *Journal of American Architects* 31 (January 1959): 47.

**1439.** "Obituary-Abram Garfield." *New York Times* (Oct. 17, 1958).

**1440.** Rudolph, Adelaide. Papers. Western Reserve Historical Society, Cleveland. 1885–1950. 2 boxes. The collection of President Garfield's niece contains some correspondence with her Garfield cousins and newspaper clippings relating to their families.

### 4. Garfield, Edward        1874–1876   Son

Nicknamed "Neddie," this seventh child died of whooping cough.

**1441.** Quinn, Sandra L., and Sanford Kanter. *America's Royalty: All the President's Children*. Westport, Conn.: Greenwood Press, 1983. 112–115. Brief discussion of the Garfield children.

### 5. Garfield, Eliza Arabella        1860–1863   Daughter

**1442.** The first of seven Garfield children, this daughter, nicknamed "Little Trot," died of diphtheria shortly after her father's election to Congress. See **1441**.

### 6. Garfield, Harry Augustus        1863–1942   Son

**1443.** Comer, Lucretia Garfield. *Harry Garfield's First Forty Years: Man of Action in a Troubled World*. New York: Vantage Press, 1965. Chaps. 1–3, 1–80. Uses her father's papers to trace his life. Contains many favorable anecdotes about her grandfather.

**1444.** Garfield, Frederick Rudolph. "Harry Augustus Garfield." *DAB* Supp 3. 292–94.

**1445.** Garfield, Harry A. Papers. Library of Congress. 1884–1942. 76 boxes. His diverse career included being a lawyer, the president of Williams College, and the U.S. fuel administrator during during World War I.

**1446.** "Obituary—Harry Garfield" *New York Times* (Dec. 13, 1942). See also **1440**.

### 7. Garfield, Irvin McDowell     1870–1951   Son

**1447.** "Obituary-Irvin Garfield" *New York Times* (July 20, 1951). A graduate of Williams College, he became a lawyer in Boston.

### 8. Garfield, James Rudolph     1865–1950   Son

**1448.** Edwards, John Carver. "Herbert Hoover's Public Lands Policy: a Struggle For Control." *Pacific Historian* 20 (1976): 34–45. Mentions his chairmanship of a special committee to study western land policy.

**1449.** Garfield, James Rudolph. Genealogical Papers. Western Reserve Historical Society, Cleveland. 1881–1948. 3 boxes.

**1450.** _____. Papers. Library of Congress. Washington, D.C. 1900–1948. 62 volumes and 89 boxes. Includes his unpublished journal, started in August, 1880.

**1451.** "Obituary—James Garfield" *New York Times* (March 25,1950).

**1452.** Thompson, Jack M. "James R. Garfield: The Career of a Roosevelt Progressive, 1895–1916." Ph.D. dissertation, University of South Carolina, 1958.

**1453.** _____. "James R. Garfield: The Making of a Progressive." *Ohio History* 74 (Spring 1965): 79–89, 143–44. Examines his role in Cleveland politics and a short-lived effort to run for Congress.

**1454.** Warner, Hoyt L. "James R. Garfield." *DAB* Supp. 4. 316–17.

### 9. Stanley-Brown, Mary ("Mollie") Garfield     1867–1947
### Daughter

**1455.** Feis, Ruth. *Mollie Garfield in the White House*. Chicago: Rand McNally & Co., 1963. Written by her daughter, this book traces her life until her marriage in 1888. Uses excerpts from the diary kept by the 14-year-old Mollie in the White House as well as her grandmother's diary for 1881.

**1456.** "Obituary-Mollie Garfield Stanley-Brown" *New York Times* (Dec. 31, 1947).

## B. Personal Habits and Travel

**1457.** Cannon, Poppy, and Patricia Brooks. *The Presidents' Cookbook: Practical Recipes from George Washington to the Present*. New York: Funk & Wagnalls Co., 1968. 302–07.

**1458.** Comer, Lucretia Garfield. *Strands from the Weaving*. New York: Vantage Press, 1959. Chap 1–4. 11–39. Daughter of Harry A. Garfield provides an interesting look at her grandfather's family's life from 1877–1881.

**1459.** Cormier, Frank. *Presidents Are People Too*. Washington: Public Affairs Press, 1966. 16, 60, 69–70. Anecdotes from secondary sources.

**1460.** Garrison, Webb. *A Treasury of White House Tales*. Nashville: Rutledge Hill Press, 1989. 174–77. Relates some quotes and the story of the attempt at air conditioning.

**1461.** Halstead, Murat. "The Tragedy of Garfield's Administration: Personal Reminiscences and Records of Conversations." *McClure's Magazine* 6 (January 1896): 269–79. Includes a conversation with Garfield the night before he was shot.

**1462.** Jeffries, Ona Griffin. *In and Out of the White House: From the Washingtons to the Eisenhowers*. New York: Wilford Funk, 1960. 221–26. Discusses the Garfields' activities, which included restoring billiards and cards to the Executive Mansion and organizing separate receptions for different political groups.

**1463.** Klapthor, Margaret Brown. *The First Ladies' Cookbook*. New York: Parents' Magazine Press, 1965. 133–39. Contains bread recipes of Lucretia Garfield as well as anecdotes about entertaining at the White House.

**1464.** Peskin, Allan. "James A. Garfield, Historian." *The Historian* (August, 1981): 483–492. Notes his interest in history and fascination with quantifiable data.

**1465.** Rysavy, Francois, and Francis S. Leighton. *A Treasury of White House Cooking*. 18, 77, 135, 257–60, 271. New York: G. P. Putnam, 1972. Food served at Garfield's Inaugural Ball reception.

**1466.** Smalley, E. V. "Characteristics of President Garfield." *Century Magazine* 23 (1881–1882): 168–76. Long-time friend provides an affectionate appraisal of Garfield.

**1467.** Stanley-Brown, Joseph. "My Friend Garfield." *American Heritage* 22 (August 1971): 49–53, 100–01. This excerpt of an unpublished autobiographical memoir by Garfield's secretary provides anecdotes on the election and administration.

**1468.** Stern, Madeleine B. "A Book from Garfield's Library: The Preface to a Preface." *Quarterly Journal of the Library of Congress* 30, no.3 (1973): 205–9. Story of his preface to a translation of a study of American law by Adolphe de Chambrun.

**1469.** Taylor, John M. *From the White House Inkwell: American Presidential Autographs*. Rutland, Vt.: Charles E. Tuttle Co., 1968. Chap. 12. Discusses the characteristics of Garfield's letters and warns that his secretary imitated his signature.

**1470.** *Wills of the United States Presidents.* New York: Communications Channels, 1976. 134–35. Garfield was one of four presidents who left no will. Probate inventory of his estate listed assets of $61,000, which were divided among his heirs.

## C. Religion

**1471.** Banks, Louis Albert. *The Religious Life of Famous Americans.* New York: American Tract Society, 1904. 53–62.

**1472.** Batdorff, Hattie Harper. *The Making of a President and Views of God's Creation.* N.p., 1972. Short sentimental review.

**1473.** Boller, Paul F., Jr. "Religion and the U.S. Presidency." *Journal of Church and State* 21 (Winter 1979): 5–21. Notes that Garfield was one of five presidents who was a "born-again Christian."

**1474.** Bonnell, John Sutherland. *Presidential Profiles: Religion in the Life of American Presidents.* Philadelphia: Westminster Press, 1971. 136–39.

**1475.** Davis, Harold E. "Religion in the Western Reserve, 1800–1825." *Ohio Archaeological and Historical Publications* 38 (1929): 475–501. Notes the origin of the Campbellites in 1830 and the conservative character of religion in the region.

**1476.** Dulce, Berton, and Edward J. Richter. *Religion and the Presidents: A Recurring Problem.* New York: Macmillan Co., 1962. 50–51. Contains surprisingly little on this preacher-president.

**1477.** Fuller, Edmund, and David E. Green. *God in the White House: The Faiths of American Presidents.* New York: Crown, 1968.1 39–45. Emphasizes Garfield's conversion and strong religious beliefs.

**1478.** Hampton, Vernon B. *The Religious Background of the White House.* Boston: Christopher, 1932. 56–71. This "preacher-president" worshipped at the Vermont Avenue Christian Church. As Congressman he also frequently took the pulpit.

**1479.** Hampton, William Judson. *The Religion of the Presidents.* Somerville, N.J.: Somerville Press, 1925. 65–67.

**1480.** Hayden, Amos Sutton. *Early History of the Disciples in the Western Reserve, Ohio.* Cincinnati: Chase & Hall, 1975. Early history written by a member of the church.

**1481.** Isely, Bliss. *Presidents: Men of Faith.* Boston: W. A. Wilde and Co., 1953. 154–67. General account includes Garfield's favorite verse—Romans 8:38–39.

**1482.** Jennings, Walter Wilson. *Origin and Early History of the Disciples of Christ: With Special References to the Period Between 1809–1835*. Cincinnati: Standard Publishing Co., 1919.

**1483.** Jones, Olga. *Churches of the President in Washington: Visits to Fifteen National Shrines*. 15–25. New York: Exposition Press, 1954. Notes Garfield's church in Washington.

**1484.** Ketchen, John C. "Hale and Strong and Utterly Wholesome of Soul: James A. Garfield as Preacher." M.A. thesis, Indiana University, 1978.

**1485.** McCollister, John. *So Help Me God: The Faith of American Presidents*. Bloomington, Minn.: Landmark Books, 1982. 98–101. Very general.

**1486.** Moore, W. T. A. *A Comprehensive History of the Disciples of Christ*. New York: Fleming H. Revell Co., 1909. Dated history of Garfield's religion.

**1487.** Olmstead, Clifton E. *History of Religion in the United States*. Englewood Cliffs, N.J.: Prentice-Hall, Inc., 1960.

**1488.** Rushford, Jerry Bryant. *Political Disciple: The Relationship Between James A. Garfield and the Disciples of Christ*. Ph.D. dissertation, University of California, 1977.

**1489.** Shaw, Henry K. *Buckeye Disciples: A History of the Disciples of Christ in Ohio*. St. Louis: Christian Board of Publication, 1952.

**1490.** Short, Howard Elmo. "President Garfield's Religious Heritage and What He Did with It." *Hayes Historical Journal* 4 (Fall 1983): 5–19. Review of Garfield's religious life.

**1491.** Steiner, Franklin. *The Religious Beliefs of Our Presidents*. Giraud, Kan.: Haldeman-Julius, 1936. 146–49.

**1492.** Sweet, William Warren. *Religion in the Development of American Culture: 1765–1840*. New York: Charles Scribner's Sons, 1952.

**1493.** Wasson, Woodrow Wilson. *James A. Garfield: His Religion and Education: A Study in the Religious and Educational Thought and Activity of an American Statesman*. Nashville: Tennessee Book Co., 1952. A documented study of Garfield's church affiliation and its impact on his thought and action.

**1494.** Wilcox, Alanson. *A History of the Disciples of Christ in Ohio*. Cincinnati: Standard Publishing Co., 1918.

**1495.** Woodward, Phillip J. *Garfield, Preacher, President*. N.p., 1900.

## D. Lawnfield

**1496.** Adelman, Edward Henry. "Ohio Presidential Sites: The Establishment, Operation and Preservation of Memorials to the United States Presidents in Ohio." M.A. thesis, Kent State University, 1989.

**1497.** Beamer, Arthur Orville. *Lawnfield: Home of President James A. Garfield.* [Cleveland]: Western Reserve Historical Society, n.d. Sixteen-page pamphlet includes descriptions of the rooms.

**1498.** Bradford, S. Sydney. "James A. Garfield Home, 'Lawnfield.' " *National Survey of Historic Sites and Buildings.* Washington: National Park Service, 1963.

**1499.** Cardinal, Eric J. "Lawnfield: The Evolution of a House." *Lake County Historical Quarterly* 23 (December 1981):1–6. Discusses the two transformations of the house.

**1500.** Eastman, John. *Who Lived Where: A Biographical Guide to Homes and Museums.* New York: Facts on File, 1983. 142, 172, 299.

**1501.** Ferris, Robert G., ed. *The Presidents ... Historic Places Commemorating the Chief Executives of the United States.* Washington: National Park Service, 1977. 505–7. Pictures and description of Lawnfield.

**1502.** *General Management and Plan Environmental Assessment: James A. Garfield National Historic Site, Ohio.* Draft. (Denver:) U.S. Dept. of the Interior, National Park Service, Denver Service Center, 1985. Sixty-page assessment of Lawnfield.

**1503.** Haas, Irvin. *Historic Homes of the American Presidents.* New York: David McKay Co., 1976. 127–31. Includes photos of the interior of Lawnfield.

**1504.** Hampton, William Judson. *Presidential Shrines: From Washington to Coolidge.* 68–81. Boston: Christopher Publications House, 1928. Description of Lawnfield and the Lakeview Cemetery memorial.

**1505.** Johanesen, Eric. "Garfield House," *National Register of Historic Places, Inventory-Nomination Form.* Cleveland: Western Reserve Historical Society, 1975. Author is the preservationist at the Western Reserve Historical Society.

**1506.** Johnson, Ronald W. *James A. Garfield National Historic Site.* Denver: Denver Service Center, Branch of Cultural Resources, National Park Service, U.S. Dept. of the Interior, 1984. Informative account of Lawnfield, which in 1936 was donated to the Western Reserve Society and in 1980 designated by Congress as a National Historic Site.

**1507.** _____. "The Memorial Library at Lawnfield: A Study in Family Participation." *Lake County Historical Quarterly* 27, no.2 (June 1981): 1–6.

**1508.** Jones, Cranston. *Homes of the American Presidents.* New York: McGraw Hill Book Co., 1962. 138–42. General account with some contemporary prints.

**1509.** U. S. Congress. House. *James A. Garfield National Historic Site. Public Law 96–607, Title XII, 28 December 1980.* Act establishing the Historic Site.

**1510.** Wood, Frederick Marcus. *The James A. Garfield Home (Lawnfield) Mentor, Ohio, Lake County.* Cleveland: Lake County Chapter of the Western Reserve Historical Society, 1950. This pamphlet has descriptions of the rooms and interior photos.

# 17
# Other Views of Garfield and His Times

**1511.** Adams, Henry. *The Education of Henry Adams: An Autobiography.* Boston: Houghton Mifflin, 1927. Has disdain for Garfield and the Gilded Age.

**1512.** Ames, Mary. 1840–84. *Ten Years in Washington: Or, Life and Scenes in the National Capital, As a Woman Sees Them, Including a Full and Authentic History of the Life and Death of President James A. Garfield.* Hartford, Conn.: Hartford Publishing Co., 1882.

**1513.** Boutwell, George S. *Reminiscences of Sixty Years in Public Affairs.* 2 vols. New York, 1902. Vol. 1, Chap. 40–41. Observations of a Massachusetts politician who was a Grant supporter.

**1514.** Butler, Joseph G., Jr. *Presidents I Have Seen and Known: Lincoln to Taft.* Cleveland: Penton Press, 1910. 25–30. Contends that Garfield "was more brilliant than able" and "suspect" on the tariff.

**1515.** Crook, William H. *Memoirs of the White House: Personal Recollections of Colonel W. H. Crook.* Ed. Henry Rood. Boston: Little, Brown & Co., 1911. Chap. 5. 142–60. Anecdotes of the Garfield family in the White House.

**1516.** Cullom, Shelby M. *Fifty Years of Public Service.* Chicago: A. C. McClurg & Co., 1911. 12. Praises his oratory as more serious than Ingersoll's.

**1517.** Gerry, Margarita Spalding, ed. *Through Five Administrations; Reminiscences of Colonel William Henry Crook—Bodyguard to President Lincoln.* New York: Harper & Brothers, 1910. Chap 14. 256–74.

**1518.** Hudson, William C. *Random Recollections of an Old Political Reporter.* New York: Cupples & Leon Co., 1911. Vol. 1. Reporter for the *Brooklyn Daily Eagle* discusses Garfield's character.

**1519.** Lamar, J. S. *Memoirs of Isaac Evert*. 2 vols. Cincinnati: Standard Publishing Co., 1893. This friend of Garfield's was a minister and the editor of the denominational *Christian Standard*.

**1520.** Stoddard, Henry L. *As I Knew Them: Presidents and Politics from Grant to Coolidge*. Port Washington, N.Y.: Kennikat Press, 1927. Chaps. 13–14, 102–16. New York editor believed that Garfield showed great promise. Reissued in 1938 as *It Costs to Be President*. New York: Harper & Brothers, 1938. 225–38.

**1521.** White, Horace. *The Life of Lyman Trumball*. Boston: Houghton, Mifflin, 1913. 402–8. Dated biography mentions his role on the Electoral Commission.

**1522.** Wheeler, Everett P. *Sixty Years of American Life*. New York: E. P. Dutton, 1917. Scattered references.

**1523.** Wise, John S. *Recollections of Thirteen Presidents*. New York: Doubleday, 1906. 145–54. Concedes Garfield's eloquence but doubts his ability and his "gander eye."

# 18
# Historical Assessments

## A. Ratings and Reviews

**1524.** Cardinal, Eric J. "Garfield in the Eyes of His Biographers: *Garfield*, by Allan Peskin, *The Garfield Orbit*, by Margaret Leech and Harry J. Brown." *Lake County Historical Quarterly* 20 (September 1979): 1–6. Review discusses new perspectives on the president and concludes the two books provide the definitive portrait of Garfield.

**1525.** Lindsey, David. "Rehabilitating the Presidents: Garfield, Arthur, McKinley." *Reviews in American History* 10 (March 1982): 72–77. Attacks old stereotypes.

**1526.** Marcus, Robert D. "James A. Garfield: Lifting the Mask." *Ohio History* 88 (Winter 1979): 78–83. Reviews Leech's and Peskin's biographies.

**1527** Murray, Robert K., and Tim H. Blessing, "The Presidential Performance Study: A Progress Report," *Journal of American History* 70 (December 1983): 535–55. This 1982 survey of eight hundred historians does not include Garfield, but is important for understanding standards used in judging presidential performance.

**1528.** Peskin, Allan. "Presidential Greatness and the Rating Game: An Evaluation of a Brief Administration." *South Atlantic Quarterly* 76 (Winter 1977): 93–102. Argues against the omission of Garfield from the presidential rating games, contending that he can be measured by his previous record and writings coupled with his brief presidential tenure.

Garfield's tenure was not included in:

Curtis Arthur Amlund, "Presidential Ranking: A Criticism," *Journal of Political Science* 8 (August 1964): 309–15; Robert E. DiClerico, *The American President* (New York: Prentice-Hall, 1979); Gary M. Maranell, "The Evaluation of Presidents: An Extension of the Schlesinger Polls," *Journal of American History* 57 (June 1970): 104–13; Arthur B. Murphy, "Evaluating the Presidents of the United States," *Presidential Studies Quarterly* 14 (Winter 1984): 117–26.

## B. Evaluations

**1529.**  Agar, Herbert. *The People's Choice: From Washington to Harding: A Study in Democracy*. Boston: Houghton Mifflin, 1933. 237–39. Balanced assessment acknowledges Garfield's education and reading.

**1530.**  Andrews, Elisha B. *History of the Last Quarter of a Century in the United States*. 2 vols. New York: Charles Scribner's, 1896. Chap. 12, 307–42. This dated account has a pro-Garfield bias.

**1531.**  Armbruster, Maxim E. *The Presidents of the United States: A New Appraisal from Washington to Kennedy*. Rev. ed. New York: Horizon Press, 1963. 214–17. Cites Garfield's lack of "assertiveness" and doubts if he would have been a great president.

**1532.**  Bailey, Thomas. *Presidential Greatness: The Image of the Man from George Washington to the Present*. New York: Appleton-Century-Crofts, 1966. 298–99. Hostile account asserts that Garfield was much overpraised.

**1533.**  _____. *Presidential Saints and Sinners*. Chap. 19, 112–17. New York: Free Press, 1981. More sympathetic assessment argues that the truncated administration showed promise of lining up "on the side of good government."

**1534.**  _____. *The Pugnacious Presidents: White House Warriors on Parade*. Chap. 10, 253–55. New York: Free Press, 1980. Acknowledges his credentials but doubts his skills.

**1535.**  Beard, Charles. *The Presidents in American History*. 33–56. 1935; rpt. New York: Julian Messner, Inc., 1957. Contends that he had merit as a candidate but not as a president.

**1536.**  Brown, Stuart Gerry. *The American Presidency: Leadership, Partnership and Popularity*. New York: Macmillan, 1966. Mentions Garfield in terms of public mourning, comparing responses to other assassinations.

**1537.**  Burns, James MacGregor. *Presidential Government: The Crucible of Leadership*. New York: Houghton Mifflin, 1973. Mentions that he "might have been an effective president if he lived."

**1538.**  Cunliffe, Marcus. *American Presidents and the Presidency*. London: Eyre & Spottiswoode, 1968. 74–80. Argues that he had "weak legitimacy" as head of a faction who had a close election.

**1539.** DeSantis, Vincent P. *The Shaping of Modern America: 1877–1916*. Boston: Allyn and Bacon, 1973. Chap. 3. Gives him the typical mixed review—an able party man but not a tested leader.

**1540.** Freidel, Frank. *The Presidents of the United States of America*. Washington: White House Historical Association, 1964. Praises Garfield for attacking political corruption and winning prestige for the presidency. Includes portrait.

**1541.** _____. *Our Country's Presidents*. National Geographic Special Publications Divisions, 8th ed. Washington: National Geographic Society, 1979. 56–63.

**1542.** Garraty, John A. *The New Commonwealth: 1877–1890*. New York, 1968. 228–29, 253–57, 264–76. Part of the New American Nation Series, this survey notes that "against his will," Garfield took action that revived the presidency.

**1543.** Hatfield, Mark O. "James A. Garfield: A Leader Sought, A People Served." *Hiram Magazine* (Spring 1981): 3–7. This address given by the Oregon senator at a 1981 Hiram symposium emphasizes Garfield's religious convictions and perspective.

**1544.** _____. "James A. Garfield: A Man." *Hayes Historical Journal* 3, no. 4 (Fall 1981): 21–30. Reprint of **1543**.

**1545.** Ketchersid, William Lester. "The Maturing of the Presidency, 1877–1889," Ph.D. dissertation, University of Georgia, 1977.

**1546.** Oberholtzer, Ellis Paxson. *A History of the United States Since the Civil War*. Vol. 4 (1878–1888) New York: Macmillan Co., 1931. 78–79, 92–95. Critical of Garfield's executive aptitude and fighting spirit.

**1547.** Pedder, Henry C. *Garfield's Place in History: An Essay*. New York: G. P. Putnam's Sons, 1882. This laudatory and sentimental biography amounts to a hundred-page memorial.

**1548.** Peskin, Allan. "A Century of Garfield." *Hayes Historical Journal* 3 (Fall 1981): 9–20. Comments on the continued neglect and misrepresentation of Garfield and his era.

**1549.** _____. "President Garfield Reconsidered." *Hayes Historical Journal* 3, nos. 1 & 2 (Spring/Fall): 35–40. His recent biographer notes that Garfield "was not remembered so much for what he did but for what he was."

**1550.** _____. "From Log Cabin to Oblivion." *American History Illustrated* 11 (May, 1975): 24–34.

**1551.** _____. "Presidents Anonymous." *Timeline* 2 (October/November, 1985): 22–35. Discusses the "present day obscurity" of Garfield and the entire generation of political leaders.

**1552.** Rhodes, James Ford. *History of the United States from the Compromise of 1850.* 7 vols. New York: Macmillan, 1893–1906. Vol. 7. Chaps. 4–6, 109–60. Mixed review.

**1553.** Rose, Galen L. "Garfield's Unfilled Promise: Is the Nation Still Paying for a President's Assassination?" *Christian Century* 92 (April 16, 1975): 387–88. Minister speculates that Garfield would have promoted civil rights.

**1554.** Stanwood, Edward. *A History of the Presidency from 1789–1884.* Cambridge: Riverside Press, 1924. Pro-Garfield interpretation notes his political courage.

**1555.** Taft, William Howard. *Our Chief Magistrate and His Powers.* New York: Columbia University Press, 1925. 62–63, 142–45. Approves of his efforts to stop the expansion of the Senate powers, but upset with his effort to expand presidential powers.

**1556.** Taylor, John M. "Garfield: Time for Rehabilitation?" *Williams Alumni Review* 59, no. 1 (Fall 1966): 8–10. Garfield historian who also investigated the life of General Hancock.

**1557.** Tugwell, Rexford. *The Enlargement of the Presidency.* Garden City: Doubleday, 1960. Chap. 26, 215–21. Argues that while the Conkling battle was important, it was based on intrigue.

**1558.** _____. *How They Became President: Thirty-five Ways to the White House.* New York: Simon & Schuster, 1964. 249–58. This hostile assessment describes him as a "demagogue of the conservative faction."

**1559.** Wiebe, Robert H. *The Search for Order, 1877–1920.* New York: Hill and Wang, 1967. 34–35. Notes the elaborate partisanship of Congress that plagued both Hayes and Garfield.

**1560.** Wilson, Woodrow. *Division and Reunion, 1829–1889.* New York: Longmans, Green & Co., 1893. 289, 293. Discussion of the Conkling contest.

**1561.** _____. *A History of the American People.* New York: Harper & Brothers, 1902. 151–63. Describes the transition from Hayes to Garfield—from a "man who did not lead to a man who had no real hold on the affections and allegiance of his party."

**1562.** Wolfe, Thomas. "The Four Lost Men." *From Death to Morning.* New York: Charles Scribner's Sons, 1935. 114–33. Sees him as one of those four "bewhiskered" presidents who now are forgotten.

## C.  General Histories of the Presidency and Nation

**1563.** Cashman, Sean Dennis. *America in the Gilded Age: From the Death of Lincoln to the Rise of Theodore Roosevelt.* New York: New York University Press, 1984. 224–27. Brief standard account.

**1564.** Cooke, Deny. *Presidents of the U.S.A.* London: David & Charles, 1981. 125–38. Brief sketch describes Garfield as "the unwitting father of the epochal civil service reform act."

**1565.** Cooke, Donald E. *Atlas of the Presidents.* Maplewood, N.J.: C. S. Hammond & Co., 1964. 52–53. Short biography with map showing important sites.

**1566.** Corwin, Edward S. *The President: Office and Powers, 1789–1947: History and Analysis of Practice and Opinion.* New York: New York University Press, 1940. Only reference to Garfield in this classic study is in the discussion of disability.

**1567.** Cunliffe, Marcus. *The American Heritage History of the Presidency.* New York: American Heritage Publishing Co., 1968. Scattered references to Garfield.

**1568.** DeGregorio, William A. *The Complete Book of the Presidents.* New York: Dembner Books, 1984. 293–306. Good description of relevant people and events in his life.

**1569.** Kane, Joseph Nathan. *Facts about the Presidents: A Compilation of Biographical and Historical Data.* New York: H. W. Wilson Co., 1974. 138–43. Facts include cabinet members and major events in his life.

**1570.** Koenig, Louis W. *The Chief Executive.* New York: Harcourt, Brace, Jovanovich, 1964. Classic study of presidential powers has a few citations on Garfield's disability.

**1571.** Lorant, Stefan. *The Glorious Burden: The American Presidency.* New York: Harper & Row, 1951. rev. ed. 1969. 345–66. This short biographical sketch concentrates on the 1880 campaign. Includes many contemporary cartoons and pictures.

**1572.** Milton, George Fort. *The Use of Presidential Power, 1789–1943.* Boston: Little Brown, 1944. Few citiations on Garfield.

**1573.** Morgan, James. *Our Presidents.* New York: Macmillan, 1924. 197–207. Short, general account of this "hard working" politician.

**1574.** Ogg, F. A. "Garfield, James A." in *Cyclopedia of American Government.* Ed. Andrew C. McLaughlin and Albert Bushnell Hart. Vol. 2: 70. New York: Peter Smith, 1948.

**1575.** Peskin, Allan. "James A. Garfield." *Encyclopedia of the United States Congress.* Ed. Donald C. Bacon, Roger H. Davidson and Morton Keller. New York: Simon & Schuster, 1994. 899–900.

**1576.** _____. "James A. Garfield." *Encyclopedia of the American Presidency.* Leonard W. Levy and Louis Fisher. New York: Simon & Shuster, 1993.

**1577.** _____. "James A. Garfield." *The Reader's Encyclopedia of American History.* Ed. Eric Foner and John A. Garraty. New York: Houghton Mifflin Company, 1991. 438–39.

**1578.** Rossiter, Clinton. *The American Presidency.* New York: Harcourt, Brace and World, 1956. 107, 208, 212, 221. This classic study of the office has few references to Garfield's disability.

**1579.** *Saturday Evening Post. The Presidents: Their Lives, Families and Great Decisions as Told by the Saturday Evening Post.* Indianapolis: Curtis Publishing Co., 1980. 72–73. Anecdotes about Garfield and his family.

**1580.** Schlesinger, Arthur M. *The Rise of Modern America: 1865–1951.* 1925; rpt. New York: Macmillan, 1951. 52, 56, 66–67. Textbook.

**1581.** Schlesinger, Arthur M., Jr. *The Imperial Presidency.* Boston: Houghton Mifflin, 1973. 213, 390. References regarding cabinet access.

**1582.** Smith, Page. *The Rise of Industrial America.* New York: McGraw-Hill, 1984. Vol. 6: 456–57. Notes his stance in the 1877 strike and his election.

**1583.** Taylor, Tim. *Book of Presidents.* New York: Arno Press, 1972. 89–104. Chronology and other facts.

**1584.** Townsend, Virginia, and Julian Devries. *Lives of the Presidents.* New York: World Publishing Company, 1940. 188–95. General description without notes.

**1585.** Weaver, G. S. *The Lives and Graves of Our Presidents.* New York: Elder Publishing Co., 1883. Chap. 21. 453–71. Sentimental biographical sketch followed by discussion of his grave.

**1586.** Whitney, David C. *The American Presidents.* New York: Doubleday, 1975. 164–69. General review of Garfield's life.

**1587.** _____. *The Presidents: Biographies of the Chief Executives from Washington through Reagan.* Garden City, N.Y.: Doubleday, 1982. 173–78. Reissue with pictures of **1586**.

**1588.** Wilson, Fred T. *Pen Pictures of the Presidents.* Nashville: Southwestern Co., 1932. 327–42. This maudlin account was written as an "inspiration to the poor boys of America."

## D. Bibliographies

**1589.** *America: History and Life.* Santa Barbara, Calif.: ABC-CLIO,1964– .

**1590.** *American Presidency: A Historical Bibliography.* Santa Barbara, Calif.: ABC-CLIO Information Service, 1984.

**1591.** *Arts and Humanities Citation Index.* Philadelphia: Institute for Scientific Information, 1978– .

**1592.** *Bibliographic Guide to North American History*, 1979 +. Boston: G. K. Hall & Co., 1979 to date.

**1593.** Blandford, Linda A., and Patricia Russell Evans, eds. *Supreme Court of the United States, 1789–1980: An Index to Opinions Arranged by Justices.* Millwood, N.Y.: Kraus, 1983. Vol. 1.

**1594.** Brown, Jessica S., ed. *The American South: A Historical Bibliography.* Vols. 1–2. Santa Barbara, Calif.: ABC-CLIO, 1986.

**1595.** Cohen, Norman S. *The American Presidents: An Annotated Bibliography.* Englewood Cliffs, N.J.: Salem Press, 1989. General resource.

**1596.** Davison, Kenneth E. *The American Presidency: A Guide to Information Sources.* Detroit: Gale Research Company, 1983. American Studies Information Guide Series.

**1597.** *Guide to the Records of the United States Senate at the National Archives, 1789–1989, Bicentennial Edition.* Washington: U.S. Senate Historical Office, 1989.

**1598.** Goehlert, Robert U., and Fenton S. Martin, eds. *The Presidency: A Research Guide.* Santa Barbara, Calif.: ABC-CLIO Information Services, 1985.

**1599.** *An Index to the Presidential Election Campaign Biographies, 1824–1972.* Ann Arbor: University Microfilms International, 1981.

**1600.** Jacob, Kathryn A., and Elizabeth A. Hornyak. *Guide to Research Collections of Former United States Senators, 1789–1982.* 97th Cong., Sen. Doc. 97–41. Washington: U.S. Senate Historical Office, 1982.

**1601.** Kennon, Donald. *The Speakers of the U.S. House of Representatives.* Baltimore: Johns Hopkins University Press, 1986.

**1602.** Kinnell, Susan K. *Military History of the United States: An Annotated Bibliography.* Santa Barbara, Calif.: ABC-CLIO, 1986.

**1603.** Martin, Fenton S., and Robert U. Goehlert. *The American Presidency: A Bibliography.* Washington: Congressional Quarterly, 1987.

**1604.** Masterson, James R., comp. *Writings on American History, 1962–73: A Subject Bibliography of Books and Monographs.* Vol. 4 (Nos. 28103–37545). White Plains, N.Y.: Kraus International Publications, 1985.

**1605.** Menendez, Albert J. *Religion and the U.S. Presidency: A Bibliography.* New York: Garland Publications, 1986. 35–36.

**1606.** Miller, Cynthia P. *Guide to Research Collections of Former Members of the United States House of Representatives, 1789–1987.* 100th Cong., House Doc. Washington: Office for the Bicentennial of the House of Representatives, 1988.

**1607.** Morris, Richard B., ed. *Encyclopedia of American History.* 6th ed. New York: Harper and Row, 1982.

**1608.** Murdock, Eugene C. *The Civil War in the North: A Selective Annotated Bibliography*. New York: Garland Publishers, Inc., 1987.

**1609.** *Presidential Chronology Series*. 35 vols. Dobbs Ferry, N.Y.: Oceana, 1967–1981. Best for high school students. Chronology, documents section, and brief annotated bibliography.

**1610.** Roller, David C., and Robert W. Twyman, eds. *The Encyclopedia of Southern History*. Baton Rouge: Louisiana State University Press, 1979.

**1611.** U.S. Congress. *Biographical Directory of the American Congress, 1774–1971*. Washington: Riverford Publishing Company, 1935.

**1612.** U.S. Library of Congress. *The Presidents of the U. S., 1789–1962: A Selected List of References*. Compiled by Donald H. Mugridge. Washington: Government Printing Office, 1963.


## E. Historical Sites

**1613.** Garfield's Home-Lawnfield (James A. Garfield National Historic Site), 8095 Mentor Avenue (U.S. 20), Mentor, Ohio.

**1614.** Garfield Memorial-Lakeview Cemetery, 12316 Euclid Avenue, Cleveland, Ohio.

# 19
# Iconography of the President

## A. Portraits and Medals

**1615.** Bassett, Margaret. *Profiles and Portraits of American Presidents and Their Wives*. Freeport, Maine: Bond Wheelwright Co., 1964. Biography, 105–8. Painting by William T. Matthews, 104.

**1616.** Durant, John, and Alice Durant. *Pictorial History of American Presidents*. New York: A. S. Barnes and Co., 1955. 168–75. Short biography with several illustrations from contemporary periodicals.

**1617.** Freidel, Frank, ed. *The Presidents of the United States*. Washington: White House Historical Association, 1975. 47. Painting of Garfield in the White House Collection.

**1618.** Jensen, Amy La Follette. *The White House and Its Thirty-Three Families: New Enlarged Edition*. New York: McGraw-Hill, 1962. 47, 55. Brief sketch includes many contemporary woodcut illustrations.

**1619.** McElroy, Richard L. *James Garfield: His Life and Times*. Canton, Ohio: Daring Books, 1986. Good collection of photographs and illustrations of Garfield, who may probably be the first president whose life can be fully documented through photography.

**1620.** Milhollen, Hirst D., and Milton Kaplan. *Presidents on Parade*. New York: Macmillan, 1948. 262–78. Good selection of illustrations of the convention, Inauguration, and other events. Also contains the Brady photograph of the Colonel and Mrs. Garfield.

**1621.** Smith, Thomas A., comp. "Garfield in Pen and Ink." *Hayes Historical Journal* 3, no. 4 (Fall 1981): 31–46. Portfolio of sketches from *Frank Leslie's Illustrated Newspaper*, *Harper's Weekly*, and *Puck*.

**1622.** *The White House Gallery of Official Portraits of the Presidents.* New York: Gravure Company, 1907. Engraving of Garfield's portrait.

**1623.** Whitney, David C. *The Graphic Story of the American Presidents.* Chicago: J. G. Ferguson, 1972. 267–75. Photographs and woodcuts.

## B. Plays and Music

**1624.** Chapple, Joe Mitchell. "James A. Garfield" in *Face to Face with Our Presidents: Covering Thirteen Administrations of Twelve Presidents, 1876–1929.* Boston: Chapple Publishing Co., 1929. Script of NBC Radio program.

**1625.** Christie, Edwin. *President Garfield's Funeral March.* Boston: O. Ditson & Co., 1881.

**1626.** Mack, E. *Gen. Garfield's Grand March.* Boston: O. Ditson & Co., 1880.

**1627.** Shaw, John. "A Shooting Star: The Life and Achievement of James A. Garfield: A Recital Drama for Five Voices." *Hayes Historical Journal* 3 (Spring 1982): 21–46. Dramatic reading for five voices is composed of documents, diaries, letters, and reminiscences by and about Garfield. First performed on February 19, 1981.

**1628.** Sondheim, Stephen. *Assassins.* New York: Theater Communications Group, 1991. Also available as RCA Victor compact disc 60737–2–RC. Guiteau was a role in this Broadway musical.

**1629.** Werner, Henry. *Garfield's Funeral March Arranged and Dedicated to the Memory of the Martyr President James A. Garfield, 20th President of the U.S.* St. Louis: Balmer & Weber, 1881.

## C. Films and Videotapes

**1630.** Eye Gate House. *Rutherford B. Hayes, James A. Garfield, and Chester Alan Arthur.* Jamaica, N.Y.: Eye Gate House, 1959. Audiovisual Filmstrip. 37 frames, captioned, color. 35 mm. Teacher's guide. Part of *Our Presidents Series* #673.

**1631.** *James A. Garfield: A Place in History.* Beachwood, Ohio: Video Genesis, Inc., 1985. 1 videocassette. 1/2 inch. 51 minutes. In this documentary Garfield's story is told by a fictional newspaper reporter who recalls events of the president's life. Flashback scenes reveal the words and actions of Garfield and his contemporaries.

**1632.** Whorf Productions, Inc. *Kaleidoscope Patriots.* Birmingham, Mich.: Whorf Productions, Inc., 1986. Recording. 4 sound cassettes: 1 7/8 ips #52

# Periodicals Consulted

*Agricultural History*
*Alienist and Neurologist*
*American Catholic Historical Society of Philadelphia*
*American Catholic Quarterly Review*
*American Heritage*
*American Historical Review*
*American History Illustrated*
*American Journal of Insanity*
*American Journal of Medical Science*
*American Journal of Neurology and Psychiatry*
*American Journal of Psychiatry*
*American Law Review*
*American Medicine*
*Atlantic Monthly*
*American Quarterly*
*Americas*

*Book Reviews*
*Boston Medical and Surgical Journal*
*Bulletin of the American Geographical Society*
*Bulletin of the History of Medicine*
*Bulletin of the Historical and Philosophical Society of Cincinnati*
*Business History Review*

*California History*
*Century Magazine*
*Chicago Medical Review*
*Cosmopolitan*

*Christian Century*
*Civil War History*
*Civil War Times Illustrated*
*Collector, The*
*Colorado Magazine*

*Frank Leslie's Illustrated Newspaper*

*Harper's Weekly*
*Hayes Historical Journal*
*Hiram College Advance*
*Hiram Magazine*
*Hispanic American Historical Review*
*Historical and Philosophical Society of Ohio Bulletin*
*Historical Reflections*
*Historian, The*
*History Teacher*

*Illinois State Historical Journal*
*Independent*
*Indiana Magazine of History*
*International Review*

*Journal of the American Geographical Society*
*Journal of American History*
*Journal of American Studies*
*Journal of Church and State*
*Journal of Interdisciplinary History*
*Journal of Modern History*
*Journal of Negro History*
*Journal of Nervous and Mental Disease*
*Journal of Political Science*
*Journal of Politics*
*Journal of Popular Culture*
*Journal of Social History*
*Journal of Southern History*
*Journalism History*

*Keynoter*

*Lancet*
*Lake County Historical Journal*
*Library of Congress Quarterly Journal of Current Acquisitions*
*Louisiana Historical Quarterly*

*Louisiana History*

*Magazine of Western History*
*Manuscripts*
*Massachusetts Historical Society Proceedings*
*McClure's Magazine*
*Medical Gazette*
*Medical News*
*Medical Record*
*Mid-America*
*Minnesota Medicine*
*Mississippi Valley Historical Review*
*Montana*

*Nation, The*
*North Carolina Historical Review*
*New England Magazine*
*New England Quarterly*
*New York Christian Advoate*
*New-York Historical Society Quarterly*
*New York History*
*North American Review*
*Northwest Quarterly*

*Ohio Archaeological and Historical Publications*
*Ohio History*
*Ohio State Archaeological and Historical Quarterly*

*Pacific Historical Review*
*Pacific Historian*
*Pearson's Magazine*
*Pennsylvania History*
*Pennsylvania Magazine of History and Biography*
*Political Science Quarterly*
*Presidential Studies Quarterly*
*Proceedings of the American Antiquarian Society*
*Proceedings of the Columbia Historical Society*
*Proceedings of the Massachusetts Historical Society*
*Proceedings of the Staff Meetings of the Mayo Clinic*
*Proceedings of the United States Naval Institute*
*Public Administration Review*

*Quarterly Journal of the Library of Congress*

*Register of the Kentucky Historical Society*
*Review of Politics*
*Reviews in American History*

*Saturday Evening Post*
*Scribner's Magazine*
*Society*
*South Atlantic Quarterly*
*South Carolina Historical Magazine*
*South West Social Science Quarterly*
*Southern Quarterly*
*St. Louis Medical and Surgical Journal*
*Surgery, Gynecology and Obstetrics*

*Time Line*

*United States Magazine*

*Vermont History*
*Virginia Law Register*

*Walsh's Retrospect*
*Western Illinois Regional Studies*
*Western Reserve Historical Society News*
*Western Reserve Magazine*
*Williams Alumni Review*
*Wilson Quarterly*
*Wisconsin Magazine of History*

# Index to Authors

Numbers are citation entry numbers, not page numbers.

# Index to Subjects

Numbers are citation entry numbers, not page numbers.

Allison, William Boyd, 59–61, 1061, 1062
African Americans:
  and Garfield, 258, 277, 278, 283, 440, 902, 906, 910–13
  and Reconstruction, 629, 644
  and Republican party, 688, 907–11, 1108, 1246
Agnew, D. Hayes, 1255, 1256
Arkansas, 1085
Arthur, Chester A., 1001–9
  biography, 1003, 1005, 1007–9
  biography, campaign, 270, 341, 346, 363, 368, 370, 797, 798
  evaluation, 1525
  filmstrip, 1630
  Hayes removal of, 1006
  monument, 1001
  papers, 31–36
  presidency: foreign policy, 976, 983, 992; press reaction to, 1004. *See also* Election of 1880
Baker, Wharton, 720, 726, 734
Barnard, Henry, 646–51
Bayard, Thomas Francis, 62, 63, 1063–65

Bell, Alexander Graham, 1259, 1291
"Black Friday." *See* Gold Panic
Black, Jeremiah Sullivan, 114, 670, 1139–42. *See also* Election of 1876; Milligan case
Blaine, James G., 1010–30
  biography, 1012, 1015, 1018, 1019, 1021, 1022, 1025–27
  biography, campaign 1013, 1014, 1023, 1024
  on black suffrage, 258
  convention of 1880, 738
  eulogy of Garfield, 1382
  papers, 37–40, 155, 1010
  Republican party and, 561, 613
  Secretary of State: foreign policy, 992, 1000, 1016, 1017, 1019, 1022, 1028, 1030; Jews in Russia, 978, 1020; Latin America policy, 973–75, 988, 1029. *See also* Presidency of James A. Garfield, foreign policy
  speeches 779, 1011
Blaine, Mrs. James G., 1010
Boynton, Henry B., 14
Boynton, William A., 14

**About the Author**

ROBERT O. RUPP is Associate Professor of history at West Virginia Wesleyan College. His interests are American politics and the American presidency. He coauthored *Andrew Jackson: A Bibliography* (Greenwood, 1990).

**Bibliographies of the**
**Presidents of the United States**

*Series Editor: Mary Ellen McElligott*

1. George Washington
2. John Adams
3. Thomas Jefferson
4. James Madison
5. James Monroe
6. John Quincy Adams
7. Andrew Jackson
8. Martin Van Buren
9. William Henry Harrison
10. John Tyler
11. James Knox Polk
12. Zachary Taylor
13. Millard Fillmore
14. Franklin Pierce
15. James Buchanan
16. Abraham Lincoln
17. Andrew Johnson
18. Ulysses S. Grant
19. Rutherford B. Hayes
20. James A. Garfield
21. Chester A. Arthur

22. Grover Cleveland
23. Benjamin Harrison
24. William McKinley
25. Theodore Roosevelt
26. William Howard Taft
27. Woodrow Wilson
28. Warren G. Harding
29. Calvin Coolidge
30. Herbert C. Hoover
31. Franklin D. Roosevelt
32. Harry S. Truman
33. Dwight D. Eisenhower
34. John F. Kennedy
35. Lyndon B. Johnson
36. Richard M. Nixon
37. Gerald R. Ford
38. Jimmy Carter
39. Ronald Reagan
40. George Bush
41. William Jefferson Clinton

ISBN 0-313-28178-5

9 780313 281785

HARDCOVER BAR CODE

# DATE DUE

| | | | |
|---|---|---|---|
| | | | |
| | | | |
| | | | |
| | | | |
| | | | |
| | | | |
| | | | |
| | | | |
| | | | |
| | | | |
| | | | |
| | | | |
| | | | |
| | | | |
| | | | |
| | | | |
| | | | |
| GAYLORD | | | PRINTED IN U.S.A. |